FOR 2002 RETURNS

ZONDERVAN | 2003

Minister's
Tax & Financial Guide
Dan Busby, CPA

GRAND RAPIDS, MICHIGAN 49530 USA

We want to hear from you. Please send your comments about this book to us in care of the address below. Thank you.

GRAND RAPIDS, MICHIGAN 49530 USA
WWW.ZONDERVAN.COM

The Zondervan Minister's Tax and Financial Guide: 2003 Edition
Copyright © 2002 by Dan Busby

For information, write to:
Zondervan, *Grand Rapids, Michigan 49530*

Publisher's note: This guide is published in recognition of the need for clarification of the income tax laws for ministers. Every effort has been made to publish a timely, accurate, and authoritative guide. The publisher, author, and the reviewers do not assume any legal responsibility for the accuracy of the text or any other contents.

Taxpayers are cautioned that this book is sold with the understanding that the publisher is not engaged in rendering legal, accounting, or other professional service. You should seek the professional advice of a tax accountant, lawyer, or preparer for specific tax questions.

References to IRS forms and tax rates are derived from preliminary proofs of the 2002 forms or 2001 forms and some adaptation for changes may be necessary. These materials should be used solely as a guide in filling out your 2002 tax return. To obtain the final forms, schedules, and tables for filing your return, contact the IRS or a public library.

ISBN 0-310-24328-9

All rights reserved. No part of this publication may be reproduced, stored in a retrieval system, or transmitted in any form or by any means—electronic, mechanical, photocopy, recording, or any other—except for brief quotations in printed reviews, without the prior permission of the publisher.

Printed in the United States of America

02 03 04 05 06 07 08 / DC / 10 9 8 7 6 5 4 3 2 1

Contents...

■ **Recent Developments** 1

■ **Form 1040 — Line by Line** 13

■ **1 Taxes for Ministers** 25
- Ministers serving local churches 26
- Evangelists and missionaries 28
- Members of religious orders 28
- Ministers in denominational service, administrative, and teaching positions 30
- Individuals not qualifying for ministerial tax treatment 33
- Social security status of ministers 33
- Income tax status of ministers 33
- Importance of the employee vs. self-employed decision 36
- Forms and schedules for the minister 37
- Recommended filing status 38

■ **2 Compensation Planning** 39
- Determine the current compensation 40
- Plan the compensation package 44
- Use fringe benefits wisely 47
- Use accountable expense reimbursements 48

3 The Pay Package 51

- Delaying a portion of your pay 51
- When do the discrimination rules apply? 52
- Tax treatment of compensation elements 53
- Reporting compensation, fringe benefits, and reimbursements 70

4 Retirement Planning 73

- Preparing for retirement 74
- The keys to social security 77
- Taking out your retirement money 78

5 Housing Allowance 81

- Types of housing arrangements 83
- Structuring the housing allowance 86
- Reporting the housing allowance to the minister 89
- Accounting for the housing allowance 90
- Other housing allowance issues 93
- Housing allowance worksheets 96

6 Business Expenses 99

- Accountable and nonaccountable expense reimbursement plans 100
- Documenting and reporting business expenses 102
- Travel and transportation expenses 104
- Auto expense deductions 108
- Home-office rules 115
- Other business and professional expenses 117
- Allocation of business expenses 121

7 Social Security Tax 123

- The two social security systems 123
- Computing the self-employment tax 125
- Both spouses are ministers 127
- Self-employment tax deductions 128
- Use of voluntary withholding agreement to pay social security taxes 128
- Opting out of social security 129
- Working after you retire 133
- Canada Pension Plan 134

8 Paying Your Taxes 135

- Tax withholding 135
- Estimated tax 136
- Excess social security withheld (FICA) 139
- Earned income credit 139
- Extension of time to file 140
- Extension of time to pay 143
- Offers in compromise 144
- Filing an amended tax return 144

Sample Returns 149

- Example No. 1
  Minister-employee for income tax purposes
  (accountable plan) 149

- Example No. 2
  Minister-employee for income tax purposes
  (nonaccountable plan) 159

Citations 175

Index 180

INTRODUCTION

The 13th edition has been thoroughly updated to even more clearly help you understand the tax laws impacting ministers. But it is much more!

The minister's housing allowance issue has been on center stage since 1998—including a challenge to the very constitutionality of these provisions. Recent tax law changes and rulings have affected minister's fringe benefits and tax deductions. Keeping you up-to-date on all of these issues and how to address them is what this book is all about.

The voluminous laws and regulations that apply to ministers are mind-boggling. Yet this book is extremely readable and understandable—defying the complexity of the topics covered. The ease-of-use of this product is what sets it apart from any other book covering these topics.

This book does include the basic rules for ministerial income taxes, determining social security tax liability, accountable expense reimbursement plans, housing allowance issues, and much more. But this book also highlights issues raised in my workshops where I have been the presenter in 37 states, speaking to thousands of ministers, plus issues from hundreds of emails and telephone calls I receive from ministers and church leaders each year. It is a veritable one-stop resource for answers to the tax and finance issues most frequently asked by ministers and churches.

Forty years ago I was a college student and my father was serving in a denominational leadership position. Dad preached for 27 years—that is, 27 years after his 65th birthday. He preached until he went to be with the Lord at age 93—preaching a total of 72 years. Even after taking one income tax class in college, I realized Dad's tax return was not being correctly prepared even though he was paying someone to prepare it. This began my mission to help ministers with tax issues.

This is still my mission today—helping ministers minimize taxes while, at the same time, filing tax returns that will enable them to sleep at night.

Dan Busby

Recent Developments

Challenge to the minister's housing allowance is dismissed

Rev. Richard Warren, pastor of Saddleback Valley Community Church in California, sued the IRS in 1998 in connection with its position that he excluded an excessive amount from his income in the form of a ministerial housing allowance designated by his church. Two primary issues were raised:

- Is the amount a minister may exclude from his or her taxable income as a housing allowance limited to the lower of the fair rental value of his or her home or the cost of providing a home?

- May all of a minister's compensation properly be designated by a church as a ministerial housing allowance?

Prior to the Warren case, the IRS's official position was that the amount that may be excluded from income was the smallest of the following:

- The amount used to provide a home (that is, the total of all housing expenses, including mortgage payments or rent, taxes, insurance, furnishings, repairs, utilities, and improvements).

- The amount officially designated by the church.

- The fair rental value of the home including utilities and furnishings.

Key Issue

The IRS had been applying the fair rental value test for ministers living in their own housing even though this limitation was not clearly etched into the tax law. When the IRS applied this test to Rev. Rick Warren's tax return, he challenged it in the Tax Court and won. But the IRS appealed the decision.

Rev. Warren's housing costs exceeded the annual fair market value rental of his home. For 1993-95, he reported as taxable compensation from the church the amount paid to him by his congregation, reduced by the amount of actual housing costs he incurred. For example, in 1994 he received $86,175 as compensation from his church. He paid $76,309 in housing expenses on his $360,000 home in Trabuco Canyon, California. Therefore, he reported $9,866 as taxable income for the year. For all but one of the years in question, the church designated the full amount of his compensation as a housing allowance.

The fair rental value of the Warrens' home for the years in question was less than the amounts designated as a housing allowance and less than what Rev. Warren spent in each year in providing a home. Accordingly, the IRS, in auditing the pastor, assessed him for taxes on the amounts by which his housing allowance exceeded the fair rental value of his home for the years in question.

Key Issue

The minister's housing exclusion was drafted in 1921 and only amended once, in 1954. No court decisions have ever been made on the constitutionality of the housing allowance. The Ninth Circuit Court of Appeals has not decided whether to rule on the issue.

The Tax Court agreed with Rev. Warren's position in 2000 that the law does not limit the exclusion for a ministerial housing allowance to the fair rental value of the minister's home. The court held that amounts designated by a church as a housing allowance for a minister may be excluded from income to the extent that the allowance is used to provide a home.

The IRS argued that it was implicit in federal law that not all of a minister's compensation may be designated as a housing allowance. The Tax Court disagreed with the IRS noting that the law did not indicate any limit on the portion of a minister's pay that may be excluded as a housing allowance. The court acknowledged that a minister with additional income from another source (Rev. Warren had income from books and tapes during the three years in question with an annual average profit of $207,602) could spend more for housing and gain a larger exclusion than a minister without additional income or assets, but this possibility has no bearing on how the statute should be interpreted.

The IRS appealed the ruling in 2001 to the Ninth Circuit Court of Appeals. In March 2002, the Ninth Circuit Court of Appeals issued an order appointing Professor Erwin Chemerinsky of the University of Southern California Law School, to serve as *amicus curiae* and both parties to submit supplemental briefs on three issues: (1) Does the court have the authority to consider the constitutionality of Section 107(2); (2) If the court has the authority, should it exercise it; and (3) Is Section 107(2) constitutional under the establishment clause? The briefs were subsequently filed.

On August 26, 2002, the Ninth Circuit Court of Appeals dismissed Chemerinsky's motion challenging the constitutionality of the housing allowance. See page 84 for a more detailed discussion of this issue.

President signs housing allowance bill

On May 20, 2002, President Bush signed the "Clergy Housing Allowance Clarification Act," Public Law 107-181. The law amended Section 107(2) of the Internal Revenue Code and states that a minister's cash housing allowance may "not exceed the fair rental value of the home, including furnishings and appurtenances such as a garage, plus the cost of utilities."

The bill, introduced by Congressman Jim Ramstad (R-Minn), cleared the House on April 16 by a vote of 408-0. On April 18, 2002, S. 2200 was introduced by Senators Baucus (D-MT) and Grassley (R-IA). The Senate bill was passed unanimously on May 2, 2002.

Proponents of the law believed it would nullify the possibility of the housing allowance being ruled unconstitutional by the Ninth Circuit Court of Appeals. Later the same day that Bush signed the act, the Department of Justice and Pastor Rick Warren filed a stipulation of dismissal of the lawsuit. The next day, Professor Erwin Chemerinsky, University of Southern California Law School Professor, filed a motion to intervene in the appeal and ask the court to ignore the stipulation. This was an effort to keep the appeal alive so the court will be able to rule on the constitutionality of the housing allowance.

The new housing allowance law clarifies the fair rental value limitation but it does not address constitutionality issues. Thus, ministers may lack the freedom to defend their rights in the courts. Challenges to the IRS by ministers may become constitutionality cases. Few ministers have the time and money to mount a constitutional case. This gives the IRS a tremendous advantage on future examination of minister's tax returns, virtually assuring that ministers will be required to let the IRS win.

The new law amended Section 107 of the Internal Revenue Code by inserting the phrase: "and to the extent such allowance does not exceed the fair rental value of the home, including furnishings and appurtenances such as a garage, plus the cost of utilities."

Key Issue

The "Clergy Housing Allowance Clarification Act" placed the fair rental value test into law. Although the Tax Court had agreed with Rev. Warren that the test was not in the law, this legislation amended the tax code to include the test. The intent of the legislation was to thwart the constitutionality challenge to the housing allowance.

The new law generally is effective with 2002 tax returns. If your 2001 return was filed before April 17, 2002:

- and you limited your housing allowance exclusion by the fair rental value, you are not eligible to file an amended return to increase your exclusion;

- and you did not limit your housing allowance exclusion by the fair rental value, you are not required to file an amended return to decrease your exclusion.

If you filed your 2001 return after April 16, 2002, your housing exclusion is limited to the smallest of:

- The amount used to provide a home (that is, the total of all housing expenses, including mortgage payments or rent, taxes, insurance, furnishings, repairs, utilities, and improvements);

- The amount officially designated by the church;

- The fair rental value of the home including utilities and furnishings.

2002 tax rate and other changes

Here are a few of the key tax rate bracket, standard deduction, personal exemption, and other changes in the tax law for 2002 (many of these provisions are phased out at upper income levels):

▶ **Earned income credit.** The new law simplifies the definition of earned income by excluding nontaxable employee compensation from the definition of earned income for earned income credit purposes for years beginning in 2002 and later. This change in the law is generally beneficial to ministers with low incomes.

For 2002, "low income" generally means families with taxable and nontaxable earned income of less than $11,060 if there is no qualifying child, less than $29,201 if there is one qualifying child, and those who earned less than $33,178 and have two or more children.

> **Caution**
>
> Prior to 2002 tax returns, amounts excluded from income as a housing allowance, the annual rental value of a parsonage, and contributions by salary reduction to either a cafeteria plan or 403(b) plan were included in the definition of earned income for earned income credit purposes. Starting with 2002, these items are excluded in earned income.

▶ **Investment income.** The amount of investment income children under age 14 can receive before it is taxed at their parents' maximum tax rate is $1,500 for 2002.

▶ **Standard deductions and personal exemptions.** The standard deduction and personal exemption amounts, if under age 65, are adjusted as follows:

	2001	2002	2003
Standard deduction:			
Married couples	$7,600	$7,850	$7,950
Head of household	6,650	6,900	7,000
Single	4,550	4,700	4,750
Dependent children (1)	750	750	750
Personal exemption	2,900	3,000	3,050

(1) The greater of $750 or $250 plus the individual's earned income up to the single standard deduction amount, whichever is greater.

▶ **Reduction in individual income tax rates.** The regular income tax rates that will most often apply to ministers is reflected in the following box:

Regular Income Tax Rate Reductions		
Year	28% rate reduced to	31% rate reduced to
2001-2003	27%	30%
2004-2005	26%	29%
2006 and later	25%	28%

The married income tax brackets for 2002 are as follows:

If taxable income is	The tax is
Not over $12,000	10% of taxable income
Over $12,000 but not over $46,700	$1,200.00 + 15% of excess over $12,000
Over $46,700 but not over $112,850	$6,405.00 + 27% of excess over $46,700
Over $112,850 but not over $171,950	$24,265.50 + 30% of excess over $112,850
Over $171,950 but not over $307,350	$41,995.50 + 35% of excess over $171,950
Over $307,050	$89,280.50 + 38.6% of excess over $307,050

➤ **Child tax credit.** The new law increases the child tax credit to $1,000 by 2010. The following table shows the increase of the child tax credit:

Year	Credit Amount per Child
2001-2004	$600
2005-2008	$700
2009	$800
2010 and later	$1,000

➤ **Long-term care premiums.** Up to $2,990 may be deducted as long-term care premiums as medical expense in 2002 for those 70 and older. For those between the ages of 60 and 70, $2,390 is deductible, $900 between ages 50 and 60, $450 between the ages of 40 and 50, and $240 if age 40 or younger.

➤ **Dependent care tax credit.** The new law increases the maximum amount of eligible employment-related expenses for 2003 and later years from $2,400 to $3,000 if there is one qualifying individual and from $4,800 to $6,000 if there are two or more qualifying individuals. The rate of the credit also increases from 30% to 35%.

➤ **Expansion of adoption tax benefits.** The new law expands the adoption tax credit and the exclusion from income for employer-provided adoption assistance beginning for 2002.

The maximum adoption credit is increased to $10,000 per eligible child. Also, the exclusion from income for employer-provided adoption assistance is increased to $10,000 per eligible child.

➤ **Coverdell education savings account.** The annual limit on contributions is increased from $500 to $2,000 effective with 2002. The definition of qualified education expenses that may be paid tax-free from an education IRA is expanded to include:

- ☐ Tuition, fees, academic tutoring, special need services, books, supplies, and other equipment incurred in connection with the enrollment or attendance of the beneficiary at a public, private, or religious school providing elementary or secondary education (kindergarten through grade 12);

- ☐ Room and board, uniforms, transportation, and supplementary items or services (including extended day programs) required or provided by such a school;

☐ The purchase of any computer technology or equipment or Internet access and related services, if the technology, equipment, or services are to be used by the beneficiary and the beneficiary's family during any of the year the beneficiary is in school.

▶ **College cost deduction.** A new $3,000 deduction starts in 2002 for college costs by itemizers and nonitemizers alike. For 2004 and 2005, the limit on the deduction will be $4,000. This provision is repealed after 2005.

Tuition paid in December 2001 for coursework that begins in January 2002 will be covered in 2002. Tuition payments postponed from 2001, but paid in 2002, will not be covered.

▶ **Reduction of the marriage penalty.** The marriage penalty means two-earner married couples have higher taxes than single filers with the same incomes. The new legislation provides relief but not until 2005 when:

☐ The standard deduction for joint filers will increase each year until 2009, when it reaches a level of twice the single standard deduction.

☐ The size of the 15% tax bracket for joint filers will increase each year until 2008, when it will double that of the 15% bracket for singles.

Standard mileage rates

The optional standard mileage rates for employees, self-employed individuals, and other taxpayers to use in computing the deductible costs paid in 2002 in connection with the operation of a passenger automobile for business, charitable, medical, or moving expense purposes are as follows (for more information, see page 109):

Type of Expense	2002 Rate (per mile)	2003 Rate (per mile)
Business	36.5 cents	36 cents
Charitable	14 cents	14 cents
Moving/Medical	13 cents	12 cents

Tip

Using the standard business mileage rate (36 cents for 2003) to reimburse a minister for church-relating, non-commuting miles is just good stewardship! Too often churches and other employers, reimburse ministers at a rate less than the maximum rate. This generally penalizes the minister since a deduction for unreimbursed miles is only a fraction of a full reimbursement.

Clean-fuel auto special tax deduction

Buyers of these clean-fuel autos can deduct up to $2,000 (up to $5,000 of the cost of a truck or van with a gross vehicle weight above 26,000 pounds) of the cost of the car on their tax returns. Buyers of Honda hybrid cars (the Insight and Civic) and the Toyota Prius qualify for the deduction. However, the proper place for the write-off is difficult to find. The deduction goes on line 34 of Form 1040. The tax break is available even if the purchaser takes the standard deduction. Larger clean-fuel vehicles get even bigger deductions, up to $5,000 for a light truck or van.

> RECENT DEVELOPMENTS

The maximum deduction is reduced by 25% in 2002, 50% in 2003, and 75% in 2004.

2002 auto depreciation deduction limits

The annual limits on depreciation deductions for automobiles first placed in service in 2002 are as follows:

Tax Year	Amount
1st Tax Year	$3,060
2nd Tax Year	4,900
3rd Tax Year	2,950
Each Succeeding Year	1,775

Effective with 2002, the first-year depreciation limit may be increased by $4,600, from $3,060 to $7,660, if the bonus depreciation is elected. Lessees of "luxury" cars for business will have imputed income on automobiles that cost more than $15,500 and are first leased in 2002. Thus, leased cars have a similar deduction limit as purchased cars.

New saver's tax credit

The tax law of 2001 provided a new tax credit that has not received much coverage in the media. The saver's tax credit is a nonrefundable income tax credit for eligible taxpayers who have adjusted gross income of $50,000 or less. Many ministers will fall in this category.

The credit is equal to a certain percentage of employee contributions made to a retirement account or IRA. The specific percentage varies depending on filing status and income. An eligible taxpayer must be at least 18 before the taxpayer's taxable year, and cannot be a full-time student or claimed as a dependent on someone else's tax return.

The maximum annual contribution eligible for the saver's tax credit is $2,000 per person. Salary reduction contributions to a 401(k) plan, section 403(b) annuities, or SIMPLE IRA plans are eligible for the credit. The credit is also available for contributions to either a traditional or a Roth IRA. The tax credit does not affect a taxpayer's use of a deduction or exclusion that would otherwise apply to the contribution.

Remember

Many ministers will qualify for the new saver's tax credit. By completing Form 8880, you can calculate your credit based on your contributions to traditional and Roth IRAs plus elective deferrals (salary reductions) to your 403(b) or 401(k) plan. Your excluded housing allowance is not considered since the credit is based on your adjusted gross income.

The amount of contributions eligible for the credit is reduced by the amount of taxable distributions received by the taxpayer from a retirement plan or an IRA during the testing period. The testing period covers the year the credit is claimed, the period after the end of that year and before the due date of the return (including extensions), and the two taxable years that precede the year for which the credit is claimed.

Since the saver's credit is based on the taxpayer's adjustable gross income, the minister's housing allowance, which is excluded from his gross income, does not have to be added into the calculation. The credit only applies for tax years 2002 through 2006.

> **Example:** Mary, a single minister, has gross compensation on $30,000 and a designated housing allowance of $13,100. Mary's W-2 shows compensation of $16,900 and has no other income. If she makes a $2,000 Section 403(b) contribution, her adjusted gross income will drop to $14,900, thus qualifying her for a 50% saver's credit or $1,000 (see table).

On a joint return, the saver's credit could be claimed for up to $2,000 of contributions for each spouse, a total of $4,000, for a maximum credit of $2,000.

Adjusted Gross Income						Applicable percentage
Joint Return		Head of Household		All Other Cases		
Over	Not over	Over	Not over	Over	Not over	
$ 0	$30,000	$ 0	$22,500	$ 0	$15,000	50
30,000	32,500	22,500	24,375	15,000	16,250	20
32,500	50,000	24,375	37,500	16,250	25,000	10
50,000		37,500		25,000		

Weight-loss programs may be tax deductible

The IRS has ruled that uncompensated amounts paid for weight-loss programs may be tax deductible if the program is treatment for a specific disease or ailment diagnosed by a physician.

The IRS ruled that obesity is medically accepted to be a disease in its own right. If a physician diagnoses a patient as obese, then the patient's participation in a weight-loss program as treatment for obesity is an amount paid for medical care. In addition, if a patient is directed by a physician to lose weight as treatment for another condition, such as hypertension, the treatment is also an amount paid for medical care. If participation in a weight-loss program is merely to improve general health and appearance, then the fees are not amounts paid for medical care. The IRS specified that an individual may not deduct any portion of the cost of purchasing reduced-calorie diet food because the food is merely a substitute for the food an individual would normally consume. The purchase of food is a nondeductible personal expense.

IRS tells teachers to save receipts for new tax deduction

The IRS has announced that teachers should save their receipts for purchases of books and classroom supplies because those out-of-pocket expenses may lower their taxes, thanks to a recent change in the law.

The new deduction is available to eligible educators in both public and private elementary and secondary schools. They must work at least 900 hours during a school year as a teacher, instructor, counselor, principal, or aide. Individuals may subtract up to $250 of qualified expenses when figuring their adjusted gross income.

Student loan interest

Student loan interest will be deductible up to $2,500 per year for 2002. This deduction is available even for those who do not itemize their deductions. For 2002 and later years, the interest deduction is available for the entire life of a student loan. The deduction cannot be claimed by someone who is claimed as a dependent on another person's tax return.

Increase in unified estate and gift tax credit

The exemption from federal estate taxes is increased from $1 million for 2002 and continues to increase through 2009 as follows (the gift tax exemption is $1,000,000 for 2002-2010):

Year	Applicable Exemption Amount
2002 and 2003	$1,000,000
2004 and 2005	1,500,000
2006 through 2008	2,000,000
2009	3,500,000

If your estate is less than $1 million, federal estate tax is not a problem. The simplest way to dispose of assets may be to place them in joint ownership with the person whom you wish to receive them, such as a spouse. If your estate is more than $1 million, estate tax planning is a must. If married, use both exempt amounts to pass up to $2 million tax-free in 2002 and 2003. There is no estate tax for those dying in 2010. Without further legislative action, the estate tax law in effect on May 26, 2001, would again become effective on January 1, 2011.

Annual gift tax exclusion

The annual exclusion for gifts for 2002 is $11,000 per year, per donee, up from $10,000 for 2001. The annual gift tax exclusion is indexed to the Consumer Price Index for periodic adjustment, rounded to the next lowest multiple of $1,000.

Foreign earned income exclusion increased

The foreign earned income credit for qualified individual U.S. citizens or residents who reside in foreign countries is $80,000 for 2002 and thereafter.

For any tax year after 2007, the $80,000 amount is increased by multiplying the dollar amount of the limitation by the cost-of-living adjustment for the calendar year in which the tax year begins. The increase will then be rounded to the next lowest multiple of $100.

2002 equipment write-off

The one-time equipment write-off, for equipment used 50% or more for business, remains $24,000 for 2002. The write-off increases again in 2003:

Year	Maximum Deduction
2002	$24,000
2003 and later	25,000

Caution for missionaries: The one-time equipment write-off does not apply to most property used outside the U.S. This will often prevent missionaries from using the Section 179 election.

Warning

The one-time equipment write-off cannot be used as part of a minister's accountable expense reimbursement plan. If a minister personally owns a computer that is partially used for his or her employer, the business portion of the computer can be reimbursed under an accountable plan based on annual depreciation. The business portion of the cost of the computer cannot be reimbursed in one year under the one-time write-off rules.

Pension reform changes

The Economic Growth and Tax Relief Reconciliation Act (EGTRRA) of 2001 contained provisions for the relaxation of some limits on pension plans relevant to nonprofit organizations:

▶ **Change to maximum exclusion allowance for 403(b) plans.** For 2002, the maximum exclusion allowance goes to $40,000 (from $35,000 in 2001) or 100% of compensation (from 25% in 2001), whichever is less.

▶ **Change in salary reduction contribution limits to 403(b) plans.** These will increase along with increases to contribution limits for 401(k) plans from $10,500 for 2001 to $11,000 in 2002. There will be a $1,000 yearly increase in these limits until they reach $15,000 in 2006. Employees over age 50 will also be able to make a "catch-up" contribution of $1,000 in 2002, increasing by $1,000 per year to $5,000 by 2006.

▶ **Revisions in "rollover" rules between certain types of plans.** The Act will allow distributions from 403(b) and IRAs to be "rolled over" into another of these types of plans or IRAs. This will improve the "portability" of pensions.

▶ **Other changes.** There are a number of other changes related to vesting for matching contributions and other aspects of pension plans contained in the 2001 Act. However, these will only be applicable to a very small number of churches and other nonprofit employers.

IRS issues guidance for health reimbursement arrangements

Paying medical insurance premiums to protect against catastrophic medical expenses is a commonly accepted practice. But even the best medical insurance policies generally do not pay all of the insured's medical expenses. These unpaid medical expenses are usually in the form of noncovered items or expenses subject to a deductible or coinsurance (or copayment) clause in a health insurance policy.

> RECENT DEVELOPMENTS

Medical expenses, not eligible for reimbursement under a health insurance plan, or otherwise reimbursed, are deductible on Schedule A as itemized deductions. But for most ministers, receiving an itemized deduction benefit from unreimbursed medical expenses is more a dream than reality. There are two major barriers to deducting medical expenses. First, many ministers use the standard deduction instead of itemized deductions. This is especially true for most ministers who live in ministry-provided housing. Second, even for those ministers and other employees who itemize their deductions, there is a 7.5% of adjusted gross income limitation on health expenses.

Medical expenses, not eligible for reimbursement under a health insurance plan, have been reimbursed to ministers by churches and other nonprofit organizations for many years. But now the IRS has introduced a phrase to describe the concept: health reimbursement arrangement (HRA). The IRS has also introduced a new concept into the reimbursement of medical expenses: HRAs can allow unused amounts to be carried forward for medical care expense reimbursements in a later year.

The IRS provides the following explanation of health reimbursement arrangements (HRAs) and how payments under HRAs qualify for the exclusion from gross income:

- An HRA is paid for solely by the ministry. It is not a salary reduction plan.

- Although the coverage period will generally be twelve months, the coverage period may be less than a year.

- Any out-of-pocket medical expenses (any medical expense that is allowable as a medical expense deduction on Schedule A) for the employee and the employee's spouse and dependents can be reimbursed under an HRA.

- The ministry must establish a maximum dollar amount for a coverage period. Any unused portion of the maximum dollar amount at the end of a coverage period is carried forwarded to increase the maximum reimbursement amount in subsequent coverage periods.

- Medical care expense submitted for reimbursement must be substantiated.

- HRAs cannot reimburse a medical care expense that is incurred before the date the HRA is in existence. Neither can a reimbursement be made for a medical care expense that is incurred before the date an employee first becomes enrolled under the HRA.

- An HRA is disqualified if any person has the right to receive cash or any other taxable or nontaxable benefit under the arrangement other than the reimbursement of medical care expenses.

- Medical care expense reimbursements may be made to current and former employees

Idea

An HRA is one option to reimburse a minister's out-of-pocket medical expenses. It must be based on a written plan and formal employee enrollment procedures. The church or other employer must provide the funding for the HRA. This is not a salary reduction concept.

11

(including retired employees), their spouses and dependents, and the spouses and dependents of deceased employees. Reimbursements may not be made to individuals whom the employer considers to be self-employed for income tax purposes.

- An HRA is subject to the nondiscrimination rules if it is self-insured (the church provides the funds for HRA payments).

The 2003 edition of *The Zondervan Church and Nonprofit Tax & Financial Guide* provides sample language for an HRA plan and employee enrollment.

2002 highly compensated employee definition

The "highly compensated employee" definition is important in determining whether certain fringe benefits are taxable to employees that fall within that category. Examples of fringe benefits that may trigger additional compensation based on favoring highly compensated employees include: qualified tuition and fee discounts, educational assistance benefits, dependent care plans, group-term life benefits, and self-insured medical plans.

Employees who have compensation for the previous year in excess of $90,000 (2002 limit) and, if an employer elects, were in the top 20% of employees by compensation meet the definition.

> **Example:** Pastor Smith received gross pay of $60,000. The church established a dependent care plan to pay for the child care of two of Pastor Smith's children. The dependent care benefit is not provided to other employees of the church. Even though the plan is clearly discriminatory, Pastor Smith does not meet the highly compensated employee definition since the gross pay is less than $90,000. Therefore, the dependent care benefit is tax-free.

2002 social security taxable limit increases

The maximum amount of taxable and creditable annual earnings subject to the social security and self-employment income tax increased to $84,900 in 2002, up from $80,400 in 2001. There is no maximum wage base for Medicare.

NEED A TAX FORM AT THE LAST MINUTE?

Try your local library. The IRS provides sets of most tax forms to libraries throughout the country.

Forms via the Internet. You can download most forms from the IRS Web site at www.irs.ustreas.gov and you can secure most IRS publications there as well. Federal and state forms are also available at www.taxweb.com/taxforms.html.

Forms by fax. Use your FAX phone and dial the IRS at 703-487-4160 and list the forms you need. They will come back to you on your fax line.

Line by Line

Form 1040

There are two short forms, the 48-line 1040A and the super-short, 12-line 1040EZ. Generally, ministers should use the 74-line Form 1040 instead. It accommodates every minister, and there's no penalty for leaving some of the lines blank. Besides, going down the 1040 line by line may jog your memory about money you received or spent in 2002. (Line numbers noted refer to the 1040 and then to Schedule A.)

- **Filing status (lines 1 to 5). Line 2:** If your spouse died in 2002, you can still file jointly and take advantage of tax rates that would be lower than if you file as a single person or as a head of household.

  Line 3: If you're married and live in one of the 42 separate-property states, compute your tax two ways—jointly and separately. Then, file the return resulting in the lower tax.

  Line 4: If you're single, you may qualify as head of household if you provided a home for someone else—like your parent. Filing as head of household rather than as a single person can save you a bundle on taxes.

  Line 5: If your spouse died in 2000 or 2001 and you have a dependent child, you can also benefit from joint-return rates as a qualifying widow(er).

- **Exemptions (lines 6a to 6d).** Remember to include a social security number for any dependent who was at least one year old on December 31, 2002. If your child does not have one, call social security at 800-772-1213 to get Form SS-5, Application for a Social Security Number. If you are unable to secure the social security number before the filing deadline, file for an extension of time to file.

- **Income (lines 7 to 22). Line 7:** If your employer considered you an employee for income tax purposes, you should receive

> **Filing Tip**
>
> **Form 1040, Line 7.** All compensation from Forms W-2 is reported on Line 7. Be sure your church has not included a formally and prospectively designated housing allowance in Box 1 of Form W-2. If so, deduct the housing allowance included in Box 1 and attach a schedule to explain the adjustment.

13

Form W-2 from the employer. The total amount of your taxable wages is shown in Box 1 of Form W-2; attach Copy B of your W-2 to your Form 1040. Include the data from other W-2s you or your spouse received on this line. If the employer erroneously included your housing allowance in Box 1, Form W-2, deduct the designated housing allowance, show the net amount on line 7, and attach an explanatory schedule.

Line 8a: Include as taxable-interest income the total amount of what you earned on savings accounts, certificates of deposit, credit union accounts, corporate bonds and corporate bond mutual funds, U.S. treasuries and U.S. government mutual funds, and interest paid to you for a belated federal or state tax refund (whether or not you have received a Form 1099-INT). If you haven't yet received any of the statements due you, call the issuer to get them. If you received more than $1,500 of taxable interest income in 2002, you must also complete Schedule B.

> **Remember**
>
> For 2002, tax returns, most ministers will no longer have to file a separate schedule if you have interest or dividend income of $1,500 or less; only the totals need to be reported on Form 1040. The new IRS standard replaces the former reporting threshold of $400.

Line 8b: Here's where you note any tax-exempt interest from municipal bonds or municipal bond funds. Don't worry—that income is not taxable. But social security recipients must count all their tax-exempt interest when computing how much of their social security benefits will be taxable.

Line 9: Enter as dividend income only ordinary dividends, not capital-gains dividends paid by mutual funds, which are reported on Schedule D. Your Form 1099-DIV statements show the amount and type of ordinary dividends you received during 2002. If you received more than $1,500 in dividend income in 2002, you must also complete Schedule B. Remember: Earnings from a money-market mutual fund are considered dividend income, not interest income.

Line 10: If you received a refund of a state or local tax in 2002 that you deducted on Schedule A in a prior year, include the refund here.

Line 12: Even when you file as an employee for income tax purposes, you will probably have some honoraria or fee income from speaking engagements, weddings, funerals, and so on. This income, less related expenses (see page 23), should be reported on Schedule C or C-EZ and entered on this line.

> **Filing Tip**
>
> **Form 1040, Line 12.** The only ministerial income that should be reported on Line 12 is: fees from weddings, funerals, speaking engagements, and similar income. Unreimbursed expenses related to this income should be deducted on Schedule C or Schedule C-EZ.

Line 13: Enter capital-gains dividends here if you had no other capital gains or losses in 2002.

Line 15a: Report as IRA distributions even amounts you rolled over tax-free in 2002 from one IRA into another. On line 15b, you will report as taxable the amount of any IRA distributions that you did not roll over minus any return of nondeductible contributions.

Line 16a: It's likely that only a portion of the total pensions and annuities you received is taxable. Your Form 1099R will show the taxable amount, which you enter on line 16b. If you received pensions and annuities from a denominationally sponsored plan, you may be eligible to exclude a portion or all of these payments as a housing allowance.

Line 20a: No more than 85% of your social security benefits can be taxed for 2002 and none at all if your income is below $32,000 on a joint return, $25,000 for singles. If your income doesn't exceed the threshold, leave this line blank. If it does, use the worksheet on Form 1099-SSA to compute taxes on your benefits.

Line 21: If your cash housing allowance designated and paid by the employer exceeds the lowest of (1) reasonable compensation, (2) the amount used to provide a home from current ministerial income, (3) the amount properly designated by the employer, or (4) the fair rental value of the home including utilities and furnishings, enter the difference on line 21.

> **Filing Tip**
>
> **Form 1040, Line 21.** If the housing allowance designated by the employer exceeds the housing allowance exclusion to which you are entitled, you must include the difference on Line 21 with a description "Excess housing allowance." Your exclusion should be limited by the lower of the fair rental value of a minister-provided home or your actual housing expenses.

- **Adjustments to income (lines 23 to 35).**
  Line 23: A teacher, instructor, counselor, principal, or aide may deduct up to $250 of unreimbursed purchases of books and classroom supplies on this line (see pages 8-9).

Line 25: Interest paid on a qualifying student loan may be deducted on this line.

Line 26: On this line, you may claim a deduction of up to $3,000 for tuition and fees paid to an institution of higher learning for the taxpayer, the taxpayer's spouse, or the taxpayer's dependent.

Line 28: If your employer paid directly or reimbursed you for your qualified moving costs incurred in 2002, these amounts would not be included as compensation on your Form W-2. Therefore, you would have no moving expenses to deduct on line 28. However, if part or all of your moving costs were not paid directly or reimbursed, deduct these expenses here.

Line 29: One-half of your social security tax that is deductible for income tax purposes is reflected on this line.

> **Filing Tip**
>
> **Form 1040, Line 26.** The tuition and fees deduction line is new for 2002 tax returns. Prior to 2002, you could deduct education expenses on Schedule A if the education maintained or improved a skill required in your trade or business, or if it was a condition of continued employment. Those limitations do not apply to this new deduction. The deduction is limited to $3,000 for 2002.

Line 31: If you have self-employment income (for income tax purposes) from the church or from other sources, you can open and contribute to an SEP (Simplified Employee Pension) plan as late as the filing deadline including extensions—and still earn a 2002 write-off. Your SEP contributions top out at 15% of your gross self-employment earnings (see page 65). Keogh contributions are also shown on this line (see page 61).

Line 34: If you are employed as a chaplain or an other minister-employee of a nonreligious organization, use this line for your deduction of 403(b) contributions that you sent directly to the plan. On the dotted line next to line 34, enter the amount of your deduction and identify it as indicated.

- **Tax computation (lines 36 to 55). Line 38:** Claim the standard deduction only if the amount exceeds what you could write off in itemizing expenses on Schedule A. For 2002, the standard deduction is $7,850 joint, $6,900 head of household, and $4,700 single (that's up from $7,600, $6,650, and $4,550 last year). The amounts are higher if you or your spouse is 65 or older or legally blind.

Line 49: Taxpayers with adjusted gross income of $50,000 or less may claim a credit on this line equal to a certain percentage of the employee contributions made to a retirement account or IRA.

> **Filing Tip**
>
> **Form 1040, Line 49.** The retirement savings contributions credit is new for 2002. If you made contributions to a 403(b) or 401(k) plan, and your adjusted gross income was $50,000 or less, you may be eligible for this credit. The credit is also available for contributions to either a traditional or a Roth IRA. The excluded portion of minister's housing does not reduce this credit.

- **Other taxes (lines 56 to 61). Line 56:** If you are a qualified minister (see pages 26-33) and have not opted out of social security, you are self-employed for social security tax purposes. Your social security is not withheld by your church but is calculated on Schedule SE if you had net earnings of $400 or more and paid with Form 1040. The tax is 15.3% of the first $84,900 of 2002 self-employment income and 2.95% of income above $84,900. If your total wages and self-employment earnings were less than $84,900, you can probably save time and headaches by filing the Short Schedule SE on the front of the SE form.

Line 58: You will owe the tax on qualified plans plus the 10% penalty on the amount you withdrew from your IRA or another retirement plan if you were under 59½, unless you meet certain exceptions.

- **Payments (lines 62 to 69). Line 62:** Did you have a voluntary withholding arrangement whereby your employing church withheld federal income tax from your compensation? Then show the amount of federal income tax the church withheld (from your W-2) along with other federal income tax withholding from other employment of you or your spouse here. Also include tax withheld on your W-2G and other Forms 1099. The amount withheld should be shown in Box 2 of Form W-2G, in Box 6 of Form 1099-SSA, and Box 4 of other Forms 1099.

Line 63: Don't get confused: Even though you made your fourth-quarter 2002 estimated tax payment in January 2003, it's counted on your 2002 return.

Line 64: Enter your earned income tax credit here or let the IRS calculate it for you. If you have a qualifying child, you must complete Schedule EIC.

- **Refund or amount you owe (lines 70 to 74).** **Line 74:** The IRS assumes you must pay the estimated tax penalty if you owe $1,000 or more beyond what you've paid through withholding or estimated tax and the amount due is more than 10% of your 2002 tax bill. You may qualify for one of several exceptions, however. Use Form 2210 to prove your case.

> **Filing Tip**
>
> **Form 1040, Line 64.** Beginning with 2002 tax returns, the excluded housing allowance, the annual rental value of parsonages, and contributions by salary reduction to 403(b) annuity plans are not required to be included on Line 64. The inclusion of this data was required for pre-2002 tax returns and limited the earned income tax credit for many ministers and completely disqualified other ministers.

Schedule A (Itemized Deductions)

If you live in church-provided housing, you often cannot itemize. But run down Schedule A just to see whether you might have more write-offs than the standard deduction will permit.

- **Medical and dental expenses (lines 1 to 4).** Don't overlook the cost of getting to and from the doctor or druggist. Write off 13 cents a mile, plus the cost of parking. If you didn't drive, deduct your bus, train, or taxi fares. The cost of trips to see out-of-town specialists and as much as $50 a day for the cost of lodging when you're out of town to get medical care count toward the 7.5%. Include all your health insurance premiums, such as the $54 a month (2002 rate) Medicare Part B premiums.

- **Taxes you paid (lines 5 to 9).** Even though your real estate taxes are a housing expense excludable under the housing allowance, you may still deduct them (even for multiple properties if not deducted elsewhere on the return) on line 6 as an itemized deduction—one of the few "double deductions" allowed in the tax law.

- **Interest you paid (lines 10 to 14). Line 10:** If you bought a house during 2002, review your escrow or settlement papers for any mortgage interest you paid that was not shown on your lender's year-end statement. If you paid interest on a second mortgage or line of credit secured by your home, include the interest expense here.

  As with real estate taxes, it is possible to deduct

> **Filing Tip**
>
> **Schedule A, Lines 6, 10-12.** These lines relate to the most significant tax break available to ministers who own their own homes. Even though real estate taxes, mortgage interest, and points are excludable under the housing allowance, subject to certain limits, the same amounts are deductible as itemized deductions.

mortgage interest as an itemized deduction even if the interest is included in housing expenses subject to a housing allowance. Interest paid on a secured mortgage is deductible on Schedule A regardless of how the proceeds of the loan are used. However, the only mortgage interest properly includable as housing expense under a housing allowance is when the loan proceeds were used to provide housing. For example, interest on a second mortgage used to finance your child's college education is deductible on Schedule A but does not qualify as a housing expense for housing allowance purposes.

Don't overlook points you paid to get the mortgage. All of the points are generally deductible as interest here. Points paid for a refinancing must be amortized over the life of the loan. But you can deduct on your 2002 return the portion of all points paid that correspond with the percentage of your refinancing used for home improvements.

- **Gifts to charity (lines 15 to 18). Line 15:** For gifts you made in 2002, you must have written acknowledgments from the charity of any single gifts of $250 or more.

  Line 16. Deduct your charitable mileage for any volunteer work at the rate of 14 cents a mile.

- **Job expenses and other miscellaneous deductions (lines 20 to 27).** Don't assume you can't surmount the 2% AGI floor on these miscellaneous deductions. A wealth of employee business, investment, and tax-related expenses—from job-hunting costs to tax preparation fees—are deductible here. And if you bought business equipment required by your employer and you were not reimbursed, you can write off its entire cost in 2002, as much as $24,000. (However, see the allocation of expense rules, pages 121-22.)

> **Filing Tip**
>
> **Schedule A, Line 20.** Since the deduction for meal and entertainment expense is limited on Form 2106, expenses claimed on Lines 20 to 22 are reduced by 2% of your adjusted gross income, and the standard deduction may be advantageous for you, using an accountable expense reimbursement plan to reduce or eliminate unreimbursed expenses is generally a wise move.

Schedule C-EZ

Nearly every minister should file Schedule C or Schedule C-EZ. While a minister should receive Form W-2 for employment compensation and report the amount in Box 1 of Form W-2 on Form 1040, line 7, most ministers have some income from honoraria or fees related to weddings or funerals. Additionally, a minister may have speaking fees unrelated to the employer, product royalties, and other self-employment income reportable on Schedule C (C-EZ).

Only expenses related to the income reported on Schedule C (C-EZ) may be deducted on the form. For example, if a minister received honoraria of $500 for speaking at a church other than where employed, the $500 is reported on Schedule C (C-EZ) and the travel and other expenses related to the speaking engagement are deductible on the form. Expenses related to a minister's primary employment (compensation that was reported on Form W-2) must be deducted on Form 2106 and carried forward to Schedule A.

- **Gross receipts. Line 1:** Include income from honoraria, fees, product royalties and other income earned as an independent contractor.

- **Total expenses. Line 2:** Only include business expenses related to the income on Line 1.

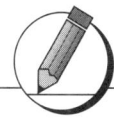

Filing Tip

Schedule C-EZ, Line 2. Only business expenses related to the income reported on Line 1 may be reported on Line 2. A minister's housing expenses are not deducted on this form (or generally any other form). Expenses related to employee compensation must be reported on Form 2106.

Form 2106-EZ

While the goal of every minister should be to minimize unreimbursed business, usually there are some unreimbursed expenses to file on Form 2106 or 2106-EZ. You may use Form 2106-EZ only if all of the following apply:

☐ You are an employee deducting expenses attributable to your job.

☐ You do not get reimbursed by your employer for any expenses (amounts your employer included in Box 1 of your Form W-2 are not considered reimbursement).

☐ If you are claiming vehicle expense, you are using the standard mileage rate for 2002.

- **Vehicle expense. Line 1:** Multiply your business miles by the 2002 standard business mileage rate of 36.5 cents per mile. Commuting miles to and from work are excluded, regardless of how many trips per days.

- **Parking fees, tolls, and transportation. Line 2:** Enter business-related parking fees, tolls, and transportation that did not involve overnight travel or commuting to and from work.

- **Travel expense while away from home overnight. Line 3:** Enter lodging and transportation expenses connected with overnight travel away from your tax home. You cannot deduct expenses for travel away from your tax home for any period of temporary employment of more than one year.

- **Business expenses not included on lines 1 through 3. Line 4:** Enter other job-related expenses not listed on any other line of this form. Include expenses for business gifts, education (tuition and books), trade publications, etc. If you are deducting depreciation or claiming a section 179 deduction on a cellular telephone or other similar telecommunications equipment, a home computer, etc., use Form 4562 to figure the depreciation and section 179 deduction to enter on line 4.

- **Meals and entertainment expenses. Line 5:** Generally, you may deduct only 50% of your business meal and entertainment expenses, including meals incurred while away from home on business.

The 1040 Challenge

Completing Form 1040 can be very challenging and take hours to complete. Although it may not seem entirely logical, the 1040 and its accompanying schedules will lead you through the process of figuring your income and deductions and computing your tax.

Exemptions reduce your income by letting you subtract a fixed amount of money for yourself, your spouse, and each of your dependents.

Total Income includes:
Compensation from the church paid to you as a minister-employee for income tax purposes shown on Form W-2.
Net earnings from Schedule C (C-EZ) for income from speaking engagements, marriages, and funerals (Schedule C will include all ministerial income and expenses if you are reporting as self-employed for income tax purposes).

Adjustments

Adjusted Gross Income (AGI)

Line 26 is new line for 2002. Use this line to claim a deduction for certain college costs (see page 6 for more information).

The 1040 Challenge

Line 49 is new line for 2002. Use this line to claim a credit on certain payments to retirement accounts or an IRA (see pages 7-8 for more information).

The 1040 Challenge

Schedule A

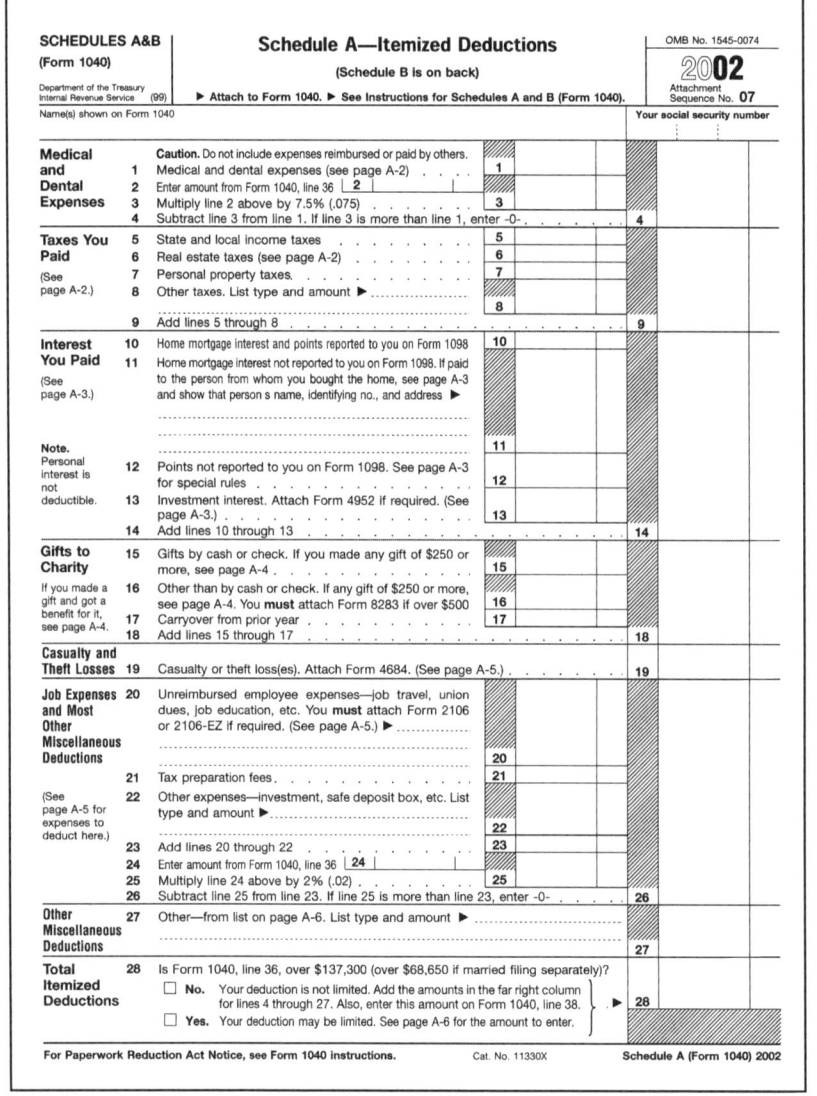

The 1040 Challenge

Schedule C-EZ

The 1040 Challenge

Form 2106-EZ

CHAPTER ONE

Taxes for Ministers

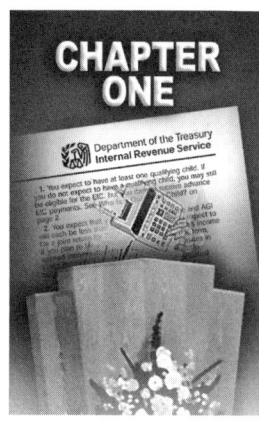

In This Chapter

- Ministers serving local churches
- Evangelists and missionaries
- Members of religious orders
- Ministers in denominational service, administrative, and teaching positions
- Individuals not qualifying for ministerial tax treatment
- Social security status of ministers
- Income tax status of ministers
- Importance of the employee vs. self-employed decision
- Forms and schedules for the minister
- Recommended filing status

Understanding how the various parts of the tax law fit together and apply to ministers is your primary challenge. With the big picture in mind, you can plan your tax liability instead of just letting it happen.

The key to understanding the federal tax system for ministers is to focus on tax rules that primarily benefit ministers (such as the housing allowance) and other provisions that are available to most individual taxpayers (like tax-free or tax-deferred fringe benefits).

There are several special tax provisions for ministers:

➤ Exclusion for income tax purposes of the housing allowance and the fair rental value of a church-owned parsonage provided rent-free to clergy;

➤ For social security tax purposes, treatment of all clergy as self-employed as it relates to income from ministerial services;

➤ Exemption of clergy from self-employment social security tax under very limited circumstances;

Remember

There is some flexibility in applying certain ministerial tax provisions. For example, a minister is exempt from mandatory income tax withholding but can enter into a voluntary income tax withholding arrangement. However, if a minister qualifies for the housing allowance, he or she is subject to self-employment social security tax (using Schedule SE), not FICA—this is not an option.

25

- ▶ Exemption of clergy compensation from mandatory income tax withholding;
- ▶ Eligibility for a voluntary income tax withholding arrangement between the minister-employee and the church;
- ▶ Potential "double deduction" of mortgage interest and real estate taxes as itemized deductions and as housing expenses for housing allowance purposes for ministers living in minister-provided housing.

The six special tax provisions listed above apply only to individuals who

- ▶ qualify as ministers of the gospel under federal tax rules, and
- ▶ are performing services that qualify in the exercise of ministry under federal tax rules.

Ministers Serving Local Churches

You may believe you are a minister, your employer may consider you a minister, your denomination may classify you as a minister, your parachurch employer may consider you a minister, but what does the IRS consider you? For tax purposes, the opinion of the IRS is the one that counts. But even the IRS does not consistently apply the same rules in determining who is a minister in a local church setting.

Deciding whether you are a minister for tax purposes is very important. It determines how you prepare your tax return for income and social security tax purposes. A qualified minister is eligible for the housing allowance. This alone can exclude thousands of dollars from income taxation. Ministers calculate social security tax on Schedule SE and pay the tax with Form 1040. Nonministers have one-half of their social security tax withheld from salary payments, and the employer pays the other half.

How can I tell whether the IRS will treat me as a minister?

If you are ordained, commissioned, or licensed, four tests are applied by the IRS to determine whether you are a minister. You

- ▶ administer sacraments (such as performing marriage and funeral services, dedicating infants, baptizing, and serving communion),
- ▶ are considered to be a religious leader by your church,
- ▶ conduct religious worship, and
- ▶ have management responsibility in the control, conduct, or maintenance of your church.

Warning

Individuals serving local churches must meet certain tests to qualify as a minister in the eyes of the IRS. The individual must always be ordained, licensed, or commissioned.

Based on guidelines issued by the IRS in 1995 related to their "Market Segment

Specialization Program" (MSSP), some of the four tests, but not necessarily all, must be met in determining ministerial status. This flexible approach will be beneficial to many ministers as some youth pastors and ministers of music, education, or administration will not meet all four tests.

Some individuals who have been ordained, licensed, or commissioned still may not qualify for ministerial tax status. The MSSP guidelines state that the duties performed by the individual are also important to the determination whether he or she is a duly ordained, commissioned, or licensed minister. Because religious disciplines vary in their formal procedures for these designations, whether an individual is duly ordained, licensed, or commissioned depends on a number of factors.

There is no requirement that you must be qualified to perform and actually perform every sacrament or rite of your religion. If you are qualified to perform certain sacraments and actually perform or could perform some of the sacraments on occasion, you will generally meet this test. A similar test applies to conducting religious worship and providing management services. If you currently conduct religious worship and provide management services, have done it in the past, or could do it in the future, the test will generally be met.

> **Caution**
>
> Determination of ministerial status is far from a precise matter. There has been considerable inconsistency in the position of the IRS and Tax Court on this issue across the years. Only a review of all the pertinent facts and circumstances for a particular minister will assist in determining whether an individual will qualify for ministerial tax status.

Job titles have little significance for tax purposes. A licensed, commissioned, or ordained minister may have a job title that implies a ministry function. However, the actual responsibilities of the position will determine if the four-factor test is met. Ministers performing services of a routine nature, such as those performed by secretaries, clerks, and janitors, generally do not qualify as ministers for tax purposes.

If your local church or parachurch organization ordains, licenses, or commissions ministers, it is very important that certain guidelines are followed. These issues are addressed in the 2003 edition of *The Zondervan Church and Nonprofit Tax & Financial Guide*.

What about licensed or commissioned ministers?

Some religious groups ordain, license, and commission ministers. Other groups only ordain, only commission, or only license and ordain ministers or provide some other combination of the three types of special recognition of ministers.

Will you be treated as a minister by the IRS if you are only licensed or commissioned? Perhaps. Your status with the IRS will depend on all the facts and circumstances, e.g., the validity of the licensing or commissioning process, and the extent to which you administer the sacraments, are considered to be a religious leader by your church, conduct worship services, and have management responsibility in the control, conduct, and maintenance of your church.

> **Example:** Rev. Smith is an ordained minister who serves as a minister of counseling at his church. He does not preach or conduct worship services and never administers sacraments. He has management responsibility for the operation of a counseling center in the local church. He occasionally makes hospital visits. While he qualifies under the "control, conduct, and maintenance of the church" test, he does not administer sacraments or conduct worship services. With professional advice, the church must decide whether he qualifies as a minister for tax purposes.

Evangelists and Missionaries

The qualifications for itinerant evangelists for the special ministerial tax provisions are generally the same as for ministers serving local churches.

Most evangelists are self-employed both for income tax and self-employment social security tax purposes. The only exception is the evangelist who has formed a corporation and is an employee of the corporation. In this instance, the evangelist is an employee for income tax purposes but remains self-employed for social security tax purposes.

Missionaries are also subject to the same rules to qualify for ministerial status for tax purposes (see pages 26-27). Qualifying for benefits such as a housing allowance is often not so important for a minister-missionary because of the foreign earned income exclusion. However, the determination of ministerial tax status is vitally important to determine if the minister is subject to social security as an employee or self-employed. The foreign earned income exclusion affects income tax but not social security tax.

Members of Religious Orders

Members of religious orders qualify for certain tax provisions afforded to ministers. The IRS has developed stringent characteristics to determine whether an organization is a religious order. They are as follows:

▶ The organization is described in section 501(c)(3) of the Internal Revenue Code.

▶ The members of the organization, after successful completion of the organization's training program and probationary period, make a long-term commitment to the organization (normally more than two years).

▶ The organization is, directly or indirectly, under the control and supervision of a church or convention or association of churches or is significantly funded by such an entity.

▶ The members of the organization normally live together as part of a community and are held to a significantly stricter level of moral and spiritual discipline than that required of church lay members.

Special Tax Provisions	Application to Religious Order Members
• Exemption of members from self-employment social security tax in very limited circumstances.	• The rules apply to religious order members and to clergy.
• Treatment of members (who do not elect social security exemption) as self-employed for social security tax purposes for income from the religious order.	• The rules apply to religious order members and to clergy.
• Exemption of member compensation from mandatory income tax withholding.	• The rules apply to religious order members and to clergy.
• Eligibility for a voluntary income tax withholding arrangement between the member-employee and the religious order.	• The rules apply to religious order members and to clergy.
• Exclusion for income tax purposes of the housing allowance and the fair rental value of religious-order-owned housing provided rent-free to a member.	• If a member is required to live on the immediate premises of the order "for the convenience of the employer," the rental value of the housing is generally tax-free for income tax purposes. If a member does not live on the immediate premises of the order, the following guidelines generally apply: **Lay members.** The rental value of religious-order-provided housing or a housing allowance is generally subject to income tax. **Ordained, licensed, or commissioned members.** If the religious order is a church or an integral agency of a church or a church denomination, the rental value of religious-order-provided housing or a housing allowance is generally tax-free for income tax purposes. If the religious order is not a church, an integral agency of a church, or a church denomination, the rental value of religious-order-provided housing or a housing allowance is generally tax-free for income tax purposes only if the work performed by the member includes sacerdotal functions.

- The members of the organization work or serve full-time on behalf of the religious, educational, or charitable goals of the organization.
- The members of the organization participate regularly in activities such as public or private prayer, religious study, teaching, care of the aging, missionary work, or church reform or renewal.

Housing for members of religious orders generally falls into the following categories:

- Housing provided by the religious order on its premises and the member is required to live in the housing.
- Other housing.
    - The member is allowed to live in religious-order-provided housing that is not located on the immediate premises of the religious order.
    - The member is allowed to live in housing other than housing provided by the religious order (i.e., housing provided by the member).

> **Warning**
>
> There are two types of members of religious orders:
> 1. members who are ordained, licensed, or commissioned by a church that is separate from the religious order, or by the religious order, if authorized by its organizing documents; and
> 2. lay members who are not ordained, licensed, or commissioned.

Ministers in Denominational Service, Administrative, and Teaching Positions

Ordained, commissioned, or licensed ministers not serving local churches may qualify as "ministers" for federal tax purposes in the following situations:

Denominational service

This category encompasses the administration of religious denominations and their integral agencies, including teaching or administration in parochial schools, colleges, or universities that are under the authority of a church or denomination.

The IRS uses the following criteria to determine if an institution is an integral agency of a church:

- Did the church incorporate the institution?
- Does the corporate name of the institution suggest a church relationship?
- Does the church continuously control, manage, and maintain the institution?
- If dissolved, will the assets be turned over to the church?

- ▶ Are the trustees or directors of the institution appointed by, or must they be approved by, the church and may they be removed by the church?
- ▶ Are annual reports of finances and general operations required to be made to the church?
- ▶ Does the church contribute to the support of the institution?

Assignment by a church

Services performed by a minister for a parachurch organization based upon a substantive assignment or designation by a church may provide the basis for ministerial tax treatment. The housing allowance should be designated by the employing organization, not the assigning church.

The following characteristics must be present for an effective assignment:

- ▶ There must be sufficient relationship between the minister and the assigning church to justify the assignment of the minister.
- ▶ There must be an adequate relationship between the assigning church and the parachurch organization to which the minister is assigned to justify the assignment.

To substantiate the relationship between the minister and the church, the church must determine "if there is sufficient authority, power, or legitimacy for the church to assign this particular minister." Such matters as being the ordaining church, providing ongoing supervision, denominational affiliation, contributing significant financial support, or being the long-term "home church" would all appear to support this relationship.

In addressing the relationship between the church and the parachurch organization, the church must answer the question of "why should the church assign a minister to this particular ministry?" Essentially, the assignment of the minister must accomplish the church's ministry purposes.

Caution

Too often, a denomination lists a minister as being assigned to a parachurch ministry, for example, in an annual directory and the minister believes he or she has been assigned for tax purposes. But effective assignments are rare because of the substantive relationship and ongoing documentation of the assignment that are needed.

In considering an assignment, it is important to distinguish between the *process* of assigning and the *documentation* of the assignment. The process of assigning expresses the church's theology, philosophy, and policy of operation: its way of doing ministry. The documentation of the assignment provides evidence that the church is doing ministry through the particular individual assigned. The keys to a proper assignment are:

- ▶ A written policy describing the specific requirements for the relationship of the church both to the minister being assigned and to the parachurch organization to which the minister is assigned. This would include the church's theological and policy goals for the assignment.

▶ A formal review to confirm that the minister and the proposed ministry with a parachurch organization qualify.

▶ A written assignment coupled with guidelines for supervision of and reporting by the minister and the parachurch organization to the church.

▶ A periodic (at least annual) formal review of the minister's activities to confirm that the assignment continues to comply with the policy.

A sample assignment letter is included in the 2003 edition of *The Zondervan Church and Nonprofit Tax & Financial Guide*.

Other service

If you are not engaged in service performed in the exercise of ministry of a local church or an integral agency of a church or a church does not assign your services, the definition of a qualifying minister becomes much narrower. Tax law and regulations provide little guidance for ministers in this category. However, Tax Court cases and IRS rulings suggest that an individual will qualify for the special tax treatments of a minister only if the individual's services for the employer substantially involve conducting religious worship or performing sacerdotal functions. This definition might include conducting Bible studies, spiritual and pastoral counseling, conducting crusades, producing religious television and radio broadcasts, and publishing religious literature.

In one important case, the Tax Court ruled that a minister fulfilled his ministry through his parachurch organization by producing missions tapes for local congregations. Testimony in this case indicated an ordained minister who "seeks to proclaim the gospel in any fashion to any person or groups of persons, or who provides church-related services to congregations" is functioning as a minister.

> **Caution**
>
> Many ministers are serving organizations other than local churches, integral agencies of churches and do not have an effective assignment by a church. The employer may be a rescue mission, a youth ministry, Christian radio or TV station, or a missionary-sending organization. Qualifying for ministerial status is based on the degree to which the individual is performing sacerdotal functions or conducting religious worship.

How much time constitutes substantial involvement in conducting worship or administering the sacraments? This is difficult to say. However, in two IRS letter rulings, the IRS determined that 5% of the minister's working hours were not sufficient to qualify for tax treatment as a minister.

What if you are a minister employed by an organization that is not a church, integral agency of a church or other religious organization? If you are an ordained, licensed, or commissioned minister conducting religious worship or performing sacerdotal functions to a substantial extent for your employer, you may qualify as a minister for tax purposes.

Based on IRS rulings, it is clear that ministers serving as chaplains in government-owned-and-operated hospitals or in state prisons fall in a special category. They are employees for social security (FICA) purposes but qualify for the housing allowance. If they have opted out of social security by filing Form 4361, the exemption does not apply to this employment.

Individuals Not Qualifying for Ministerial Tax Treatment

You do not qualify as a "minister" for federal income tax purposes if you are

- a theological student who does not otherwise qualify as a minister,
- an unordained, uncommissioned, or unlicensed church official,
- an ordained, commissioned, or licensed minister working as an administrator or on the faculty of a nonchurch-related college or seminary,
- an ordained, commissioned, or licensed minister working as an executive of a nonreligious, nonchurch-related organization,
- a civilian chaplain at a VA hospital (the tax treatment of ministers who are chaplains in the armed forces is the same as for other members of the armed forces), and
- an ordained, licensed, or commissioned minister employed by a parachurch organization but who does not meet the sacerdotal function or conducting religious worship tests.

Social Security Status of Ministers

Ministers engaged in the exercise of ministry are always treated as self-employed for social security purposes. This is true whether you are an employee of your church or self-employed for income tax purposes.

Ministers pay social security under the Self-Employment Contributions Act (SECA) instead of under the Federal Insurance Contributions Act (FICA). If you are a qualified minister, you should never have FICA-type social security tax withheld from your pay. It is possible to become exempt from SECA if you meet strict exemption requirements (see pages 130-33).

Your earnings that are not from the exercise of ministry are generally subject to social security tax under FICA or SECA as applied to all workers.

Caution

Social security is one of the most confusing issues for many ministers. FICA-type social security never applies to an individual who qualifies as a minister for tax purposes. Stated another way, if a housing allowance has been designated for you, FICA tax should not be deducted from your pay—you are responsible to determine your social security tax by completing Schedule SE each year.

Income Tax Status of Ministers

Are ministers employees or self-employed (independent contractors) for income tax purposes? The IRS considers virtually all ministers to be employees for income tax purposes. The income tax filing decision has many ramifications for what and how a church and the minister reports to the IRS.

Employees report their compensation on Form 1040, line 7. Self-employed individuals report compensation on Schedule C or C-EZ. Employees receive Form W-2 each year, while Form 1099-MISC is used to report compensation received by a self-employed individual. (Also see pages 36 and 38 for the employee vs. self-employed impact on the taxability of certain fringe benefits.)

Employees deduct unreimbursed business expenses, and expenses reimbursed under a nonaccountable plan, on Form 2106 (2106-EZ) with the amount carried forward to Schedule A as an itemized deduction. The expense is subject to a 2% of adjusted gross income limitation, and only 50% of business meals and entertainment expenses may be included. Self-employed individuals deduct expenses on Schedule C or C-EZ whether or not they are eligible to itemize deductions. Expenses are not subject to the 2% of adjusted gross income limitation, but the 50% of business meals and entertainment limit still applies. Whether expenses are deducted on Schedule A, Schedule C or C-EZ, they are subject to the allocation rules explained on pages 121-22.

The IRS applies a common-law test to ministers (and nonministers) to determine whether they are employees or self-employed for income tax purposes. Ministers are generally considered employees for income tax purposes if they

- must follow the church's work instructions;
- receive on-the-job training;
- provide services that must be rendered personally;
- provide services that are integral to the church;
- hire, supervise, and pay assistants for the church;
- have an ongoing work relationship with the church;
- must follow set hours of work;
- work full-time for the church;
- work on the church's premises;
- must do their work in a church-determined sequence;
- receive business expense reimbursements;

Key Issue

The defining court case on the topic of income tax status for ministers was a case in which a Methodist minister (Weber) took the position he was self-employed for income tax purposes. The Tax Court held that he was an employee for income tax purposes. The decision was elevated when a federal appeals court upheld the decision.

- receive routine payments of regular amounts;
- need the church to furnish tools and materials;
- don't have a major investment in job facilities;
- cannot suffer a loss from their services;
- work for one church at a time;
- do not offer their services to the general public;
- can be fired by the church;
- may quit work at any time without penalty.

Caution

With rare exceptions, ministers should receive Form W-2 from their church or other employer. Few ministers qualify as an independent contractor for income tax purposes (even though considered self-employed for social security tax purposes). A church or other employer generally has sufficient control over the minister to qualify for W-2 treatment.

Some of the above factors are often given greater weight than others. Generally a minister is an employee if the church has the legal right to control both what and how work is done, even if the minister has considerable discretion and freedom of action. The threshold level of control necessary to find employee status is generally lower when applied to professional services than when applied to nonprofessional services.

The most recent Tax Court cases have adopted the following seven-factor test to determine if you are an employee or self-employed for income tax purposes:

- How much control does the church exercise over your work?
    - ☐ Do you have the authority to establish your own church?
    - ☐ Are you required to give an account of your pastoral ministries to an annual convention or conference at a district, state, or regional level?
    - ☐ Are you amenable to a local church board?
- Does the church or the minister invest in the facilities used in the work?
    - ☐ Who provides the church facilities?
    - ☐ Who provides an office, equipment, library, and so on?
- Does the minister have the opportunity for profit or loss?
    - ☐ Is the minister paid a fixed salary?
- Does the church have the right to discharge the minister?
    - ☐ Can the minister be removed if the church believes the minister is unacceptable?
- Is the work performed by the minister a part of the regular business of the church?
    - ☐ Is the work of the minister an integral part of the work of the church?
- How permanent is the relationship between the church and the minister?
    - ☐ Does the minister offer his or her services to the general public as would an independent contractor?

- Does the church provide retirement benefits (such as contributions to a pension plan) for the minister?

➤ What relationship does the church and the minister believe they have created?

- Does the church withhold federal income tax from the minister's salary and provide Form W-2?

- Does the church provide the minister with a home or a cash housing allowance to provide his or her own home?

Based on this seven-factor test, most ministers serving local congregations will be determined by the IRS to be employees for income tax purposes.

Importance of the Employee vs. Self-Employed Decision

Determining if you are an employee or self-employed for income tax purposes will resolve several other tax-related issues:

➤ Minister-employees must be given Form W-2 and report their compensation on page 1 of Form 1040. They are eligible to claim unreimbursed business expenses and expenses reimbursed under a nonaccountable plan on Schedule A (non-accountable plan reimbursements must be included in compensation on Form W-2). If you itemize deductions, business and professional expenses are deductible only to the extent that such expenses exceed 2% of adjusted gross income (AGI). Deductible business meals and entertainment expenses are limited to 50%.

Key Issue

It is vital for churches and other employers to treat ministers as employees (Form W-2) for income tax purposes in nearly every instance. If the minister is not considered an employee for income tax purposes, it jeopardizes the tax-free treatment of fringe benefits like health, accident and long-term care insurance premiums, group-term life premiums, and certain other fringe benefits.

Ministers who are self-employed for income tax purposes receive a Form 1099-MISC and report compensation and business expenses on Schedule C or C-EZ. Business expenses are deductible regardless of itemized deductions and are not subject to the 2%-of-AGI floor. The 50% limitation on business meals and entertainment applies to expenses claimed on Schedule C or C-EZ.

➤ Health, accident, and long-term care insurance premiums paid directly by an employer or reimbursed by an employer, after the minister provides substantiation, are not reportable as income to the minister-employee but must be reported as taxable income to the self-employed minister.

Minister-employees may deduct health, accident, and long-term care insurance

CHAPTER 1 ▶ TAXES FOR MINISTERS

Forms and Schedules for the Minister

You may need to file a variety of other forms in addition to the 1040. Here are some of the forms ministers typically need to file.

Form 2106 or 2106-EZ is filed with Schedule A to document your unreimbursed business expenses for ministers reporting as employees for income tax purposes.

Schedule A lists the itemized deductions you can take. You may deduct home mortgage interest and property taxes even though the same expenses are used to justify your housing allowance.

Schedule SE is used to calculate the social security and Medicare tax on your ministerial income. Be sure to include your housing allowance or fair rental value of a church-provided parsonage on this schedule.

Schedule B reports interest and dividend income. You should have received Form 1099 for each item you include.

Schedule EIC is used to calculate your earned income credit.

Schedule C or C-EZ is completed by nearly every minister. Income from speaking engagements, marriage and funeral fees, and related expenses go on this form. If you are reporting as a self-employed minister for income tax purposes, all of your ministerial income and expenses are reported here.

Schedule D reports capital gains and losses on securities and real estate transactions.

Schedule E is used to report your income from rents, royalties, partnerships, estates, trusts, and other sources.

37

premiums paid personally, and not reimbursed by the church, on Schedule A as a medical and dental expense, subject to a 7.5% limitation of adjusted gross income.

▶ Health reimbursement arrangements (see pages 10-12) are only available to those ministers who are employees for income tax purposes.

▶ Group-term life insurance, provided by an employer, of $50,000 or less is tax-free to employees but represents taxable income for the self-employed.

▶ A voluntary arrangement to withhold income tax may be used by a minister-employee but may not be used by the self-employed.

Recommended Filing Status

Most local church ministers qualify as employees for income tax purposes. It is wise to file as an employee for income tax purposes unless you can clearly demonstrate that you qualify for self-employed status. Few ministers can sufficiently substantiate filing as other than an employee for income tax purposes.

Churches must provide a Form W-2 to ministers it considers to be employees. Yet the minister may take an exception to the reporting of the church. For example, if the church gives the minister a Form 1099-MISC or provides no Form W-2, the minister may report as an employee on line 7, page 1, Form 1040 and attach a statement to explain that the church did not provide a W-2.

Even though the minister might take an exception to the reporting of the church, the church still has a responsibility under the law to determine the proper filing method and proceed accordingly.

 **Action Steps**

- Determine if the special tax provisions for ministers are applicable to you.
- Determine whether the church considers you an employee or self-employed for income tax purposes. The IRS considers almost all ministers to be employees.
- If you qualify as a minister, pay your social security tax (SECA) based on the annual completion of Schedule SE. The church should never withhold FICA tax from your pay.
- If you are a qualified minister, request that an appropriate amount be designated as a parsonage or housing allowance whether you provide your own housing or live in church-provided housing.

Chapter Two
Compensation Planning

In This Chapter

- Determine the current compensation
- Plan your compensation
- Use fringe benefits wisely
- Use accountable expense reimbursements

Pastoral compensation reached a new high last year according to the Barna Research Group, with the median compensation of just over $40,000. The study reported that the average pastoral compensation package represents just less than one-third (31%) of the median annual operating budget for Protestant churches.

The survey indicated that certain types of pastors receive larger compensation packages than do others. Education makes a substantial difference in compensation: seminary graduates receive an average of 38% more compensation than do senior pastors who did not graduate from a seminary. Pastoral experience makes a difference, too, but not until a pastor enters his or her second decade of ministry.

One of the largest gaps is that which distinguishes pastors in urban and suburban churches from those in rural congregations. Pastors of urban and suburban churches average about one-third more each year than do their rural peers. Packages given to pastors vary significantly according to the size of the church. Pastors of churches that attract 100 to 250 adults get 50% more than churches that have an average of less than 100 adults in attendance.

> **Key Issue**
>
> If a church does not increase the pastor's pay each year, it has reduced the pay. Inflation is in single digits, but it is still there, even at about three or four percent. It does cost more each year to live. And just as laypersons expect their employer to provide them with a cost-of-living pay increase each year, a pastor should expect the same.

Even with pastoral salaries higher than ever before, the amounts are unreasonably low. For example, recent Census Bureau studies reported higher salary levels for other well-educated professionals such as corporate executives and managers (38% higher than the pastoral average), management consultants (46% higher), and public school administrators (88% higher). Plus, the Census Bureau data only includes salary but the Barna study included the value of the entire compensation package: salary, fringe benefits, and expense reimbursements.

When taking time to compare apples to apples, the tragic truth is that pastors are paid far below reasonable levels. This is true across the U.S., across denominational lines, in independent churches, in rural and suburban areas.

Most church members in the U.S. do not know what the true compensation of their pastor really is. Even when a church financial report is presented, the data is mangled to such a degree that there typically is no clear communication of salary as contrasted with fringe benefits and expense reimbursements. Too often, all of these expense elements are added together so the appearance is that the pastor is making much more than he or she really is.

Key Issue

In trying to determine which pastor has the best pay plan, one pastor often compares notes with another pastor by asking: "How much does your church pay you per week?" But this data doesn't begin to tell which pay plan is better. Determining what a minister is really paid is a challenging task but worth the effort.

Determine the Current Compensation

Ask a pastor how much he or she is paid and the response will often be: "My check from the church is $500 a week." But that tells us very little. Let's look at a few examples:

Example 1: Churches A and B pay their pastors cash salary of $40,000 and $45,000, respectively, for the year. A parsonage is not provided in either instance. Which minister has the best salary and are they compensated adequately? We do not have enough information to answer either question.

Since $45,000 is more than $40,000, why isn't the $45,000 salary the best? The cost of living may be enough higher in the Church B community and lower in the Church A community that the pastor at Church A may be able to buy more with his cash salary than the pastor at Church B.

Example 2: Pastor A receives cash salary of $45,000 but the church does not directly pay or reimburse his health insurance premiums of

Idea

Start by documenting the minister's pay. Use the worksheet on page 42. This exercise will reveal how well your employer has provided for fringe benefits and expense reimbursements. And it will show the gross pay (including housing allowance or parsonage value) that can be evaluated for adequacy.

CHAPTER 2 ➤ COMPENSATION PLANNING

Reporting Ministerial Compensation

Common reporting practice to avoid

	Church-Provided Housing	Minister-Provided Housing
Pastor's cash salary	$ 20,000	$ 30,000
Parsonage utilities	3,000	
Pension	1,000	1,000
Social security reimbursement	4,000	4,000
Health, disability, and group life insurance	8,000	8,000
Professional expense reimbursements	5,000	5,000
	$ 41,000	$ 48,000

Better reporting approach

Salary and equivalent compensation		
Cash salary	$ 20,000	$ 30,000
Fair rental value of parsonage provided	9,000	
Social security reimbursement (in excess of 50% of total social security)	2,000	2,000
	$ 31,000	$ 32,000
Fringe benefits		
Pension	1,000	1,000
Social security reimbursement (up to 50% of total social security)	2,000	2,000
Health, disability, and group life insurance	8,000	8,000
	$ 11,000	$ 11,000
Professional expense reimbursements	$ 5,000	$ 5,000

Confusion over how much the pastor is paid all starts with the church's financial reporting approach. In reporting to the congregation, many churches include the pastor's expense reimbursements and fringe benefits in the same section of the report with cash salary. In these examples, the common reporting practice makes it appear the pastor is being paid $41,000 or $48,000, depending on church-provided or minister-provided housing. Actually, the compensation is only $31,000 or $32,000 respectively. Use the worksheet on page 42 to determine what and how you are paid.

$10,000. Pastor B receives cash salary of $35,000 but the church directly pays his $10,000 health insurance premiums. Which pastor has the better compensation plan based on just these factors?

Minister's Compensation Worksheet

		This Year	Next Year

Salary and Equivalent Compensation:
- A. Cash salary, less designated housing/furnishings allowance $_____ $_____
- B. If parsonage owned by church, fair rental value including utilities and any housing/furnishings allowance _____ _____
- C. If parsonage not owned by church, cash housing allowance provided (plus utilities, maintenance, or any other housing expenses paid directly by church) _____ _____
- D. Tax-deferred payments (TSA/403[b], 401[k], IRA) _____ _____
- E. Cash bonus _____ _____
- F. Social security reimbursement (in excess of 50% of SECA) _____ _____
- G. Other _____ _____
- **Total Salary** $_____ $_____

Fringe Benefits:
- A. Denominational pension fund $_____ $_____
- B. Social security reimbursement (up to 50% of SECA) _____ _____
- C. Health reimbursement arrangement _____ _____
- D. Insurance premiums paid or reimbursed by church
    1. Health _____ _____
    2. Disability _____ _____
    3. Long-term care _____ _____
    4. Group-term life _____ _____
    5. Dental/vision _____ _____
    6. Professional liability _____ _____
    7. Malpractice _____ _____
- E. Other _____ _____
- **Total Fringe Benefits** $_____ $_____

Professional Expense Reimbursements:
(limited to ordinary, necessary, and actual expenses)
- A. Auto/travel $_____ $_____
- B. Books/subscriptions/tapes _____ _____
- C. Continuing education _____ _____
- D. Conventions/conferences _____ _____
- E. Professional dues _____ _____
- F. Church-related entertainment _____ _____
- G. Child care _____ _____
- H. Other _____ _____
- **Total Professional Expense Reimbursements** $_____ $_____

Tax-deferred payments are shown under the salary category on this form. This presentation seems to be appropriate because it is often an option of the minister to receive the funds as salary or have them paid into a deferred plan.

Pastor B has the best plan in nearly every instance. Why? Health insurance premiums paid by a pastor have absolutely no tax value to a minister who uses the standard deduction, as does nearly every pastor who lives in church-provided housing. And even ministers who do itemize their deductions on Schedule A only receive tax benefits from the premiums when their medical expenses, including health insurance, are greater than 7.5% of their adjusted gross income.

Example 3: Is it better stewardship for a church to pay its pastor cash salary of $40,000 and provide a professional expense allowance (nonaccountable plan) of $8,000 or pay its pastor cash salary of $40,000 and reimburse up to $8,000 of professional expenses under an accountable plan?

The church is going to spend the same amount of money either way: $48,000. But the pastor will almost always have less money in his or her pocket at the end of the year with the nonaccountable plan. Why? Because the $8,000 of professional expense allowance under a nonaccountable plan must be added to the pastor's Form W-2 as taxable compensation (see chapter 6 for more information on accountable and nonaccountable plans).

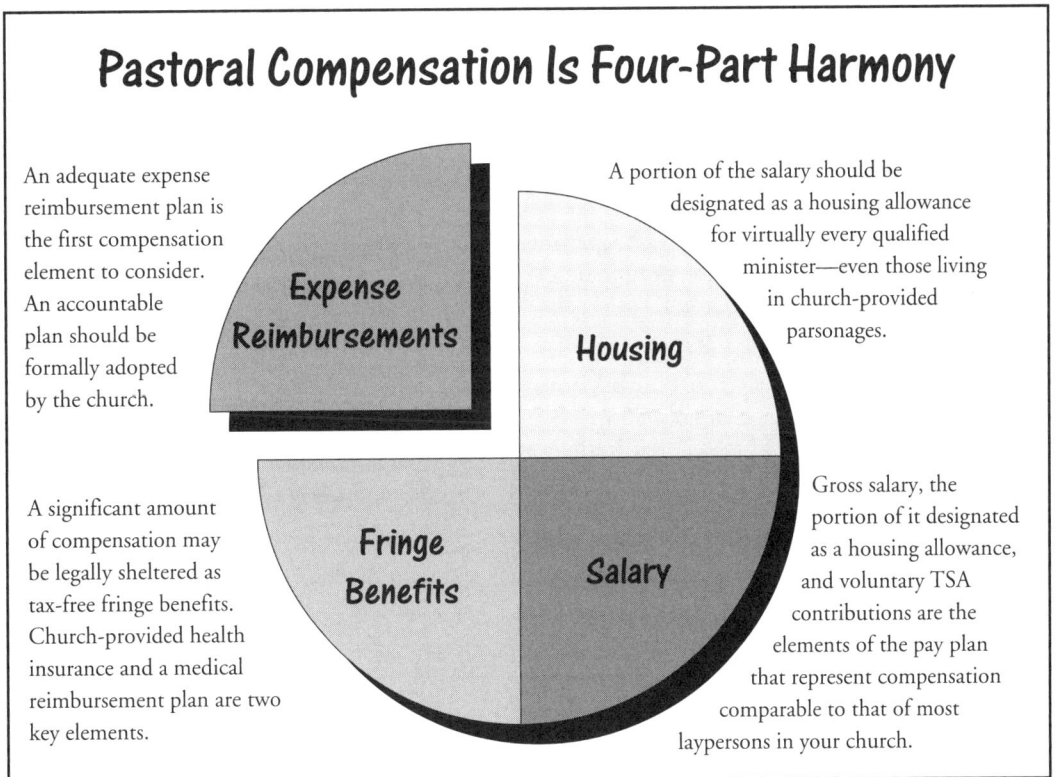

Pastoral Compensation Is Four-Part Harmony

An adequate expense reimbursement plan is the first compensation element to consider. An accountable plan should be formally adopted by the church.

Expense Reimbursements

A portion of the salary should be designated as a housing allowance for virtually every qualified minister—even those living in church-provided parsonages.

Housing

A significant amount of compensation may be legally sheltered as tax-free fringe benefits. Church-provided health insurance and a medical reimbursement plan are two key elements.

Fringe Benefits

Salary

Gross salary, the portion of it designated as a housing allowance, and voluntary TSA contributions are the elements of the pay plan that represent compensation comparable to that of most laypersons in your church.

Then, the pastor must deduct the expenses not reimbursed under an accountable plan. If the pastor could not itemize his deductions before considering this $8,000 of unreimbursed expenses, there will be deductions lost just to get up to the itemized deduction level. And even if the minister was already beyond the itemizing threshold for the year, only 50% of meals and entertainment are deductible (versus 100% eligible for reimbursement) and the first 2% times adjusted gross income of miscellaneous expenses are not deductible.

Plan the Compensation Package

The participation of the pastor with an individual or a small group for compensation discussions is crucial. The entire congregation may ultimately approve the annual budget that includes pastoral pay, benefits, and reimbursements. But the pay package needs to be carefully developed before it reaches the congregational approval stage. Even the entire church board is too large a forum for the initial compensation discussions.

An annual review of a pastor's pay is vital. The pastor should know exactly what to expect from the congregation during the coming year. It is inexcusable to wait until the new church year begins or later to decide the new pay plan for the pastor.

Late in 2002 is a good time for the committee responsible for recommending compensation matters to get busy to put a plan together for the new church year that might begin in early to mid-2003. A representative or a small committee from the church board should meet with the pastor, talk about pay expectations, review past pay patterns, discuss the tax consequences of compensation components, then make recommendations to the appropriate body.

The church board should act on the recommendations by March for a fiscal year beginning in mid-2003. Then the compensation package may be included in the congregational budget for the next year. The detail elements of the pay plan, while fully disclosed to the church board, are often summarized for presentation to the congregation.

> **Remember**
>
> All of the elements of a minister's compensation plan should be annually evaluated. A thorough evaluation is much more than just tacking on an inflationary increase to gross pay. If the gross pay was inadequate before the increase, it is still too low after the inflationary increase.

Consider goals and objectives

Does your church have goals and objectives for the church? Perhaps the goals include a percentage increase of Sunday school and worship attendance, growth in giving to missions, paying down or off the mortgage, or raising money for a building expansion.

Have your stated the specific objectives of your pastoral compensation policy? Here are a few examples:

➤ **Attraction.** Our goal is to attract a pastor who has a record of leading spiritually and numerically growing churches.

➤ **Retention.** Our goal is to increase the average time a pastor stays at our church to more than ten years.

➤ **Motivation and reward.** Our goal is to motivate our pastor to do what is necessary to cause our church to meet its objectives as a congregation.

Remember

Ministers who live in church-provided housing are penalized when residential real estate values are increasing. Even if real estate is modestly increasing, it is important for a church to provide an equity allowance. This annual payment in lieu of home ownership permits the pastor to invest the amount that might have been received through growth in the real estate market.

Taking your overall church goals and objectives and your pastoral compensation objectives into account, it may be helpful to establish a written compensation policy for the pastor or pastoral staff.

Example: Our compensation policy will attract, retain, reward, and motivate a pastor in a fair and equitable manner, when considering the compensation of other pastors in our denomination but particularly pastors in our local community, the compensation of citizens of our community, and the members of this congregation.

Compare the job description to benchmarks of other jobs

The pastor's job description should be compared to other jobs based on the following requirements: knowledge base, problem-solving ability, and the personal accountability for results. How much are other well-educated professionals paid in the community or the area? Surely a pastor should be paid as much as an elementary school principal, middle school principal, or high school principal in your area. This data is public information and can be readily obtained.

Key Issue

Compensation paid to the minister should be fair and a reasonable indication of the congregation's evaluation of the minister's worth. Above all, compensation should reflect the congregation's assessment of how well the minister handles a multitude of challenges and effectively serves a diverse congregation. Pay should relate to the responsibilities, the size of the congregation, the economic level of the locale, and the experience of the pastor.

Recognize the motivational factors and job description

It is important to recognize factors that commonly motivate pastors. These include extrinsic factors (God's call to preach the Word), intrinsic factors (the pastoral role, relationships with church attendees and those in the community), and external factors (salary and benefits).

But it is the job description for most pastors that is astounding! Typically, the job includes preaching the Word, equipping the saints for the work of ministry, administering the sacraments, visiting the sick and the needy, comforting those who mourn, correcting, rebuking and encouraging, caring for the departments of the church, giving leadership to evangelism and education programs of the church, supervising the preparation of statistical reports, and so much more.

Elements of the package to review

In too many congregations, the church leadership may say, "We can pay you $40,000. How do you want the money divided among salary, housing allowance, fringe benefits, and expense reimbursements?" Your salary may be considered as $40,000 when it is really considerably less. Salary is just one component of compensation. And, this approach lacks good stewardship as it almost always results in the minister paying more taxes than is necessary.

In another church, the church leadership may set your salary at $30,000, professional reimbursements at $4,000, and pension contributions at $2,000. Thus, your salary may be viewed as $36,000, not what it really is: $30,000.

Some congregations may choose to boost your salary 4% this year, leaving other elements of the pay package as they are. This practice presumes that your base salary for the previous year was adequate. This may or may not have been true.

Churches should consider salary ranges rather than fixed amounts. Show the pastor that based on experience, longevity, and education, he or she will start at a higher rate and receive better periodic increases.

An accountable expense reimbursement plan should be provided to every minister. An ideal policy provides for the full reimbursement for all professional expenses. Alternately, the plan should provide for reimbursements up to a specified annual limit. It is generally counterproductive to set expense plan limits by segments of expense like automobile, meals and entertainment, dues, and so on. If an expense limit is set, use one limit for all business and professional expenses. (See chapter 6.)

Key Issue

Few churches in America compensate ministers adequately. First, consider the minister's job description. Then, compare the job description to benchmarks of other jobs in the community based on the knowledge base, problem-solving ability, and personal accountability required for the minister.

After the reimbursement policy and the fringe benefit items are decided, housing and salary should be reviewed. Housing and salary are the true "compensation" items of the pay plan. Reimbursements are not a part of salary. Reimbursements are simply a form of church operating expenses. Fringe benefits are not salary even if they are taxable. They are simply benefits.

Just as laypersons do not include the payments made by their employers to pension or health plans as part of their salary, a congregation should not add those costs as part of the pastor's salary. True, they are a real cost for having a pastor, but they are benefits, not salary. *Housing, salary, church-funded IRA payments, and voluntary tax-sheltered annuity (403[b]) contributions are generally the only elements that represent compensation comparable to most laypersons in your church.*

Use Fringe Benefits Wisely

Fringe benefit plans should be established by a church separately from housing allowance resolutions, accountable expense reimbursement arrangements, and compensation resolutions. There are different tax rules that apply to gross pay, the housing allowance, and the various fringe benefits. Too often, churches try to wrap too many plans into one resolution. This can result in improperly establishing important elements in the compensation plan.

There are several key fringe benefits that many churches consider for ministers:

> **Tax-deferred accounts.** Contribute as much as you can (see chapter 3 for limitations) to tax-deferred accounts such as tax-sheltered annuities (TSAs) or 401(k) plans. Also, encourage your church to pay in the maximum to a denominational pension plan if one is available to you. Caution: Do not exceed retirement plan limits (see page 66-67).

> **Idea**
>
> A sound fringe benefit package almost always starts with the church or other employer paying for the minister's health insurance. This is vital because the health insurance payments are tax-free. If the minister has to pay the health insurance premiums, they can be claimed on Schedule A but rarely produces a tax benefit.

> **Health insurance.** This benefit is tax-free to a minister-employee if the church pays the premiums directly to the insurance carrier. And a reimbursement to a minister-employee for health insurance premiums is tax-free if based on substantiation. The reimbursement may include premiums paid by a spouse via payroll deduction.

>> **Example:** Is it better stewardship for a church to pay a salary of $45,000 and let the minister pay his or her own health insurance premiums of $10,000 or pay $35,000 and reimburse the minister's health insurance premiums? Pay $35,000 and reimburse the premiums. If the minister must

> **Caution**
>
> An allowance to cover the minister's self-employment social security tax provides absolutely no tax benefit since the amount is fully taxable. However, paying at least one-half of the minister's social security tax is important so this amount can be properly shown as a fringe benefit for compensation analysis purposes.

47

pay the premiums, the only possible deduction is on Schedule A and then only if the minister itemizes. Even so, most of the $10,000 deduction will usually be lost because of the 7.5% times adjusted gross income limitation on medical expenses.

▶ **Social security reimbursement.** All ministers pay self-employment social security tax of 15.3% on the first $84,900 of income in 2002. The Medicaid tax of 2.9% is due for all income above this limit. The only exception is for the few ministers who qualify, file, and are approved for social security exemption.

Churches often provide a reimbursement or allowance to assist the pastor in paying a portion or all of the social security tax. The payments are taxable for income and social security tax purposes whether paid directly to the minister or the IRS.

Use Accountable Expense Reimbursements

Since all ministers incur travel expenses while conducting the ministry of the local church, an adequate accountable reimbursement plan is vital. Auto expenses are generally a minister's most significant ministry-related expense. If payments to the minister with respect to these and other ministry expenses are not made subject to the accountable plan rules, the payments simply represent additional taxable compensation.

Ministers also incur other business expenses such as entertainment, professional books and magazines, membership dues, and supplies. Some churches reimburse their ministers in full for these expenses. Other churches reimburse the minister for these expenses up to certain limits.

All churches should establish a fair and equitable reimbursement plan, comparable to most business situations. The reimbursement plan should meet the rules for accountable plans explained in chapter 6. Full reimbursement of reasonable professional expenses should be the goal. If the church does not reimburse you for 100% of professional expenses, the unreimbursed expenses probably will not be fully deductible for tax purposes and perhaps not deductible at all. Anything less than 100% reimbursement of church-related expenses is poor stewardship of the money entrusted to a church.

> **Remember**
> Expense allowances have no tax value to a minister—they simply represent fully taxable compensation and the minister must try to deduct as many church-related expenses as possible. It is only through an accountable expense reimbursement plan that the reimbursement of expenses can be tax-free.

In addition to the adoption of an accountable reimbursement plan by the church, you must keep proper records and provide substantiation to the church for the expenditure of funds. The failure to account adequately for the expenses may be very expensive to you in terms of income taxes.

CHAPTER 2 ▸ COMPENSATION PLANNING

Income Tax Reporting and Expense Reimbursements

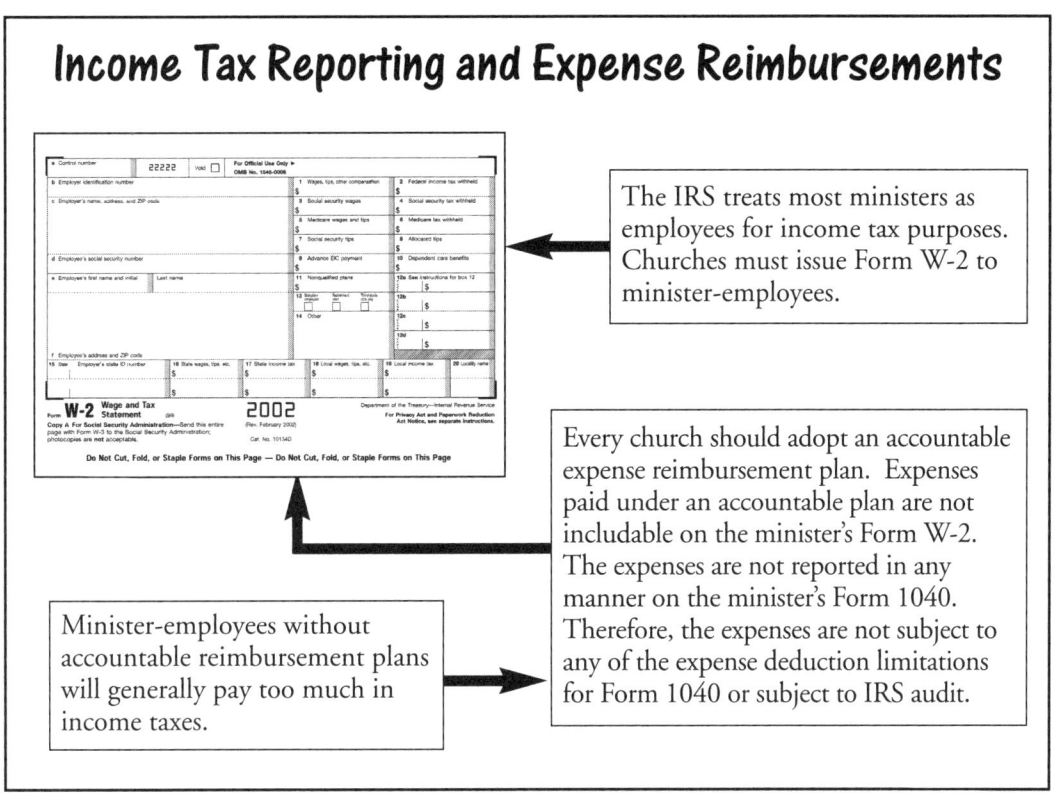

The IRS treats most ministers as employees for income tax purposes. Churches must issue Form W-2 to minister-employees.

Every church should adopt an accountable expense reimbursement plan. Expenses paid under an accountable plan are not includable on the minister's Form W-2. The expenses are not reported in any manner on the minister's Form 1040. Therefore, the expenses are not subject to any of the expense deduction limitations for Form 1040 or subject to IRS audit.

Minister-employees without accountable reimbursement plans will generally pay too much in income taxes.

Avoid recharacterization of income

Some churches fund expense reimbursements through a salary reduction arrangement falsely believing this creates a tax benefit for the minister. Under this method, which should be avoided, the church determines the combined cash salary and the reimbursable-expense dollar limit. Then substantiated expenses are subtracted from compensation.

Example: The church provides a combined cash salary and reimbursable-expense limit of $30,000. The minister substantiates $8,000 of church-related business expenses. The church reduces the $30,000 combined total by the $8,000 of expenses and provides the minister with a Form W-2 reflecting $22,000 of compensation. This is generally improper reporting since specific salary and expense plan amounts were not separately stated by the church when the compensation plan was drawn; Form W-2 must show compensation of $30,000. The minister may deduct the $8,000 of expenses on Form 2106/Schedule A or Schedule C (C-EZ), subject to limitations.

Reimbursements through salary reduction are generally not an effective method to reduce gross compensation. The valid approaches for funding expense reimbursements are as follows:

➤ The church may reimburse substantiated business expenses without limitation under the "accountable plan" rules discussed in chapter 6.

Example: The church agrees to provide the minister-employee with a salary of $30,000 per year plus an unlimited reimbursement of business expenses. Following the "accountable reimbursement rules," the minister substantiates expenses of $8,473 during the year. The church gives the minister a Form W-2 reflecting compensation of $30,000. The expenses of $8,473 are not reported by the church or the minister to the IRS.

➤ The church may reimburse substantiated business expenses up to certain limits under the "accountable plan" rules discussed in chapter 6.

Example: The church agrees to provide the minister-employee with a salary of $30,000 per year and reimburse business expenses up to $8,500 per year. Following the "accountable reimbursement rules," the minister substantiates $8,500 of expenses during the year. Additionally, the minister incurs $385 of business expenses beyond the $8,500 plan limit. The $385 of expenses are not reimbursed. The church gives the minister a Form W-2 showing compensation of $30,000. The $8,500 of reimbursed expenses are not reported by the church or the minister to the IRS. The $385 of unreimbursed business expenses may be claimed by the minister on Form 2106 (2106-EZ) and carried forward to Schedule A, miscellaneous deductions.

As a part of a church plan to reimburse a minister for business expenses, the church also may establish guidelines about the rate for auto mileage or apply per diem rates instead of paying actual expenses for meals and lodging (see chapter 6).

 **Action Steps**

- Encourage your church board to perform an annual review of the entire pay package.
- Segregate salary, fringe benefits, and reimbursements when the pay package is designed.
- Encourage church leaders to adopt an accountable expense reimbursement plan.
- Have an adequate housing allowance designated, even if you live in church-provided housing.
- File as an employee for income tax purposes in virtually every instance.
- Shift as much taxable income as possible into tax-free or tax-deferred fringe benefits, assuming you have income to defer.
- Keep detailed records of auto miles and business expenses.

CHAPTER THREE
The Pay Package

In This Chapter

- Delaying a portion of your pay
- When do the discrimination rules apply?
- Tax treatment of compensation elements
- Reporting compensation, fringe benefits, and reimbursements

Ask most ministers about their compensation and they will tell you the amount of their salary and housing allowance. Usually there is more to it than that. Not only is your salary subject to tax, but so are many fringe benefits that you may receive.

What are fringe benefits? A fringe benefit is any cash, property, or service that an employee receives from an employer in addition to salary. The term "fringe benefits" is really a misnomer because employees have come to depend on them as a part of the total compensation package. All fringe benefits are taxable income to employees unless specifically exempted by the Internal Revenue Code.

Many fringe benefits can be provided by a church to a minister without any dollar limitation (health insurance is an example), while other fringe benefits are subject to annual limits (dependent care is an example). The annual limits by fringe benefit type are reflected in this chapter.

Delaying a Portion of Your Pay

Following conventional advice, a minister should generally defer as much income as possible. Deferring income postpones reckoning with taxes until a future year.

You should come out ahead if you invest 100% of your money, pay no current taxes on earnings, and then pay taxes on both the principal and earnings a number of years later. Your option is to pay the taxes on all your income, including earnings, as you go.

But the principle of deferring income and taxes relies on one key assumption: the playing field remains level over the time period the income is deferred. If tax rates stay the same or go down, deferring income is generally wise. However, if tax rates go up, you could actually lose money by using this technique. If the foreign earned income exclusion is available to you, it may be unwise to defer income. Any significant change in the favorable tax rules available to ministers today would also impact the benefit of deferring income.

Many ministers have an extra potential benefit from deferring certain types of income over nonministers. If a minister has funds placed in a denominationally sponsored pension, tax-sheltered annuity, or 401(k) plan, the benefits received at retirement are eligible for exclusion under the housing allowance rules and they are not subject to social security tax.

When Do the Discrimination Rules Apply?

To qualify for exclusion from income, many fringe benefits must be nondiscriminatory. In other words, the benefits must be offered to all employees or all employees in certain classes. A fringe benefit subject to the nondiscrimination rules that is offered by a church only to the senior pastor, when other individuals are employed by the church, could trigger the nondiscrimination rules. This is particularly true for some benefits for certain key employees.

Failure to comply with the nondiscrimination rules does not disqualify a fringe benefit plan entirely. Only the highly compensated employees lose the tax-free benefit. Other employees will still receive the benefit tax-free.

The nondiscrimination rules apply to several types of fringe benefit plans including

- qualified tuition and fee discounts (see page 68),
- eating facilities on or near the employer's premises (see page 62),
- educational assistance benefits (see page 57),
- dependent care assistance plans (see page 55),
- group-term life benefits (see pages 61-62),
- self-insured medical plans (see page 60), and
- cafeteria plans (see page 58), including health reimbursement arrangements (see pages 59-60).

Tip

Churches can discriminate between employees for many fringe benefits. For example, a church can offer health insurance tax-free to one employee and not offer the coverage to another. It may be inequitable and could be inadvisable, but it's legal. There are only a handful of fringe benefits that are covered under the nondiscrimination rules.

A "highly compensated employee" for 2002 is

- paid more than $90,000 for the previous year, or
- if the employer elects, was in the top 20% of employees by compensation for the previous year.

Tax Treatment of Compensation Elements

▶ **Awards.** Ministers rarely receive awards based on performance. But such awards are generally taxable income unless the value is insignificant. If an award is made to the minister in goods or services, such as a vacation trip (see page 105 for trips to the Holy Land), the fair market value of the goods or services is includable in income.

▶ **Bonuses.** A bonus received by a minister is taxable income.

▶ **Books.** A church may reimburse a minister for ministry-related books with a short life as a tax-free benefit under an accountable plan. For example, a current best-selling book generally has a short life, but a commentary has a much longer life. Therefore, the best-seller could be reimbursed under an accountable plan but a commentary could not. However, the commentary could be deducted under the Section 179 rules (see page 120).

Idea

To avoid confusion, it is wise for churches to have a policy covering who owns the books paid for by the church. Without a policy, books purchased out of the church budget belong to the church. The issue is not as clear for books for which the church reimbursed the minister under an accountable expense reimbursement plan.

▶ **Business and professional expense payments without adequate accounting.** Many churches pay periodic allowances or reimbursements to the minister for business expenses with no requirement to account adequately for the expenses. These payments do not meet the requirements of an accountable expense reimbursement plan.

Allowances or reimbursements under a nonaccountable plan must be included in the taxable income of the minister. For an employee, the expenses related to a nonaccountable reimbursement plan are deductible only if the minister itemizes expenses on Schedule A. Even then, the business expenses, combined with other miscellaneous deductions, must exceed 2% of adjusted gross income.

A portion of unreimbursed expenses are subject to disallowance when they relate to a housing allowance according to the IRS (see pages 121-22).

▶ **Business and professional expenses reimbursed with adequate accounting.** If the church reimburses the minister under an *accountable* plan for employment-related professional or business expenses (for example, auto, other travel, subscriptions, entertainment, and so on), the reimbursement is not taxable compensation and is not reported to the IRS by the church or the minister (see pages 100-102). Per diem allowances up to IRS-approved limits also qualify as excludable reimbursements (see page 106).

▶ **Clothing.** Ordinary clothing worn in the exercise of your duties for the church are personal expenses and not deductible as business expenses or reimbursable by the church under an accountable plan.

If you wear clothing for your ministry that is not adaptable to general use, such as vestments, it is deductible or reimbursable as a business expense.

▶ **Computers.** The value of the business use of a church-provided computer for home use may be excludable from your gross income as a "working condition" fringe benefit (see pages 119-20). In order for the exclusion to apply, your business use of the computer must

☐ relate to the work of the church,

☐ entitle you to a business deduction if you purchased the computer personally, and

☐ be more than 50% of your total use.

You must include the value of the benefit of a church-provided computer in income if

☐ your use is nonbusiness,

☐ your use does not qualify as a working condition fringe benefit (see the three requirements shown above), or

☐ you do not keep records to substantiate business use.

Idea

The goal of every minister should generally be to have all or most employment-related expenses reimbursed by the employer. If your expenses are not fully reimbursed, instead of getting a pay increase, you will come out ahead to get the additional money in your accountable expense reimbursement plan.

Even if your church-provided computer use qualifies as a "working condition" fringe benefit, you must allocate the value of your personal use of the computer and add it to your income.

▶ **Conventions.** Expenses incurred for you to attend a ministry-related convention or seminar are generally deductible. (See chapter 6 for rules for the expenses of your spouse and children.)

If the convention is held outside North America, expenses are deductible only if the attendance is ministry-related and it is as reasonable for the convention to be held outside North America as within it.

When a minister travels away from home to attend a convention and combines personal activities with ministry activities, the deduction for convention expenses may be subject to certain limitations. When a minister attends a convention on a cruise ship, expenses incurred in connection with the convention are deductible only if the convention is ministry-related, the cruise ship is registered in the United States, and the ship does not stop at a port outside the United States or one of its possessions. Additionally, there is a $2,000 limit on expenses that may be deducted for a convention of this type.

▶ **Deferred compensation.** A church may maintain a retirement or other deferred compensation plan for employees that is not qualified under the Internal Revenue Code and is not a tax-sheltered annuity (see pages 66-67) or a "rabbi trust" (see page 65). If the plan is unfunded (the church makes a promise, not represented by a note, to pay at some time in the future), contributions to the plan are generally not taxable currently.

Funds placed in an investment account (other than in a tax-sheltered annuity or "rabbi trust") under the church's control to provide retirement funds for the minister have no tax consequence to the minister until the funds are paid or available to the minister.

Nonqualified deferred compensation plans generally limit deferrals of compensation to amounts deferred before they are earned and to the lesser of $11,000 (2002 rate) or 25% of the employee's includable compensation (reduced by amounts deferred under a 403[b], 401[k], or SEP-IRA plan).

Tip

With the 403(b) plan contribution limits increased for 2002, relatively few ministers will need to look for other retirement plan options. If the church funds an unqualified plan (such as purchasing an annuity contract) that is not a tax-sheltered annuity or a rabbi trust, the contributions are generally taxable currently.

▶ **Dependent care.** If the church provides you with child care (for dependents under age 13) or disabled dependent care services to allow you to work, you can exclude the amount of this benefit from income within certain limits. The amount excludable is limited to the smaller of

☐ your earned income,

☐ your spouse's earned income, or

☐ $5,000 ($2,500 if married filing separately).

The dependent care assistance must be provided under a separate written plan of your employer that does not favor highly compensated employees and that meets other qualifications.

Dependent care assistance payments are excluded from income if the payments cover expenses that would be deductible if the expenses were not reimbursed. If the minister is married, both spouses must be employed. There are special rules if one spouse is a student or incapable of self-care.

For a sample dependent care assistance plan, see the 2003 edition of *The Zondervan Church and Nonprofit Tax & Financial Guide*.

▶ **Dependent educational benefits.** The church may provide educational benefits for the minister's children when they attend college or a pre-college private school. When the church makes the payment to the college, the funds are taxable income to the minister. If the church withholds money from your pay and forwards the funds to a college for the education of your child, the amount withheld does not reduce your taxable compensation. See the 2003 edition of *The Zondervan Church and Nonprofit Tax & Financial Guide* for more information on scholarship funds established by churches.

▶ **Disability insurance.** If the church pays the disability insurance premiums (and the minister is the beneficiary) as a part of your compensation package, the premiums are excluded from your income. Any disability policy proceeds must be included in your gross income. This is based on who paid the premiums for the policy covering the year when the disability started. If the premiums are shared between the church and the minister, then the benefits are taxable in the same proportion as the payment of the premiums.

Conversely, if you pay the disability insurance premiums or have the church withhold the premiums from your salary, you receive no current deduction and any disability benefits paid under the policy are not taxable to you.

A third option is for the church to pay the disability premiums. But, instead of treating the premiums as tax-free, the church treats the premiums as additional employee compensation. Benefits you receive under this option are tax-free.

Idea

Statistics suggest that a minister is seven times more likely to need disability insurance than life insurance before age 65. When a church provides the maximum disability insurance as a tax-free benefit, it could reduce the awkwardness of a pastoral transition should the minister become disabled while the serving the congregation.

How do you determine whether disability benefits are taxable if the disability insurance premiums are paid by the church for some years and by the minister for other years? Taxability of the benefits generally depends on who paid the premiums for the policy year in which the disability benefit payments begin.

▶ **Discretionary fund.** Churches often establish a fund to be disbursed upon the discretion of the pastor. If the funds are used for church business or the needs of individuals associated with the church in a benevolent manner, and a proper accounting is made, there is no tax impact on the minister. If there is no accounting to the church, and if it is permissible to distribute some of the funds to the minister, money placed in the fund becomes additional taxable income to the minister in the year the money is transferred by the church to the discretionary fund.

Caution

Discretionary funds often serve a useful purpose for the pastoral staff—giving them the flexibility to provide immediate financial assistance, generally in small amounts, to those in need (larger amounts should be handled through a formal benevolence fund). However, an adequate accounting (dates, names, amounts, and need) must be maintained and made available for audit.

▶ **Dues and memberships.** Club dues are not deductible or reimbursable. This includes any club organized for business, pleasure, recreation, or other social purposes. The disallowance provision for club dues does not extend to professional organizations (such as a ministerial association) or public service organizations (such as Kiwanis, Rotary, and Lions clubs). If the church pays the health, fitness, or athletic facility dues for a minister, the amounts paid are generally fully includable in the minister's income as additional compensation.

▶ **Educational assistance benefit plans.** An educational assistance program is a separate written plan of a church to provide educational assistance to employees. The church must annually file Form 5500, Schedule F. A program may include courses whether or not they are job related. Graduate-level courses are covered under the program effective with 2002. The program must be nondiscriminatory.

No benefits may be provided to the employee's spouse or dependents. The church should exclude from income the first $5,250 of any qualified educational assistance paid for you during the year.

➤ **Educational reimbursement plans.** If your church requires you to take educational courses or you take job-related courses, and your church either pays the expenses directly to the educational organization or reimburses you for the expenses after you make a full accounting, you may not have to include in income the amount paid by your church.

While there are no specific dollar limits on educational expenses paid under a nonqualified reimbursement plan, the general ordinary and necessary business expense rules do apply. These types of payments may be discriminatory.

Though the education may lead to a degree, expenses may qualify as excludable if the education

- is required by your church to keep your salary, status, or job (and serves a business purpose of your church), or
- maintains or improves skills required in your present work.

Even if you meet the above qualification, education expenses do not qualify if the education is

- needed to meet the minimum educational requirements of your present work, or
- part of a program of study that can qualify you for a new trade or business, even if you have no plans to enter that trade or business.

> **Idea**
>
> A new $3,000 deduction starts in 2002 for college costs by itemizers and non-itemizers alike. For 2004, the limit on the deduction will be $4,000. To take this deduction, the education need not be necessary for you to keep your position. The education can even qualify you for a new occupation.

It may be possible for you to deduct as itemized deductions unreimbursed educational expenses or those reimbursed under a nonaccountable plan.

➤ **Equity allowance.** If the church owns the parsonage, only the church is building up equity. If the church provides a cash allowance for the minister to purchase a home, the minister may establish some equity.

An equity allowance is an amount paid to the minister living in a church-owned parsonage. This allowance may partially or fully offset the equity that the minister would have accumulated in a personally owned home.

An equity allowance that you are paid is fully taxable and not excludable as a housing allowance. However, the church could make the equity payments to a tax-sheltered annuity (TSA) or 401(k) plan. This would be consistent with the desire of a congregation to provide funds for housing at retirement. Under current law, the funds received at retirement from church-sponsored TSA or 401(k) plans may be eligible for tax-free treatment as a housing allowance (see pages 94-95).

▶ **Entertainment expenses.** A minister may deduct ministry-related entertainment expenses. Entertainment expenses must be directly related to or associated with the work of the church. Entertainment expenses are not deductible if they are lavish or extravagant.

If business meal and entertainment expenses are not reimbursed under an accountable plan, only 50% of the expenses are deductible. If the church reimburses the expenses, a 100% reimbursement may be made.

▶ **Flexible spending arrangements.** "Cafeteria" or flexible spending plans are separately written plans that allow employee participants to choose between two or more qualified fringe benefits.

The only taxable benefit that a cafeteria or flexible spending plan can offer is cash. A nontaxable benefit to the participant includes any benefit that is not currently taxable upon receipt. Examples of these benefits are group-term life insurance up to $50,000, coverage under an accident or health plan, and coverage under a dependent care assistance program.

A cafeteria or flexible spending plan cannot discriminate in favor of highly compensated participants for contributions, benefits, or eligibility to participate in the plan. Churches with fewer than 25 employees generally do not find these plans feasible.

▶ **401(k) plans.** A church may offer a 401(k) plan to its employees. Under a 401(k) plan, an employee can elect to have the church make tax-deferred contributions (up to $11,000 for 2002). See the 2003 edition of *The Zondervan Church and Nonprofit Tax & Financial Guide* for a comparison between 401(k) and tax-sheltered annuity plans.

▶ **Frequent flyer awards.** Free travel awards used personally that are received as frequent flyer miles on business travel paid by the church are not taxable when the awards are used. However, if these awards are converted to cash, they are taxable.

▶ **Gifts/personal.** Money that a minister receives directly from an individual is usually considered a personal gift and may be excluded from income if the payments are intended for the personal benefit of the minister and not in consideration of any services rendered. If the gift is a check, it should be made payable

Idea

For several years, the IRS has taken the position that an individual has tax liability because he or she has received or used frequent flyer miles or other promotional benefits related to the individual's business travel. In 2002, the IRS threw in the towel, saying these benefits are generally tax-free.

directly to the minister to qualify for tax exclusion for the minister. A personal gift of this nature will not qualify as a charitable contribution by the donor.

➤ **Gifts/special occasion.** Christmas, anniversary, birthday, retirement, and similar gifts paid by a church to its minister are typically taxable compensation. This is true if the gift came from the general fund of the church or from an offering in which tax-deductible contributions were made to the church for the benefit of the minister.

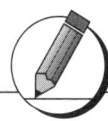

Filing Tip

Checks payable to the church designated for the benefit of the minister typically represent taxable income when paid to the minister. Such payments may not qualify as charitable contributions because of their possible appearance as conduit payments. It is highly preferable for payments of this nature to be made directly to the minister instead of "running them through the church" to try to get a tax deduction.

To qualify as a nontaxable gift, the payment must be based on detached and disinterested generosity, out of affection, respect, admiration, charity, or like impulses. The transferor's intention is the most critical factor. Also, it must be made without consideration of services rendered.

The church may announce an all-cash offering with a clear understanding that all proceeds will be paid directly and personally to the minister and that amounts given will not be receipted as charitable contributions. If the amounts given are not entered on the church books as contributions, they may qualify as tax-free gifts to the minister.

If the church gives you a turkey, ham, or other item of nominal value at Christmas or other holidays, the value of the gift is not income. But if the church gives you cash or an item that you can easily exchange for cash, such as a gift certificate, the gift is extra compensation regardless of the amount involved.

➤ **Health insurance.** If the church pays the medical insurance premiums directly to the insurance carrier or reimburses the minister-employee for the premiums based on substantiation, the premiums are tax-free to the minister. However, if similar payments are made for a minister that the church considers to be self-employed for income tax purposes, the payments represent additional taxable income.

Churches are *exempt* from the requirements imposed on other employers to refrain from discriminating in favor of more highly paid individuals for health insurance programs handled through an insurance carrier.

➤ **Health reimbursement arrangement.** A properly designed, *written* employee health reimbursement arrangement (HRA) under which the church pays the medical expenses

Caution

Certain noninsurance arrangements, often called "newsletter" plans, are used by some ministers. Since such plans make strong claims about not being insurance, the payments by a church to these plans (or to reimburse a minister's payments to these plans) is a fully taxable benefit reportable on the employee's Form W-2.

of the minister, spouse, and dependents, not covered by health insurance, may be nontaxable to the minister-employee. The IRS provided new guidance (see pages 10-12) on HRAs in 2002. (Also see the 2003 edition of *The Zondervan Church and Nonprofit Tax & Financial Guide* for a sample plan and other requirements for an HRA.)

HRAs may only be funded by church provided funds. Funding by a salary reduction election is not permitted. Excess money in a church-funded HRA can be carried over to a future year without any tax implications to the minister. Because benefits can be carried over indefinitely, the only danger of losing the balance in an HRA account is at retirement or other separation of employment.

Caution

An HRA may reimburse health care expenses under a plan where the employer decides how much will be available for each employee. This amount is generally the same for all eligible employees because the nondiscrimination rules apply. Account balances may be carried forward to increase the maximum reimbursement amount in subsequent coverage periods.

Typical expenses covered by such a plan are deductibles, coinsurance, and noncovered amounts paid by the individual. An HRA may be an excellent supplement to a high-deductible health insurance plan.

HRAs may not discriminate in favor of highly compensated employees, with regard to either benefits or eligibility. HRAs are only available to employees.

▶ **Home office.** If their home is the principal place of business, certain taxpayers can deduct a portion of their home expenses (for example, depreciation, utilities, and repairs). However, a home provided by a minister does not generate any home-office deductions if the church designates a housing allowance and all housing expenses are excluded. With the exclusion of the housing allowance from salary, the housing expenses—including the housing element of home-office expenses—have already been treated as tax-free.

The status of a home office as a regular or principal place of business may have a direct bearing on the status of commuting vs. business transportation expenses (see pages 115-17).

▶ **Housing allowance.** A properly designated housing allowance may be excluded from income subject to certain limitations. The fair rental value of a parsonage provided to a minister is not taxable for income tax purposes but is includable for social security tax purposes.

Any housing allowance paid to a minister that is more than the excludable amount is taxable compensation. The excess must be determined by the minister and reported on Form 1040, page 1. The church does not have a reporting requirement to the minister or the IRS regarding any portion of the designated housing allowance that exceeds the amount actually excluded.

▶ **Individual Retirement Accounts.** Amounts contributed by a church for a minister-employee's Individual Retirement Account (IRA) are includable in the employee's compensation on the Form W-2 and are subject to self-employment tax. IRA contributions may fall into one of the following categories:

- ☐ **Contributions to a regular IRA.** Each spouse may, in the great majority of cases, make deductible contributions to his or her IRA up to the dollar limitation (e.g., $2,000 reduced by adjusted gross income limits). The adjusted gross income phaseout ranges for 2002 are $54,000 to $64,000 for married taxpayers and $34,000 to $44,000 for singles. (The phaseout amounts are different if you are not an active participant but your spouse is.)

- ☐ **Contributions to a Roth IRA.** Nondeductible contributions may be made to a Roth IRA. The buildup of interest and dividends within the account may be tax-free depending on how and when you withdraw the money from the account.

▶ **Keogh plans.** If a minister has self-employment income for income tax purposes, a Keogh plan may be used. Amounts contributed to a Keogh plan are not taxed until distribution if the contribution limits are observed. If you withdraw money from your Keogh plan before you reach the age of $59\frac{1}{2}$, you will be subject to a 10% early withdrawal penalty.

▶ **Life insurance/group-term.** If the group life coverage provided under a nondiscriminatory plan does not exceed $50,000 for the minister, the life insurance premiums are generally tax-free to the minister-employee. Group-term life insurance coverage of more than $50,000 provided to the minister-employee by the church is taxable under somewhat favorable IRS tables. Group-term life insurance is term life insurance protection that

- ☐ provides a general death benefit that can be excluded from income,
- ☐ covers a group of employees (a "group" may consist of only one employee),
- ☐ is provided under a policy carried by the employer, and
- ☐ provides an amount of insurance for each employee based on a formula that prevents individual selection.

> **Caution**
>
> If the church pays the premium on a whole life or universal life policy on the life of the minister and the minister names personal beneficiaries, all the premiums paid are taxable income to the minister.

If you pay any part of the cost of the insurance, your entire payment reduces, dollar for dollar, the amount the church would otherwise include in income.

If your group-term life insurance policy includes permanent benefits such as a paid-up or cash surrender value, you must include in income the cost of the permanent benefits, reduced by the amount you pay for them.

If you are a retired minister, you also should include in income any payments for group-term life insurance coverage over $50,000 made by a former employing church, unless you otherwise qualify to exclude the payments.

▶ **Loan-grants.** Churches may provide a loan-grant to a minister relating to moving expenses, the purchase of a car, or the purchase of other property. In these instances, compensation is reported on Form W-2 for the minister based on the amount of the loan forgiven in a calendar year. The rules on compensation-related loans (see below) apply to loan-grants over $10,000.

▶ **Loans.** If the church provides a below-market compensation-related loan to a minister-employee or to a self-employed minister, additional compensation for the foregone interest may be required to be added to the minister's Form W-2.

If the loan proceeds are used for housing, the loan is secured, properly recorded, and you itemize your deductions, you may be able to deduct the imputed interest as mortgage interest. However, term loan interest must be prorated over the term of the loan. The interest is also eligible for inclusion in housing expenses for housing allowance purposes.

A "compensation-related" loan is any direct or indirect loan of over $10,000 made below market interest rates that relates to the performance of services between a church and a minister. There is also an exception for certain employee-relocation loans.

For term loans, additional compensation equal to the foregone interest over the entire term of the loan is considered as received on the date the loan was made. For demand loans, the foregone interest is added to compensation each year that the loan is outstanding.

Loans to ministers may be prohibited by state law. Employers should check with legal counsel before making such a loan.

▶ **Long-term care insurance.** Long-term care or nursing home insurance premiums paid or reimbursed by the church are tax-free. If the premiums are paid by the minister and not reimbursed by the church, they are deductible as medical expenses subject to annual limits based on your age.

▶ **Meals.** If meals provided to you by the church are a means of giving you more pay and there is no other business reason for providing them, their value is extra income to you.

If the meals are furnished by the church for the church's convenience (e.g., such as having a minister on call) and as a condition of employment, a minister-employee does not include their value in income if the benefits are nondiscriminatory. However, the benefits are taxable for social security purposes.

▶ **Minimal fringe benefits.** If the fringe benefits are so small *(de minimis)* in value that it would be unreasonable or impractical to account for them, the minister does not have to include their value in income. If the value of the benefit is not small, you must include its entire value in your income.

De minimis fringe benefits include traditional holiday gifts with a low fair market value, occasional typing of personal letters by the church secretary, or occasional personal use of the church copy machine.

> **Example:** You use the church copy machine for personal items. The machine is used at least 85% of the time for business purposes since the church restricts personal use of the copy machine. Though you use the machine for personal purposes more than other employees, your use is *de minimis* and not taxable.

▶ **Moving expenses** (paid by the church). Moving expenses paid directly or reimbursed by the church are excludable from gross income (reported on Form W-2, only in Box 12, using Code P to identify them as nontaxable reimbursements) for minister-employees. Amounts are excludable only to the extent that they would be deductible as moving expenses, i.e., only the cost of moving household goods and travel, other than meals, from the old residence to the new residence. Distance and timing tests must also be met.

Moving expenses do not qualify as business expenses. Therefore, moving expenses are not deductible in computing self-employment tax on Schedule SE for ministers considered to be self-employed for income tax purposes. For ministers filing as employees for income tax purposes, there is no requirement to add moving expense reimbursements, excluded on Form W-2, to Schedule SE income.

> **Caution**
>
> Churches and other employers should review the distance and timing tests to determine if moving expenses paid or reimbursed or includable in or excludable from gross pay. For example, the new principal place of work must be at least 50 miles farther from the minister's old residence than the old residence was from the minister's old place of work.

▶ **Parking.** You do not have to include in income the value of free parking facilities provided to you on or near the church premises if it is $185 or less per month for 2002. This also applies for reimbursements from the church for renting a parking space on or near the church premises.

A church can also sell transit passes or tokens to ministers at discounts of up to $100 per month tax free or give cash up to $100 for passes and tokens tax-free.

▶ **Pension plans.** Contributions to certain pension and retirement plans are excludable or deductible by a minister for income tax purposes. In these instances, there is generally no tax consequence until the funds are distributed to the minister.

☐ **Denominational plans.** When the church makes contributions to a denominational pension plan for you, the contributions are not included in your taxable income. Upon retirement, the benefits represent taxable income for income tax purposes unless excluded as a parsonage allowance. Pension benefits are tax-free for social security purposes.

☐ **Nonqualified deferred compensation plans.** (See Deferred compensation.)

☐ **Pension payroll deductions.** The amounts provided by salary reductions to

403(b) tax-sheltered annuities or 401(k) plans are excluded from income for income tax purposes. However, you cannot generally exclude from income amounts that you pay directly or pay into a pension plan through payroll deductions.

- ☐ **Other.** (See Individual Retirement Accounts, Keogh plans, Simplified Employee Pension plans, and Tax-sheltered annuities.)

▶ **Pre-employment expense reimbursements.** Prospective ministers may be reimbursed for expenses related to seeking a position with a particular church. Substantiated expenses related to interviews (meals, lodging, and travel) are not includable in the prospective employee's gross income whether or not the minister is subsequently employed.

▶ **Property transfers/restricted.** To reward good work, a church may transfer property to a minister subject to certain restrictions. The ultimate transfer of the property will occur only if the restrictions are met at a later date.

Property that is subject to substantial risk of forfeiture and is nontransferable is substantially not vested. No tax liability will occur until title to the property is vested with the minister. This simply represents a deferral of the tax consequences.

When restricted property becomes substantially vested, the minister must include in income, for both income and social security tax purposes, an amount equal to the excess of the fair market value of the property at the time it becomes substantially vested, over the amount the minister pays for the property. The church should report the additional income on the minister's Form W-2 or 1099-MISC.

For tax planning purposes, the "vesting" of a restricted property transfer to a minister may be staggered over several years. The reporting of a sizable restricted gift in one year may have significant tax consequences.

Example: A church transfers a house to a minister subject to the completion of twenty years of pastoral service to the church. The minister does not report any taxable income from the gift until the year that includes the twentieth anniversary of the agreement.

▶ **Property transfers/unrestricted.** If a church transfers property (for example, a car, equipment, or other property) to a minister at no charge, this constitutes taxable income to the minister. The amount of income is generally the fair market value of the property transferred as of the date of the transfer.

If you buy property from the church at a price below its fair market value, you must include in compensation the difference between the property's fair market value and the amount you paid for it and liabilities that you assumed.

Caution

If property is transferred by the church to a minister at no charge or less than fair market value, the church should report the additional income on the minister's Form W-2 or 1099-MISC.

- **Rabbi trust.** Deferred compensation plans that use a trust are commonly referred to as "rabbi trusts." If the model trust issued by the IRS is used, contributions to the trust will generally not be taxed currently.

- **Recreational expenses.** A minister may incur expenses that are primarily recreational, e.g., softball or basketball league fees, greens fees, and so on. Even if there is an element of ministry purpose, the deduction or reimbursement of such fees as business expenses is generally not justified.

- **Retirement gifts.** Gifts made to a minister at retirement by the employing church are usually taxable compensation. This is particularly true for minister-employees. Retirement gifts made by an individual directly to a minister may be tax-free to the minister, but they will not qualify as charitable contributions by the donor.

- **Salary.** The cash salary (less the properly designated and excludable housing allowance amount) is taxable income.

- **Sabbatical pay.** Unless payments qualify as a tax-free scholarship, sabbatical pay generally represents taxable income. To achieve treatment as a scholarship, the recipient must be a candidate for a degree at an educational institution and the scholarship must be used for tuition.

- **Severance pay.** A lump-sum payment for cancellation of your employment contract is income in the tax year you receive it and must be reported with your other compensation.

- **Sick or disability pay.** Amounts you receive from your employer while you are sick or disabled are part of your compensation (sick or disability pay is distinguished from payments for injury provided under Workers' Compensation insurance, which are normally not taxable). You must also include in income any payments made by an insurance company if the employer paid the premiums.

    If you paid the premiums on an accident or health insurance policy or if the premiums paid by your employer were treated as part of your taxable compensation, the benefits you receive under the policy are not taxable.

- **Simplified Employee Pension plans (SEPs).** Through an SEP, your employer may contribute amounts to your IRA if you are an employee or self-employed for income tax purposes. But there are many nondiscriminatory limitations on SEP contributions that most churches will find insurmountable.

- **Social security tax reimbursement.** Churches and other employers commonly reimburse ministers for a portion or all of their self-employment social security (SECA) tax liability. Any social security reimbursement must be reported as taxable income.

    Because of the deductibility of the self-employment tax in both the income tax and self-employment tax computations, a full reimbursement is effectively less than the gross 15.3% rate:

Your Marginal Tax Rate	Effective SECA Rate
0%	14.13%
10	13.42
15	13.07
27	12.22
30	12.01

It is usually best to reimburse the minister for self-employment tax on a monthly or quarterly basis. An annual reimbursement may leave room for misunderstanding between the church and the minister if the minister moves to another church before the reimbursement is made.

Caution

An allowance to cover the minister's self-employment social security tax provides absolutely no tax benefit since the amount is fully taxable. However, paying at least one-half of the minister's social security tax is important so this amount can be properly shown as a fringe benefit for compensation analysis purposes.

For missionaries who are not eligible for the income tax deduction of one-half of the self-employment tax due to the foreign earned income exclusion, the full reimbursement rate is effectively 14.13%.

▶ **Subscriptions.** A church may reimburse a minister for ministry-related magazine subscriptions as a tax-free benefit. Unreimbursed subscriptions may be deducted on Schedule A or C.

▶ **Tax-sheltered annuities (TSAs).** Ministers who are employees for income tax purposes may have a Section 403(b) salary reduction arrangement based on a written plan. Payments to a TSA contract by chaplains filing as self-employed for income tax purposes must be deducted on Form 1040, line 31. Such payments are not eligible for pretax treatment.

Compliance with special nondiscrimination rules may be a condition to a minister benefiting from the Section 403(b) exclusion allowance (see page 52 for more information on these rules). Churches and elementary or secondary schools controlled, operated, or principally supported by a church or convention or association of churches are not subject to the nondiscrimination rules.

Both nonelective (for example, payments by your church into a denominational TSA pension plan other than funded through a salary reduction agreement) and elective (funded through a salary reduction agreement) contributions for a minister to a TSA are excludable for income and social security tax (SECA) purposes. While permissible, after-tax employee contributions are the exception in TSAs.

Filing Tip

The limits on contributions to 403(b) tax-sheltered annuity plans are significantly relaxed starting with 2002. Not only have contribution limits increased but the limits have become much simpler to determine.

There are two separate, yet interrelated limitations on the amount of contributions to a TSA that are excludable from gross income:

- **Salary reduction limitation.** This limitation is $11,000 for 2002. There will be a $1,000 yearly increase in this limit until it reaches $15,000 in 2006. Employees over age 50 will also be able to make a "catch-up" contribution of $1,000 in 2002, increasing by $1,000 per year to $5,000 by 2006.

- **Maximum exclusion allowance.** For 2002, the maximum exclusion allowance is $40,000 (up from $35,000 in 2001) or 100% of compensation (up from 25% in 2001), whichever is less.

A minister can roll funds tax-free from one TSA to another TSA and from a TSA to an IRA. Rollovers are not subject to annual limits.

Withdrawals from a denominationally sponsored TSA plan qualify for designation as a housing allowance and are not subject to social security (SECA) tax (see pages 94-95).

For a comparison between TSAs and 401(k) plans, see the 2003 edition of *The Zondervan Church and Nonprofit Tax & Financial Guide.*

▶ **Telephone/cellular.** If a cellular telephone is provided by the church and you meet the working condition fringe benefit test, you still must allocate the value of your personal use of the cellular telephone and add it to your income (see pages 120-21).

▶ **Travel expenses.** Travel expenses of a minister are deductible as business expenses if they are ordinary and necessary and incurred while traveling away from the minister's tax home for business-related reasons. Expenses that are for personal or vacation purposes, or that are lavish or extravagant, may not be deducted.

Travel expenses incurred outside the United States may be subject to a special business vs. personal travel expense allocation of the transportation costs to and from the business destination. This allocation can apply even when foreign travel expenses are incurred primarily for business purposes. Expenses incurred for travel as a form of education, such as a tour of the Holy Land, are generally not deductible (see pages 105).

Caution

The travel expenses of an employee's spouse and children often do not qualify for tax-free reimbursement or as a business tax deduction. There must be a bona fide business purpose for the spousal and children travel in addition to substantiation of expenses.

If a minister incurs travel expenses for a spouse or child, the minister may deduct or receive a tax-free reimbursement for the spouse's and children's expenses if they qualify for employee treatment and

- the travel is for a bona fide business purpose; and

- the minister-employee substantiates the time, place, amount, and business purpose of the travel under an accountable business expense reimbursement plan.

▶ **Tuition and fee discounts.** If you are an employee of a church-operated elementary, secondary, or undergraduate institution, certain tuition and fee discounts provided to a minister, spouse, or dependent children are generally tax-free. The discounts must be nondiscriminatory and relate to an educational program.

If you are employed by the church and not by the church-related or church-operated private school, tuition and fee discounts that you receive are taxable income.

Tip

Tax-free tuition and fee discounts are only available to the dependents of an employee of a school. Discounts provided to church employees are taxable. This is true if the school is operated as part of the church, is a subsidiary corporation under the church, or is separately incorporated.

▶ **Vacation pay.** Payments made by the church to you for vacations are taxable income.

▶ **Vehicles/personal use of church-owned vehicle.** One of the most attractive fringe benefits for a minister is for the church to own or lease a vehicle for the minister. The church generally makes the lease payments or car loan payments, if any, plus paying for all gas, oil, insurance, repairs and other related expenses. Unless the vehicle is always parked on the church premises (e.g., where business trips start) and never used for personal purposes, the minister must maintain a log to document personal use of the vehicle.

The fair market value of the personal use must be included in the minister's gross income unless the minister fully reimburses the value to the church.

Example: Your church provides a vehicle for your use for a full year. The vehicle cost was $16,000 and the annual lease value for the year is $4,600 (see table in the 2003 edition of *The Zondervan Church and Nonprofit Tax & Financial Guide*). You drive 6,000 miles during the year for the church and 2,000 miles for personal use. The value of the working condition fringe is 6,000 (business miles) divided by 8,000 (total miles) times $4,600 (total value) equals $3,450. The $3,450 value of the working condition fringe is excluded from income. The remaining $1,150 value is for the personal use of the vehicle and must be included in your income. You must also add 5.5 cents per mile unless you paid for the fuel when the vehicle was used for personal purposes.

Many churches use the annual lease value rule to set a value on the use of a church-provided vehicle. (There are also several other valuation rules that are available.) If the church provides the fuel, 5.5 cents per mile must be added to the annual lease value. See IRS Publication 535 for more information.

▶ **Vehicle use/nonpersonal.** The total value of the use of a qualified nonpersonal-use vehicle is excluded from income as a working condition fringe. The term "qualified nonpersonal-use vehicle" means any vehicle that is not likely to be used more than a small amount for personal purposes because of its nature or design.

> **Example:** A church provides you with a vehicle to use for church business. You do not qualify for a home office and leave the car parked at the church when it is not being driven for business purposes. There is a written agreement with the church that prohibits your personal use of the vehicle. Only in an emergency is the car driven for personal benefit. This vehicle should qualify under the nonpersonal-use provision, and the entire value of the vehicle would be excluded from your income.

▶ **Wage continuation.** Generally, payments to an employee from a wage continuation plan are treated as compensation for income tax purposes. For the treatment of special types of wage continuation plans, see the explanations under Disability insurance (see pages 55-56) and Workers' Compensation (below).

▶ **Withholding.** Amounts withheld from your pay or put into your bank account under a voluntary withholding agreement for income tax or savings bonds are compensation as though paid directly to you. These amounts must be included on your Form W-2 in the year they were withheld. The same generally is true of amounts withheld for taxable fringe benefits.

If the church uses your wages to pay your debts, or if your wages are garnisheed, the full amount is compensation to you.

▶ **Workers' Compensation.** A minister who receives Workers' Compensation benefits due to his job-related injuries or sickness may generally exclude the benefits from gross income. In addition, the minister is not taxed on the value of the insurance premium paid by the church.

Minister-employees are subject to Workers' Compensation laws in many states. It is often important to cover ministers under Workers' Compensation insurance even if it is not a state requirement. For work-related injuries of minister-employees, many health benefit plans will not pay medical expenses unless the minister is covered by Workers' Compensation insurance.

 **Action Steps**

- Understand the different treatment of certain fringe benefits depending on whether you are an employee or self-employed for income tax purposes.
- Determine which fringe benefits are taxable, tax-free, and tax-deferred. Structure your pay package to include as many tax-free and tax-deferred fringe benefits as possible while minimizing your taxable salary.
- Be aware of the nondiscrimination rules for certain fringe benefits. Many fringe benefits for ministers are taxable under these rules.

Reporting Compensation, Fringe Benefits, and Reimbursements for Income Tax Purposes

Compensation, fringe benefits, or reimbursement	Minister-Employee
Bonus or gift from church	Taxable income/Form W-2
Business and professional expenses reimbursed with adequate accounting	Tax-free
Business and professional expense payments without adequate accounting	Deduction on Schedule A, Miscellaneous Deductions. Subject to 2% of AGI and 50% meals and entertainment limits
Club dues paid by the church	Taxable income/Form W-2 (exception for dues for civic and public service groups)
Compensation reported to minister by church	Form W-2
Dependent care assistance payments	Tax-free
Earned income tax credit (EITC)	May be eligible for EITC
Educational assistance programs	May be eligible to exclude up to $5,250 of qualified assistance
401(k) plan	Eligible for 401(k)
Gifts/personal (not handled through church)	Tax-free
Housing allowance	Excludable. Subject to limitations
IRA payments by church	Taxable income/Form W-2

Reporting Compensation, Fringe Benefits, and Reimbursements for Income Tax Purposes

Compensation, fringe benefits, or reimbursement	Minister-Employee
Insurance, disability, paid by church, minister is beneficiary	Premiums are tax-free, but proceeds are taxable
Insurance, disability, paid by minister, minister is beneficiary	Proceeds are tax-free
Insurance, group-term life, paid by church	First $50,000 of coverage is tax-free
Insurance, health	Tax-free if directly paid by church or reimbursed to minister upon substantiation. If paid by minister and not reimbursed by church, deduct on Schedule A
Insurance, life, whole or universal, church is beneficiary	Tax-free
Insurance, life, whole or universal, minister designates beneficiary	Taxable income/Form W-2
Insurance, long-term care	Tax-free if directly paid by church or reimbursed to minister on substantiation. If paid by minister and not reimbursed by church, deduct on Schedule A subject to limitations
Loans, certain low-interest or interest-free to minister over $10,000	Imputed interest is taxable income/Form W-2
Medical expense reimbursement plan	May be tax-free
Moving expenses paid by the church (only applies to certain qualified expenses)	Tax-free if directly paid by church or reimbursed to minister on substantiation. Reported on Form W-2, only in Box 12, using Code P

Reporting Compensation, Fringe Benefits, and Reimbursements for Income Tax Purposes

Compensation, fringe benefits, or reimbursement	Minister-Employee
Pension payments to a denominational plan for the minister by the church	Tax-deferred. No reporting required until the funds are withdrawn or pension benefits are paid
Per diem payments for meals, lodging, and incidental expenses	May be used for travel away from home under an accountable reimbursement plan
Professional income (weddings, funerals)	Taxable income/Schedule C (C-EZ)
Property transferred to minister at no cost or less than fair market value	Taxable income/Form W-2
Retirement or farewell gift to minister from church	Taxable income/Form W-2
Salary from church	Report salary on page 1, Form 1040
Social security reimbursed by church to minister	Taxable income/Form W-2
TSA, Sec. 403(b) tax-sheltered annuity	Eligible for TSA
Travel paid for minister's spouse by the church	May be tax-free if there is a business purpose
Tuition and fee discounts	May be tax-free in certain situations
Value of home provided to minister	Tax-free
Vehicles/personal use of church-owned auto	Taxable income/Form W-2
Voluntary withholding	Eligible for voluntary withholding agreement

CHAPTER FOUR
Retirement Planning

In This Chapter

- Preparing for retirement
- The keys to social security
- Taking out your retirement money

Age 65 was entrenched as the finish line for our careers. But this false endpoint is gradually being removed. We are living longer, the social security retirement age is increasing, and stock market fluctuations have significantly impacted our retirement plans. In fact, the stock market slump has left many ministers focused on their nest eggs to the exclusion of all else in their retirement planning.

Medicare still becomes effective at age 65. But this program for the elderly and disabled doesn't pay for prescription drugs, and it does not pay for long-term care costs.

For many ministers, the word "retirement" means freedom. Retirement is the end to stressful deadline pressure and setting your alarm clock. But it's also the end to regular paychecks. For ministers who have lived in church-owned parsonages all their lives, retirement brings significant housing challenges.

Retirement is a transition period. God never intended for retirement to be an end in itself. And instead of kicking back at age 60 or 65, starting a second career, shifting to part-time work, or simply continuing to work full-time can allow your retirement portfolio to expand by compounding for a greater period of time.

There is a danger in trying to be too precise in planning your nest egg with elaborate worksheets or powerful computer programs. Life isn't that precise. Think about what will constitute a successful retirement for you. Most people would be better off investing more of their efforts in the things money cannot buy:

➤ Relationship with the Lord,

➤ Building and expanding relationships with family and friends,

➤ Remaining in good health—weight and stress management are vital, and

➤ Participating in gratifying and fulfilling activities.

Preparing for Retirement

How much income will you need?

Being financially prepared for retirement is simply a function of time and money: The less you have of one, the more you need of the other.

What is the biggest excuse ministers use who are not saving for retirement? They say they need every penny to pay their bills now—but they'll start saving once the bills are paid off. Paying off your debts is a worthy goal, but most people never pay them all off.

Most ministers cannot save a fortune by the time they reach retirement. On a minister's pay, it is difficult to squirrel away as much as many experts insist is needed for a comfortable retirement. But there is one inescapable truth: the sooner you start saving, the better. Saving for retirement isn't like climbing one great peak. It's really like climbing several smaller ones.

Many financial planners suggest that you will need 70% to 80% of your preretirement income. But you may be able to significantly reduce your income requirement just by moving from an area with a high cost of living to a lower-cost one.

How long is retirement going to be?

The major concern of retirees today is the fear of outliving their income. Today, a 66-year-old male is expected to live 18 more years, and a female is expected to live 24 more years. But life expectancies are averages, and planning on an "average" retirement can be dangerously shortsighted for anyone in good health. It makes sense for healthy people from long-lived families to plan for a retirement stretching at least to age 85, and women are likely to live longer than men.

Investing for retirement

The best advice for ministers is the simplest—put as much into your 403(b)/tax-sheltered annuity plan as you can. Whether the payments are church-funded or funded by a salary reduction from your pay, the contributions are tax-deferred for income tax purposes and they are not subject to self-employment social security taxes. When you receive benefits from your tax-sheltered annuity plan in retirement, the payments are not subject to self-employment social security taxes.

If your plan was sponsored by a church denomination, your benefits qualify for housing allowance treatment, subject to the regular housing allowance limitations (see pages 94-95). Most financial planners recommend paying off your mortgage before you retire. But if you are a good money

> **Idea**
>
> Few ministers contribute up to the limits of their retirement plans. With the changes in retirement plan contribution limits beginning in 2002, ministers can contribute more than ever before. Check out these new rules on pages 66-67.

manager, you may want to arrange your indebtedness so you have mortgage payments during at least the early years of your retirement.

What if you have already contributed the maximum to your tax-sheltered annuity plan? A $2,000 per year contribution to a nondeductible Roth IRA or a regular deductible IRA is a good option for your next retirement savings dollars. How do you decide? Young ministers will tend to benefit more from a Roth IRA because it thrives on long-term compounding. If you are nearing retirement and in a 27% or higher income tax bracket but believe you will drop to the 15% bracket when you retire, stay with a deductible IRA.

When you've exhausted these options, consider a taxable investment. The key to choosing taxable investments for your retirement savings is to keep your expenses down and get the most benefit from the 20% maximum capital gains rate (10% if you are in the 15% income tax bracket).

Variable annuities may make sense for a fixed-income asset such as bonds or cash, if you are saving for at least 12 years. In that case, the gains from compounding your interest free of income tax eventually outweigh the fees charged by most variable annuities.

Asset allocation—the division of your savings among different investment vehicles—is a key part of any retirement strategy. Not only do you have to decide what kind of investment account to use, you also have to decide which of your specific investments go into which account.

Proper diversification entails much more than simply spreading your contributions evenly among the choices open to you. It is influenced strongly by how long you will continue to work and how much you already have invested elsewhere. In general, the more time you have, the more aggressive you can afford to be in your asset allocation.

Insurance choices as you approach retirement

When you are approaching retirement, your insurance needs often are different from when you were in your 30s and 40s. Here are some insurance policies that you may need and policies you can probably do without:

➤ **Life insurance.** The need for life insurance usually declines or disappears once you are in or near retirement. Your children are probably financially independent. And by now you may have accumulated enough assets to cover your spouse's future needs. This means you might want to drop some of your insurance coverage.

If you need life insurance for estate planning, or to protect dependents financially for at least 15 years, you should probably buy cash-value insurance so you can lock in the premium. If you own a term life policy you no longer need, you can stop paying premiums and let the policy lapse.

➤ **Long-term care insurance.** Long-term care (LTC) insurance is a way to pay for nursing home costs while protecting your financial assets. LTC policies have improved significantly in recent years, but they are expensive, averaging more than

Countdown to Retirement

This table can help you make the timely decisions that ensure a comfortable retirement. Since only you know when you plan to call it quits, it is organized according to the number of years you have until then. If you have to move up your plans, you can compress this checklist into the time you have available.

CATEGORY	FIVE YEARS BEFORE RETIREMENT	TWO YEARS BEFORE RETIREMENT	THREE MONTHS BEFORE RETIREMENT	IN RETIREMENT
BUDGET	Draw up two budgets, current expenses and expected expenses in retirement. Plan to pay off debts by retirement.	Update your current and future budgets.	Merge your two budgets, deleting career expenses and adding any new retiree expenses.	Fine-tune your budget every year so that your projected spending matches your actual spending.
PENSION Defined-benefit plan	Ask your pension office to project your pension monthly and in a lump sum.	Decide how to take your pension; if as a lump sum, decide how to invest it.	Set up the investments you have chosen for your lump sum.	Invest your lump sum immediately to avoid the tax consequences.
403(b), 401(k) plans	Put the maximum in your plan. Wait as long as possible to tap the money so earnings grow tax deferred.	Keep contributing the maximum. If you will take a lump sum, ask an accountant how to minimize taxes.	Decide how to take your money. At 59½ you may start penalty-free lump-sum withdrawals.	At 70½ you may have to start minimum withdrawals from tax-deferred retirement plans.
SOCIAL SECURITY	Send Form 7004 to your local social security office to check your earnings and be sure your employers contributed the right amounts.	Double-check your account by sending your local social security office another Form 7004.	Decide when after age 62 to start receiving social security.	At retirement age (currently 65), there is no limit on the income you can earn without reducing your social security benefits.
INVESTMENTS	Meet with a financial planner to discuss your goals and adjust your asset mix to meet them.	Adjust the balance between growth and income investments to reduce your market risk and increase income.	Make further reductions in market risk.	Generally, keep some of your money in stocks to offset inflation.
EMERGENCY FUND	Stash an amount equal to three months' expenses in a money-market fund.	Set up (or renew) a home-equity line of credit that you can tap in case of an emergency.	Your cash and home-equity line of credit should amount to one full year of expenses.	Keep one year's expenses in the fund; tap it only when you must.
HOUSE Sell vs. keep	Decide whether to keep your present house or sell it. If you sell, decide whether to buy another or rent.	If you plan to move after retiring, visit potential locations during vacations.	If you are selling, put your house on the market three to six months before retirement.	Your gain on the house is tax-free up to $500,000 (married), $250,000 (single).
Repairs and improvements	Renovate now; it's easier to borrow if you're employed.	Budget now for any big-ticket repairs you may need after you retire.		
MEDICAL INSURANCE	Ask your pension office what your medical benefits will be in retirement.	If you need individual coverage, start shopping for it now.	Apply for the coverage one month prior to retiring.	Medicare starts at 65. Six months before then, shop for Medigap insurance.

$2,000 a year for policies purchased at age 65.

Long-term care policies cover nursing home stays only, home care only, or both. A good LTC policy will cover skilled or intermediate care, or custodial help in any type of facility, with no prior hospitalization required.

➤ **Medical insurance.** Your medical insurance may stop when you become eligible for Medicare at your full retirement age, currently age 65. If you're old enough for Medicare, call social security to enroll. You may be eligible to remain in your group policy for 18 months after you leave your current employment, if the plan is based on COBRA rules.

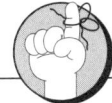

Remember

Nursing home stays are typically short but the need for home health care is often longer. Consider long-term care plans that provide the same coverage for home health care and nursing facilities. Your employer can pay or reimburse your LTC premiums tax-free. The premiums are generally your responsibility from after-tax dollars after you retire.

The Keys to Social Security

Ignore scare stories about social security not being there when you retire. The truth is, the benefits for most ministers will survive largely intact for many years. And Congress is likely to take steps to shore up the program in the next few years.

The age for collecting your full social security benefit used to be 65—but no longer. Full retirement gradually increases from age 65 to 67. Here, by year of birth, is the age at which you can expect to collect your full social security retirement benefit:

Year of Birth	Age for Collecting Full Retirement Benefit
Before 1938	65
1938	65 and two months
1939	65 and four months
1940	65 and six months
1941	65 and eight months
1942	65 and 10 months
1943-1954	66
1955	66 and two months
1956	66 and four months
1957	66 and six months
1958	66 and eight months
1959	66 and 10 months
1960 and later	67

Filing Tip

If you work while receiving social security benefits, you still pay social security and Medicare taxes regardless of your age. Additional earnings can result in increasing your benefit if the earnings are higher than those of an earlier year used in the previous calculation.

Income taxes on benefits

Social security benefits are income tax free for the majority of beneficiaries. However, those with high total incomes must include up to 85% of their benefits as income for federal income tax purposes. Special step-rate "thresholds" determine the amount on which you may be taxed:

- Single persons: $25,000 and $34,000
- Married couples filing a joint return: $32,000 and $44,000

Working after you reach retirement age

Beneficiaries ages 62 through 64 lose $1 of social security benefits for every $2 they earn over a certain limit, which increases annually (it was $11,280 in 2002). Once you are retirement age, you can earn as much as you like with no cut in benefits. The earnings test looks only at money you earn from a job or self-employment, not income from investments or other sources. Dollars from income excluded because of the housing allowance are included in the earnings test.

Checking on your benefits

Complete a Request for Earnings and Benefit Estimate Statement (Form SSA-7004) every three years. You can order a free copy of the form by calling 800-772-1213. Complete the form and the SSA will mail you a statement of your earnings along with a projection of your future benefits. Notify the SSA of any discrepancies.

And don't overlook the possibility of errors in your church retirement plan, either. Get a summary plan description from your church pension board, and look over your annual statement summary.

Taking Out Your Retirement Money

Ministers spend their entire lives putting money into retirement plans. When and how you withdraw money from your tax-deferred retirement plans are among the most important financial decisions of your life.

Capital builds up in your retirement plans, free of taxes. But the federal, state, and local governments are looking for their share when you pull out your money. And Congress has devised a host of hurdles and penalties:

- You cannot start withdrawing until you retire at age 55 or reach 59½. If you do, you have to pay a 10% tax penalty on top of the standard income tax rates. The Roth IRA is an exception because money can be withdrawn without penalty if you leave the funds in the Roth IRA for at least five years.

How long will $100,000 last?

Withdrawals starting at*	Years money will last invested at the following yields				
	4%	6%	8%	10%	12%
$ 2,000	50	151	FOREVER		
$ 6,000	17	20	25	43	FOREVER
$10,000	10	11	12	14	17
$14,000	7	8	8	9	10

*Single withdrawal at first of year, increasing each year by 4% to cover inflation

➤ For church plans, you must start withdrawals at age 70½ or your date of retirement, whichever is later. For other retirement plans, you must start withdrawals when you reach age 70½. If you don't, you have to pay a walloping 50% penalty tax. There is no age requirement for starting to withdraw funds from your Roth IRA.

What, then, can you do to plan a sensible, tax-saving strategy for withdrawing from your retirement funds? Ask your denominational pension plan representative or financial advisor these key questions:

➤ How much money do I now have in my plans?

➤ Given a reasonable growth rate, how much will I accumulate in all those plans in future years?

➤ How long, and how much, should I continue to contribute to those plans?

➤ When does it make sense for me to start withdrawing from those plans?

➤ Given my life expectancy, my tax situation, my expected pension, and other retirement benefits, plus the amount of money I will need to live on, how much should I withdraw each year?

Decide how you want to take your money

Leave your retirement plan money alone to enjoy tax-deferred compounding. This is the best move if you don't need it right away. If you are eligible for a lump-sum distribution from your retirement plan and you believe you can achieve better investment results on your own, you may want to roll over the assets to a self-directed IRA. Your plan assets will continue to grow unhampered by taxes. Should you need a large sum of money right away, you can take part of your stash directly and put the rest into an IRA. Any cash you collect directly, of course, will be taxed as ordinary income in the year you take it.

Choosing between a lump sum and an annuity is an important decision for a minister. If you take money out of your retirement plan in a series of lifelong payments, this is referred to as annuitizing. While assuring you will not outlive the monthly payments, this method may prevent your family from inheriting the money in your retirement plan. After your death the remaining money goes to the insurance company or the pension plan. If you do not annuitize, your plan money that is not spent can be bequeathed to heirs.

Here is a rundown on the pluses and minuses of common payout options:

➤ **Lump sum.** Your pension may be made up of some money you have contributed and some funds contributed by the churches you served during your ministry. One option is to take a lump sum of your funds and receive the church's contributions piece-by-piece in the years to come.

Withdrawing the portion represented by your contributions is often a wise choice. The time value of money could allow you to invest it and come out ahead of spreading the payments out over your lifetime. However, there is both opportunity and risk associated with taking a lump-sum payment.

➤ **Straight-life (single-life) benefit.** Whether or not you take your own contributions in a lump sum, you still need to decide how you will receive the rest of the pension. One option is called a straight-life or single-life benefit. This option offers the highest monthly payout, but it would pay only as long as you live. No benefit is available to anyone after your death. While this can be a valid choice for a single person, it is generally unwise for a married couple.

➤ **Fifteen-year certain payout.** This option guarantees payments for 15 years, even if you die before that. However, if you were to die after 15 years, no benefit would be available to your spouse. The payout is barely more than the joint-survivorship benefit, which would continue paying the surviving spouse the same benefit for life. This option is rarely a wise choice.

➤ **Joint-survivorship benefit, with same payout to surviving spouse life.** This is the payout option that is best for most situations. The payout is about 90% of the single-life payout, but significantly less risky.

 **Action Steps**

- Set your goals and start saving early.
- Make maximum tax-deferred contributions to your retirement plans.
- Decide what you would like to do in retirement.
- Figure out how much money you will need.
- Plan for more years than you think will be necessary.
- Maximize your housing allowance benefit, even during retirement.
- Improvise if you cannot close the money gap.

CHAPTER FIVE

Housing Allowance

In This Chapter

- Types of housing arrangements
- Structuring the housing allowance
- Reporting the housing allowance to the minister
- Accounting for the housing allowance
- Other housing allowance issues
- Housing allowance worksheets

Ministers are eligible to receive lodging from the church free of *income* tax liability. Maximizing housing benefits requires careful planning. Used properly, the housing allowance can truly be the minister's best tax friend.

Every minister should have a portion of salary designated as a housing allowance. For ministers living in church-owned housing, a housing allowance covering expenses such as furnishings, personal property insurance on contents, and utilities could save several hundred dollars of income taxes annually. A properly designated housing allowance may be worth thousands of dollars in income tax savings for ministers living in their own homes or rented quarters.

The housing allowance provides an opportunity to *exclude* dollars from gross income. The designated housing allowance should be subtracted from compensation before the church completes the data on Form W-2. The excluded portion of the housing allowance is not entered on Form 1040 or related schedules, except Schedule SE, since it is not a deduction for income tax purposes.

If the church properly designates a portion of your cash salary for expenses of a home you provide, the exclusion is commonly referred to as a *housing* allowance. If the church properly designates a portion of your cash salary for expenses you incur in relation to a church-owned home, the exclusion is often called a *parsonage* allowance. In either instance, it is an exclusion from income tax, not self-employment tax.

Ministers are eligible to exclude the fair rental value of church-provided housing, for income tax purposes, without any official action by the church. However, a cash housing allowance related to church-provided or minister-provided housing is only excludable under the following rules:

Employer-Provided Housing

The fair rental value of the housing plus utilities (if paid by employer) is

- Excludable for federal income tax purposes
- Includable for social security (SECA) purposes

A housing allowance may be provided a minister living in employer-provided housing. It is a designation of the cash salary. The housing allowance may cover certain housing expenses paid by the minister (see the worksheet on page 96).

Minister-Provided Housing

The excludable portion of a housing allowance is not taxable for federal income tax purposes. The entire housing allowance is taxable for social security tax (SECA) purposes. See the worksheets on pages 97-98 for excludable expenses.

The excludable housing allowance is the lowest of these factors:
- Reasonable compensation
- Amount used from current ministerial income to provide the home
- Amount prospectively and officially designated by the employer
- The fair rental value of the home including utilities and furnishings

If a designated housing allowance exceeds these four factors, the excess is reportable as additional income for income tax purposes.

➤ The allowance must be officially designated by the church. The designation should be stated in writing, preferably by resolution of the top governing body, in an employment contract, or, at a minimum, in the church budget and payroll records. If the only reference to the housing allowance is in the church budget, the budget should be formally approved by the top governing body of the church. See the 2003 edition of *The Zondervan Church and Nonprofit Tax & Financial Guide* for examples of housing allowance resolutions.

Tax law does not specifically say an oral designation of the housing allowance is unacceptable. In certain instances, the IRS accepted an oral housing designation. Still, the use of a written designation is preferable and highly recommended. The lack of a written designation significantly weakens the defense for the housing exclusion upon audit.

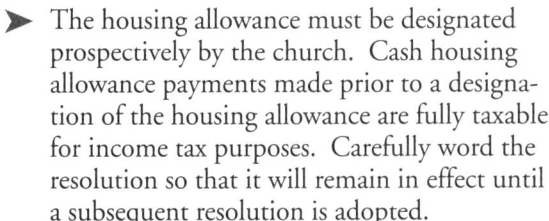

Key Issue

Understanding the distinction between a housing allowance designation and the housing exclusion is fundamental. The designation is officially made by the church or other employer. The exclusion is the amount the minister actually excludes for income tax purposes after applying the limitations outlined in this chapter.

➤ The housing allowance must be designated prospectively by the church. Cash housing allowance payments made prior to a designation of the housing allowance are fully taxable for income tax purposes. Carefully word the resolution so that it will remain in effect until a subsequent resolution is adopted.

➤ Only actual expenses can be excluded from income. The source of the funds used to pay for a minister's housing expenses must be compensation earned by the minister in the exercise of ministry in the current year.

➤ Only an annual comparison of housing expenses to the housing allowance is required. For example, if the housing allowance designation is stated in terms of a weekly or monthly amount, only a comparison of actual housing expenses to the annualized housing allowance is required.

➤ The housing allowance exclusion cannot exceed the fair rental value of the housing including utilities and furnishings. (See pages 84 for a discussion of the Warren case and pages 91-92 for 2002 legislation that impacted this limitation.)

Types of Housing Arrangements

Minister living in church-provided housing

If you live in a church-owned parsonage or housing rented by the church, the fair rental value of the housing is not reported for income tax purposes. The fair rental value is subject only to self-employment tax.

Legal Challenge of Housing Allowance Dismissed

For years, the IRS has applied the fair rental value limitation to the housing allowance exclusion. The limitation was difficult to apply because the IRS provided little guidance on determining the fair rental value. It was also a challenge to determine the fair rental value of a home owned by the minister when there is not a comparable furnished home in a nearby area. The fair rental value limitation was particularly difficult for ministers living in relatively expensive housing, making a purchase down payment, or paying off a mortgage early.

Rev. Rick Warren, senior pastor at Saddleback Valley Community Church in California, decided to make the first court challenge of the fair rental value test in 1998; and in 2000, the U.S. Tax Court ruled in his favor, saying that the fair rental value is not a limitation for purposes of the housing exclusion. The court ruled that a housing allowance was excludable from income simply because it was approved by the church board in advance and it was all spent on housing. Many ministers rejoiced at the ruling and it appeared that Rev. Warren's name would be long remembered in a favorable light in connection with this historic case. However, the celebration was short-lived.

The IRS decided to appeal the issue in February 2001 to the Ninth Circuit Court of Appeals. In the Ninth Circuit, things took a surprising turn. A panel of the Ninth Circuit requested an answer to a question not raised by the parties: whether the parsonage exclusion violated the Constitution's Establishment Clause. (The constitutionality issue was only raised regarding minister-provided housing, not church-provided housing.) The court appointed University of Southern California Professor Erwin Chemerinsky to submit an *amicus curiae* brief on the constitutionality issue. His brief asserted that the exemption was clearly unconstitutional because it accorded clergy a benefit not given to others.

Attempting to short-circuit the fair rental value issue in the Warren case before the Ninth Circuit, Congress passed the Clergy Housing Allowance Clarification Act of 2002 and on May 20, 2002, President Bush signed it into law. Effective January 1, 2002, the housing exclusion is limited by the fair rental value of the property for ministers who provide their own home. The law effectively sides with the long-held position of the IRS.

After the fair rental value test became law, both parties filed to dismiss the case on May 22, 2002, before the Ninth Circuit. They said the IRS was precluded under the new legislation from continuing the case. However, Chemerinsky filed a motion to intervene as a private taxpayer on May 29, 2002, and opposed the dismissal. On August 26, 2002, the Ninth Circuit Court of Appeals dismissed Chemerinsky's motion challenging the constitutionality of the minister's housing allowance. This dismissal effectively ends the current challenge to the housing allowance. Another lawsuit would be required to address the constitutionality issue.

With the constitutionality issue behind us for the moment, ministers who provide their own homes should turn their attention to complying with the Clergy Housing Allowance Clarification Act of 2002.

You may request a housing allowance to cover expenses incurred in maintaining the church-owned or church-rented housing. The cash housing allowance excludable, for income tax purposes, is the *lowest* of (1) reasonable compensation, (2) actual housing expenses paid from current ministerial income, (3) the amount prospectively and officially designated, or (4) the fair rental value of the home including utilities and furnishings. Examples of allowable expenses are utilities, repairs, furnishings, and appliances. If the actual expenses exceed the housing allowance declared by the church, the excess amount cannot be excluded from income. The expenses shown on the worksheet on page 96 qualify as part of the housing allowance for a minister living in housing owned or rented by the church.

Tip

The designation of a housing allowance for a minister living in church-provided housing is often overlooked. While the largest housing allowance benefits go to ministers with mortgage payments on their own homes, a housing allowance of a few thousand dollars is often beneficial to a pastor in a church-provided home.

It is appropriate for the minister's out-of-pocket expenses for the maintenance of a church-owned parsonage to be reimbursed by the church if a full accounting is made. Such reimbursements do not relate to a housing allowance. If such expenses are not reimbursed, they could be excludable from income under a housing allowance.

If the church owns the parsonage, the church may wish to provide an equity allowance to help compensate the minister for equity not accumulated through home ownership. An equity allowance is taxable both for income and social security tax purposes *unless* directed to a 403(b) tax-sheltered annuity, 401(k) plan, or certain other retirement programs.

Minister owning or renting own home

If you own or rent your own home, you may exclude, for income tax purposes, a cash housing allowance that is the *lowest* of (1) reasonable compensation, (2) the amount used to provide a home from current ministerial income, (3) the amount prospectively and officially designated, or (4) the fair rental value of the home including utilities and furnishings.

The expenses shown on the worksheet on page 97 qualify as part of the housing allowance for a minister owning or buying a home. Page 98 shows a similar worksheet for a minister renting a home.

Many ministers make the mistake of automatically excluding from income (for income tax purposes) the total designated housing allowance, even though actual housing expenses are less than the designation. This practice may cause a significant underpayment of income taxes.

The housing expenses related to a minister-owned house should not be reimbursed by the church. These expenses should be covered by the minister under a cash housing allowance paid by the church.

Example: A minister lives in a personally owned home. The church

85

prospectively designates $18,000 of the salary as housing allowance. The minister spends $17,000 for housing-related items.

Since the amount spent is lower than the designated housing allowance, the excludable housing is $17,000. Therefore, $1,000 ($18,000 less $17,000) must be added by the minister to taxable income on Form 1040, page 1, line 21. Unless the minister has opted out of social security, the entire $18,000 is reportable for social security purposes on Schedule SE.

Structuring the Housing Allowance

Before paying compensation

The employer should take the following steps to designate a housing allowance *before* paying compensation:

- Verify the qualified status of the minister. Does the minister meet the tests found on pages 26-32?

- Verify the qualified nature of the minister's services, e.g., administering sacraments, conducting religious worship, performing management responsibilities for a church, a denomination, or an integral agency (see pages 30-31) of a church or denomination (see pages 31-32 for ministers employed by a parachurch or other organization).

- Determine the extent to which payment of housing expenses will be the responsibility of the minister. For example, will the utilities for a church-owned parsonage be paid by the church or the minister?

- Request that the minister estimate the housing-related expenses expected in the coming year.

- Adopt a written designation based on the minister's estimate. This designation may be included in minutes or resolutions of the top governing body, an employment contract, annual budget, or another appropriate document if official action on the document is recorded.

Warning

It is the responsibility of the church or other employer—not the minister—to determine if an individual qualifies as a minister in the eyes of the IRS and, therefore, qualifies for a housing allowance designation. Simply being ordained, licensed, or commissioned is often not enough to qualify for this status.

During the calendar year

The following actions should be taken during the year (after designating the housing allowance):

- The minister should keep records of allowable housing expenses incurred.

- The minister should make payments to the IRS to cover the self-employment tax (SECA) on the entire housing allowance (and other income subject to SECA) plus federal income tax on any anticipated unexpended portion of the allowance and other taxable income. This may be accomplished by submitting quarterly tax installments with Form 1040-ES, voluntary income tax withholding by the minister's employer, or spousal income tax withholding.

- The minister should identify any significant change in housing expenses and estimate the amount by which the total actual expenses may exceed the amount designated as the housing allowance.

- When housing expenses are running higher than anticipated or are expected to do so, the minister should ask the church to *prospectively* increase the housing allowance designation. A *retroactive* housing allowance increase is ineffective.

- The church should *prospectively* amend the minister's housing allowance as appropriate to reflect the anticipated change in housing expenses.

After each calendar year

The following steps should be taken after the close of each calendar year with respect to the housing allowance:

- The church should provide the minister with copies of Form W-2. An approved housing allowance paid to the minister may be included on Form W-2 in Box 14 with the explanation: "Housing Allowance." As an option, the church could provide the minister with a separate statement showing the amount of any housing allowance *paid* to or for the minister and omit the data from Form W-2.

- The minister who provides his or her own housing should compare reasonable compensation, the amount designated for housing, and actual housing expenses. The *lowest* of these amounts is excluded for income tax purposes.

  Ministers living in church-provided housing must compare the amount designated and actual housing expenses, and exclude the lowest of these amounts.

Designation limits

The IRS does not place a limit on how much of a minister's compensation may be *designated* as a housing allowance by the employing church. In a few instances, as much as 100% of the compensation may be designated. But practical and reasonable limits usually apply.

A housing allowance must not represent "unreasonable compensation" to the minister. Unfortunately, neither the IRS nor the courts have provided a clear definition of unreasonable compensation. The IRS considers the total compensation package, including the housing allowance and taxable and nontaxable fringe benefits. This amount is often compared with the church's annual budget and may be compared with other similar-sized churches.

Unless the amount is justified based on anticipated expenses, it may be unwise for the employing church to exclude 100% of compensation. A 100% exclusion may result in very unusual reporting to the IRS that may draw questions and an audit. Officers of financial organizations often give extra scrutiny to loan or home mortgage applications of ministers where the income reflected on Form W-2 is unusually low.

Caution

How high is too high? Can even 100% of a minister's cash salary be designated as a housing allowance? Yes, but only in a few situations. The fair rental value and actual housing expense limitations usually make the 100% designation inappropriate.

Example 1: A minister receives a salary of $10,000 per year and provides his home. Actual housing costs are $12,000. If the church sets the housing allowance at 100% of compensation, or $10,000, the minister may exclude $10,000 for federal income tax purposes. If the church had set the housing allowance at 50% of compensation, or $5,000, only $5,000 could be excluded.

Example 2: A minister-employee has a voluntary withholding arrangement with the church, and the church sets the housing allowance at 100% of compensation. Form W-2 would show no salary (ignoring other compensation factors) but would reflect federal income tax and possibly state income tax withheld. While Form W-2 would be correctly stated, its appearance would be most unusual.

It is often best to overdesignate your parsonage allowance by a reasonable amount to allow for unexpected expenses and increases in utility costs. Any excess housing allowance designated should be shown as income on line 21 of Form 1040 for minister-employees.

Amending the housing designation

If a minister's actual housing expenses are or will be higher than initially estimated and designated, the church may *prospectively* amend the designation during the year.

Remember

The housing allowance designation may be prospectively amended at any time during the year regardless of whether the church or other employer uses a calendar or fiscal year. Changing the designation to cover expenses that have already been paid (almost all ministers use the cash basis for tax purposes) is not acceptable.

Example: The church sets the housing allowance at $1,000 per month on January 1, but housing expenses are averaging $1,200 per month. On July 1, the church approves an increase in the housing allowance to $1,600 per month. Therefore, the housing allowance for the year totals $15,600 ($6,000 for the first six months and $9,600 for the other six months). Actual housing costs are $14,400 ($1,200 for each month). The minister excludes $13,200 for federal income tax purposes: $6,000 for the first six months (limited by the designation) and $7,200 for the last six months (limited by the actual housing costs).

Housing allowance as a percentage of salary

Some churches set the housing allowance by applying a percentage to the total cash salary. Housing allowance percentages are often in a range of 40% to 60% of the total cash salary. Setting the housing designation based on an estimate of housing expenses for each minister is highly preferred to the percentage method. By using the percentage approach, the church may unintentionally permit an excessive housing exclusion from income or preclude a legitimate exclusion.

Housing allowance adopted by denomination

If the local congregation employs and pays you, a resolution by a national or area office of your denomination does not constitute a housing allowance designation for you. The local congregation must officially designate a part of your salary as a housing allowance.

But a resolution of your denomination can designate your housing allowance if you are employed *and* paid by a national or area office or if you are a retired minister receiving retirement funds from a denominational retirement plan.

Reporting the Housing Allowance to the Minister

The designated housing allowance may be reflected on Form W-2 in Box 14 with the notation, "Housing Allowance." Though not required, this reporting method is suggested by Publication 517.

Or, a church can report the designated housing allowance to a minister by providing a statement separate from Form W-2. This may be in a memo or letter. The statement should not be attached to your income tax returns.

Your church may erroneously include the housing allowance on your Form W-2, Box 1. If this happens, the church should prepare a corrected form. If a corrected form is not prepared, you should deduct your actual housing expenses, subject to the housing allowance limitations, on line 21 of Form 1040.

Tip

The designated housing allowance should always be excluded from Form W-2, Box 1, as compensation. Including the housing allowance in this box could cause unnecessary communication between the IRS and the minister.

There is no requirement for the minister to account to the church for the actual housing expenses. Many ministers consider this as an intrusion into their personal finances. However, if the church requires this reporting, based on administrative discretion, the church would prepare Form W-2 with the adjusted housing allowance excluded. Under this approach, the excluded housing is always equal to or less than the housing designation.

Accounting for the Housing Allowance

Determining fair rental value

The determination of the fair rental value of church-provided housing for self-employment social security purposes is totally the responsibility of the minister. The church is not responsible to set the value. The fair rental value should be based on comparable rental values of other similar residences in the immediate neighborhood or community, comparably furnished.

Caution

Even though the fair rental value test is now etched into law (see pages 91-92), there has been change in the sketchy guidance provided by the IRS as to how to determine the fair rental value.

One of the best methods to use in establishing the fair rental value of your housing is to request a local realtor to estimate the value in writing. Place the estimate in your tax file and annually adjust the value for inflation and other local real estate valuation factors.

Housing allowance in excess of actual expenses or fair rental value

Some ministers erroneously believe that they may exclude every dollar of the housing *designation* adopted by the church without limitation. The housing designation is merely the starting point. If reasonable compensation, actual expenses, or the fair rental value is lower, the lowest amount is eligible for exclusion from income.

> **Example:** A minister living in a home owned personally receives cash compensation from the church of $25,000. The church prospectively designates $20,000 as a housing allowance. The fair rental value is $21,000. Actual housing expenses for the year are $14,000. The amount excludable from income is limited to the actual housing expenses of $14,000.

Determining actual expenses

The actual amount expended for housing and furnishings is limited to amounts expended in the current calendar year. Amounts expended in a prior year cannot be carried forward to a following year through depreciation or by carrying forward actual current year expenses that exceeded amounts designated in a prior year. Housing expenses that are not used to justify a housing allowance exclusion simply have no value in future years.

Clergy Housing Allowance Clarification Act of 2002

On May 20, 2002, President Bush signed the "Clergy Housing Allowance Clarification Act of 2002," Public Law 107-181:

A. In General. Section 107 of the Internal Revenue Code of 1986 is amended by inserting before the period at the end of paragraph (2) "and to the extent such allowance does not exceed the fair rental value of the home, including furnishings and appurtenances such as a garage, plus the cost of utilities."

B. Effective Date.

(1) In General. The amendment made by this section shall apply to taxable years beginning after December 31, 2001.

(2) Returns Positions. The amendment made by this section also shall apply to any taxable year beginning before January 1, 2002, for which the taxpayer

  (a) on a return filed before April 17, 2002, limited the exclusion under Section 107 of the Internal Revenue Code of 1986 as provided in such amendment, or

  (b) filed a return after April 16, 2002.

(3) Other Years Before 2002. Except as provided in paragraph (2), notwithstanding any prior regulation, revenue ruling, or other guidance issued by the Internal Revenue Service, no person shall be subject to the limitations added to Section 107 of such Code by this Act for any taxable year beginning before January 1, 2002.

The law only applies to minister-provided housing and not church-provided housing. Here is how the law will impact ministers who provide their own homes:

➤ **2001 tax returns.** If a minister filed his or her 2001 return by April 16, 2002, and did not apply the fair rental value test, the new law does not apply. If the minister did apply the fair rental value test, the return may not be amended to ignore the test.

Example 1: Minister A filed his 2001 tax return on or before April 16, 2002. The church had designated a housing allowance of $30,000 for 2001. Actual housing expenses were $32,000 and the fair rental value of the home was $20,000. The minister excluded $30,000 of housing expenses for income tax purposes. Must the minister file an amended tax return and reduce his housing exclusion to $20,000, the amount of the fair rental value? No. The new law will not apply to him until 2002.

Example 2: Minister B filed his 2001 tax return on or before April 16, 2002. The church had designated a housing allowance of $30,000 for 2001. Actual housing expenses were $32,000 and the fair rental value of the home was $20,000. Minister B excluded $20,000 of housing expenses for income tax purposes. Can Minister B file an amended tax return and increase his housing exclusion to $30,000, the amount designated for housing? No.

> **Example 3:** Minister C filed an extension for his 2001 tax return and filed his tax return on June 1, within the time allowed by the extension. The church had designated a housing allowance of $30,000 for 2001. Actual housing expenses were $32,000 and the fair rental value of the home was $20,000. Minister C excluded $20,000 of housing expenses for income tax purposes. Can he file an amended tax return and increase his housing exclusion to $30,000, the amount designated for housing? No. Since he filed his return after April 16, 2002, he is limited by the fair rental value.

➤ **2002 tax returns.** The fair rental value test applies to 2002 returns, in addition to the other tests. If you own or rent your own home, you may exclude, for income tax purposes, a cash housing allowance that is the lowest of (1) reasonable compensation, (2) the amount used to provide a home from current ministerial income, (3) the amount prospectively and officially designated, or (4) the fair rental value of the home including utilities and furnishings.

> **Example:** For 2002, the church designated a housing allowance of $20,000, the minister spent $17,000 on housing and the fair rental value of the home was $16,000. How should the minister report this data on Form 1040? The exclusion is limited to $16,000. The difference between the housing designation of $20,000 and the exclusion of $16,000, or $4,000 must be reported on Form 1040, Line 21 as income from the "Excess Housing Allowance." The entire $20,000 should be included on Schedule SE for social security purposes.

➤ **Housing designations.** How should a church or other employer decide how much should be designated as a housing allowance? Ask the minister to prospectively estimate the lower of the actual housing expenses or the fair rental value of the home including utilities and furnishings. If this amount seems reasonable, use the amount as the basis of the prospective and formal designation. If the amount requested seems unreasonably high, ask for an explanation of the amount and then decide what is reasonable.

> **Example:** A minister provides her own housing. The fair rental value is $15,000. She anticipates spending $18,000 on housing. Should the church designate a housing allowance of $15,000 or at least $18,000? A designation of $15,000 should be made since the minister cannot exclude more than this amount.

Home equity loans and second mortgages

Without a home mortgage, a minister has no mortgage principal and interest amounts to exclude under a housing allowance. Also, there is no double deduction of the mortgage interest as an itemized deduction and as housing expense for purposes of the housing allowance exclusion if there is no mortgage.

What is the treatment of principal and interest payments on a second mortgage or a mortgage that has been refinanced to increase the indebtedness? This issue has not been addressed by the IRS or a court. However, it appears that an allocation of the loan payments between excludable housing expenses and nonexcludable personal expenses would be required based on the use of the additional loan proceeds.

Warning

Loan payments on home equity loans and second mortgages qualify as housing expenses only in certain instances. The use of the loan proceeds as housing expenses vs. nonhousing expenses determines whether the loan payments may be excluded for income tax purposes.

Do principal and interest payments on a home equity loan qualify as excludable housing expenses? The IRS and the Tax Court have ruled that the loan or mortgage payments are excludable as housing expenses *only* if the loan proceeds are used for housing expenses. The exclusion is not available if the loan proceeds are used for personal expenses such as the purchase of an auto or for a child's college education. The interest is only deductible on Schedule A if the note is secured.

> **Example:** In 2001, a home equity loan of $20,000 was obtained by a minister, secured by the residence. The money was used in 2001 as follows: $10,000 for a new car and $10,000 to add a deck and screened-in porch to the minister's home. The home equity loan payments relating to funds used to purchase the new car are not excludable as housing expenses. Since the other $10,000 was used for housing, the payments relating to this portion of the loan qualify as housing expenses.

Other Housing Allowance Issues

Payment of the housing allowance to the minister

It is immaterial whether the payment of a properly designated cash housing allowance is a separate payment or is part of a payment that also includes other compensation. A cash housing allowance usually is included with the minister's salary check.

Cost of the housing allowance to the church

Some churches mistakenly believe that providing a housing allowance to their minister will increase the church budget. This is not true. If a portion of the minister's compensation is designated as a housing allowance, it costs the church nothing.

> **Example:** A church is paying a minister $30,000 per year but does not presently designate a housing allowance. The minister provides the home. The minister requests that the church designate a housing allowance of

$10,000 per year. The church adopts a resolution reflecting compensation of $30,000 per year, of which $10,000 is a designated housing allowance. Before the designation, Form W-2 for the minister would have shown compensation of $30,000. After the designation, Form W-2 would reflect compensation of $20,000. The cash spent by the church is the same before and after the designation.

Double deduction of interest and taxes

Ministers who own their homes and itemize their deductions are eligible to deduct mortgage interest and property taxes on Schedule A even though these items are excluded from taxable income as part of the housing allowance. This is often referred to as a "double deduction."

Housing allowances for retired ministers

Pension payments, retirement allowances, or disability payments paid to a retired minister from an established plan are generally taxable as pension income. However, denominations generally designate a housing allowance for retired ministers to compensate them for past services to local churches of the denomination or to the denomination or in denominational administrative positions. The housing allowance designated relates only to payments from the denominationally sponsored retirement program.

Withdrawals from a denominationally sponsored tax-sheltered annuity (TSA) or 401(k) plan qualify for designation as a housing allowance. Withdrawals from a TSA or 401(k) plan that is not sponsored by a local church are not eligible for designation as a housing allowance. Benefits from a TIAA-CREF plan for a minister formerly employed by a church-related college *do not* qualify for the housing allowance.

Also, retired ministers may exclude the rental value of a home furnished by a church or a rental allowance paid by a church as compensation for past services.

> **Remember**
>
> Payments from denominational retirement plans are generally subject to a housing allowance designation. This means the money going into the plan is generally tax-deferred for income tax purposes and not subject to social security tax. And the money coming out of the plan may qualify for exclusion for income tax purposes and is not subject to social security tax.

If a denomination reports the gross amount of pension or TSA payments on Form 1099-R and designates the housing allowance, the recipient may offset the housing expenses and insert the net amount on page 1, Form 1040. A supplementary schedule such as the following example should be attached to the tax return:

Pensions and annuity income (Form 1040, line 16a)	$10,000
Less housing exclusion	8,000
Form 1040, line 16b	$2,000

The amount excluded is limited to the lowest of (1) the amount used to provide a home, or (2) the properly designated housing allowance.

A surviving spouse of a retired minister *cannot* exclude a housing allowance from income. If a minister's surviving spouse receives a rental allowance, it is includable in gross income.

Housing allowances for evangelists

Traveling evangelists may treat a portion of an honorarium received as an excludable housing allowance to the extent that the paying church designates all or a portion of the honorarium as a housing allowance in advance of payment. Honoraria payments of $600 or more in a calendar year to an evangelist require the church to issue Form 1099-MISC. The $600 reporting threshold is after excluding any properly designated housing allowances and net of expense reimbursements based on adequate substantiation.

> **Example:** William Dalton, an ordained evangelist, preaches at Westside Church for ten days. Westside Church paid Mr. Dalton $1,500 consisting of $300 documented travel expenses, a properly designated housing allowance of $500, and a $700 honorarium. Since the honorarium exceeded $600, the church issued Mr. Dalton a Form 1099-MISC for $700.

Some itinerant evangelists form nonprofit corporations for their ministries. The nonprofit corporation may designate a housing allowance for the evangelist. This eliminates the need for each church to provide the housing designation. If an evangelist purchases a house and rents it out while traveling, only the housing expenses relating to the time at home are excludable.

Action Steps

- The church should adopt a written housing designation based on the minister's estimate of housing expenses after considering the possible impact of the Warren Tax Court case.
- The minister should request a housing designation even if living in church-provided housing.
- The church should never approve a retroactive adjustment in the housing designation.
- The minister should keep a record of actual allowable housing expenses.
- Include in income any housing allowance paid that is more than the *lowest* of (1) the amount used to provide the home from current ministerial income, (2) the amount properly designated by the church, or (3) reasonable compensation.
- Include the entire housing designation in the computation of your social security tax on Schedule SE unless you have opted out of social security.
- Determine if it is appropriate for you to revoke your election to opt out of social security.

Housing Allowance Worksheet
Minister Living in a Parsonage
Owned by or Rented by the Church

Minister's Name: _____ _____

For the period _____, 200__ to _____, 200__

Date designation approved _____, 200__

Allowable Housing Expenses *(expenses paid by minister from current income)*

	Estimated Expenses	Actual
Utilities *(gas, electricity, water)* and trash collection	$ _____	$ _____
Local telephone expense *(base charge)*	_____	_____
Decoration and redecoration	_____	_____
Structural maintenance and repair	_____	_____
Landscaping, gardening, and pest control	_____	_____
Furnishings *(purchase, repair, replacement)*	_____	_____
Personal property insurance on minister-owned contents	_____	_____
Personal property taxes on contents	_____	_____
Umbrella liability insurance	_____	_____
Subtotal	_____	
10% allowance for unexpected expenses	_____	
TOTAL	$ _____	$ _____ (A)
Properly designated housing allowance		$ _____ (B)

The amount excludable from income for federal income tax purposes is the *lowest* of A or B.

CHAPTER 5 ➤ HOUSING ALLOWANCE

Housing Allowance Worksheet
Minister Living in Home
Minister Owns or Is Buying

Minister's Name: _____

For the period _____, 200__ to _____, 200__

Date designation approved _____, 200__

Allowable Housing Expenses *(expenses paid by minister from current income)*

	Estimated Expenses	Actual
Down payment on purchase of housing	$ _____	$ _____
Housing loan principal and interest payments	_____	_____
Real estate commission, escrow fees	_____	_____
Real property taxes	_____	_____
Personal property taxes on contents	_____	_____
Homeowner's insurance	_____	_____
Personal property insurance on contents	_____	_____
Umbrella liability insurance	_____	_____
Structural maintenance and repair	_____	_____
Landscaping, gardening, and pest control	_____	_____
Furnishings *(purchase, repair, replacement)*	_____	_____
Decoration and redecoration	_____	_____
Utilities *(gas, electricity, water)* and trash collection	_____	_____
Local telephone expense *(base charge)*	_____	_____
Homeowner's association dues/condominium fees	_____	_____

Subtotal _____

10% allowance for unexpected expenses _____

TOTAL $_____ $_____ (A)

Properly designated housing allowance $_____ (B)

Fair rental value of home $_____ (C)

The amount excludable from income for federal income tax purposes is the *lowest* of A, B, or C.

Housing Allowance Worksheet
Minister Living in Home
Minister Is Renting

Minister's Name: _____

For the period _____, 200__ to _____, 200__

Date designation approved _____, 200__

Allowable Housing Expenses *(expenses paid by minister from current income)*

	Estimated Expenses	Actual
Housing rental payments	$ _____	$ _____
Personal property insurance on minister-owned contents	_____	_____
Personal property taxes on contents	_____	_____
Umbrella liability	_____	_____
Structural maintenance and repair	_____	_____
Landscaping, gardening, and pest control	_____	_____
Furnishings *(purchase, repair, replacement)*	_____	_____
Decoration and redecoration	_____	_____
Utilities *(gas, electricity, water)* and trash collection	_____	_____
Local telephone expense *(base charge)*	_____	_____
Mobile home space rental	_____	_____
Subtotal	_____	
10% allowance for unexpected expenses	_____	
TOTAL	$ _____	$ _____ (A)
Properly designated housing allowance		$ _____ (B)

The amount excludable from income for federal income tax purposes is the *lower* of A or B.

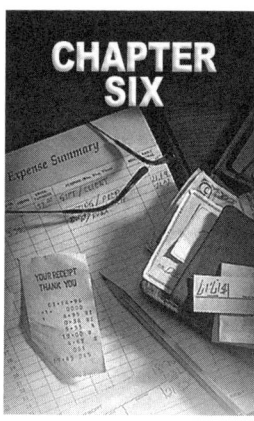

CHAPTER SIX

Business Expenses

In This Chapter

- Accountable and nonaccountable expense reimbursement plans
- Documenting and reporting business expenses
- Travel and transportation expenses
- Auto expense deductions
- Home-office rules
- Other business and professional expenses
- Allocation of business expenses

Most ministers spend several thousands of dollars each year on church-related business expenses. For example, the ministry-related portion of auto expenses is often a major cost. You only have two choices: try to deduct the expenses for tax purposes or have the expenses reimbursed by the church. You will almost always save tax dollars if your expenses are reimbursed.

Business and professional expenses fall into three basic categories: expenses reimbursed under an accountable plan, expenses reimbursed under a nonaccountable plan, and unreimbursed expenses. The last two categories are treated the same for tax purposes.

The reimbursement of an expense never changes the character of the item from personal to business. Business expenses are business whether or not they are reimbursed. Personal expenses are always nondeductible and nonreimbursable. If a personal expense is inadvertently reimbursed by the employer, the minister should immediately refund the money to the employer.

Key Issue

Combining an accountable expense reimbursement plan with a housing allowance or health reimbursement arrangement is not permissible. These concepts are each covered under separate sections of the tax law and cannot be commingled.

To be deductible or reimbursable, a business expense must be both ordinary and necessary. An *ordinary* expense is one that is common and accepted in your field. A *necessary* expense is one that is helpful and appropriate for your field. An expense does not have to be indispensable to be considered necessary.

Accountable and Nonaccountable Expense Reimbursement Plans

An accountable plan is a reimbursement or expense allowance arrangement, established by your church, that requires (1) a business purpose for the expenses, (2) substantiation of expenses to the church, and (3) the return of any excess reimbursements.

The substantiation of expenses and the return of excess reimbursements must be handled within a reasonable time. The following methods meet the "reasonable time" definition:

▶ The fixed date method applies if

  ☐ an advance is made within 30 days of when an expense is paid or incurred;

  ☐ an expense is substantiated to the church within 60 days after the expense is paid or incurred; and

  ☐ any excess amount is returned to the church within 120 days after the expense is paid or incurred.

▶ The periodic statement method applies if

  ☐ the church provides employees with a periodic statement that sets forth the amount paid under the arrangement that is more than substantiated expenses;

  ☐ the statements are provided at least quarterly; and

  ☐ the church requests that the employee provide substantiation for any additional expenses that have not yet been substantiated and/or return any amounts remaining unsubstantiated within 120 days of the statement.

Caution

Documentation for business expenses must be submitted to the church or other employer on a timely basis—within 60 days after the expense was paid or incurred. While the 60 days is a timeliness "safe harbor" vs. a fixed time limit, it is clear that documentation semiannually or annually should not be reimbursed under an accountable plan.

If you substantiate your business expenses and any unused payments are returned, expense reimbursements have no impact on your taxes. The expenses reimbursed are not included on Form W-2 or deducted on your tax return.

Example 1: Your church adopts an accountable reimbursement plan using the "fixed date method." The church authorizes salary of $26,000 and agrees to pay business expenses up to $10,000.

During the year, you substantiate $9,000 of expenses under the accountable guidelines. The church provides you with a Form W-2 reflecting compensation of $26,000. The substantiated expenses of $9,000 are not reported to the IRS by the church or on your tax return.

The church retains the $1,000 difference between the amount budgeted by the church and the amount reimbursed to the minister. (See page 102 for an example where the church pays the balance in the expense budget to the minister.)

Example 2: Your church authorizes a salary of $23,000 plus an auto allowance of $5,000 and $3,000 for other business expenses. The church does not require or receive any substantiation for the auto or other business expenses. This is a nonaccountable reimbursement plan.

The church should provide you with a Form W-2 reflecting compensation of $31,000. The auto and other business expenses you incur could be claimed on Form 2106 (2106-EZ) and Schedule A as miscellaneous deductions if you are reporting as an employee for income tax purposes.

The IRS disallows deductions for a portion of unreimbursed business expenses on the premise that the expenses are allocable to your excludable housing allowance (see allocation of business expenses on pages 121-22). This is another reason that every minister should comply with the accountable expense reimbursement rules. The goal should be to eliminate all unreimbursed business expenses.

Accountable expense reimbursement plans cannot be combined with other fringe benefit plans or a housing allowance. Too often, ministers have been advised that the employing church can establish a general reimbursement account to cover church-related business expenses, housing expenses, dependent care expenses, out-of-pocket medical expenses, and educational expenses. While all of these items can be handled in a tax beneficial manner for a minister, they are subject to separate rules in the tax law. Some of the items are subject to the nondiscrimination rules, others are not.

> **Caution**
>
> Contrary to erroneous advice often shared in the church community, the accountable expense reimbursement of business expenses must not be commingled with other fringe benefit plans. Overlapping of benefit plans runs the risk of nullifying all of the plans.

Dollar limits must be separately established in some instances, and not in others. Housing expenses for a minister-owned home are not reimbursable at all.

Nonaccountable expense reimbursement plans

If your business expenses are not reimbursed, if you do not substantiate your expenses to the church, or if the amount of the reimbursement exceeds your actual expenses and the excess is not returned to the church within a reasonable period, your tax life becomes more complicated.

Nonaccountable reimbursements and excess reimbursements over IRS mileage or per diem limits must be included in your gross income and reported as wages on Form W-2. If your church pays you an "allowance" for certain business expenses, it represents taxable compensation. An allowance not based upon actual expenses does not meet the adequate accounting requirements for an accountable plan and must be included in your income.

Unreimbursed expenses or expenses reimbursed under a nonaccountable plan can be deducted only as itemized miscellaneous deductions and only to the extent that they, with your other miscellaneous deductions, exceed 2% of your adjusted gross income. Unreimbursed expenses are not deductible if you are an employee for income tax purposes and do not itemize.

Warning

Many ministers are paid expense "allowances." These payments accomplish nothing in terms of good stewardship. "Allowances" are fully taxable for income and social security tax purposes. Ministers must then resort to trying to deduct their expenses—much of which will be limited by the tax law—instead of receiving a full reimbursement.

Excess reimbursement retained as a "bonus"

If your church allows you to keep excess reimbursements by calling them a "bonus," the expense reimbursement plan becomes nonaccountable. This is also referred to as a "recharacterization of income." All payments under a nonaccountable plan are reportable as compensation on Form W-2.

Example: Your church sets your salary at $25,000 and agrees to reimburse your business expenses under an accountable plan for up to $10,000. Your reimbursed expenses are $9,000 and the church gave you a bonus for the $1,000 difference. Because of the "bonus" arrangement, all reimbursements made under the plan become nonaccountable. The entire $35,000 must be reported by the church as compensation on Form W-2.

Idea

The best expense reimbursement plans for a minister is one that pays 100% of church-related expenses. Too often, churches place dollar limits on these plans. With a dollar limit, any money left in the plan at the end of the year must stay with the church for the reimbursements to be tax-free. If the balance is paid to the minister, all payments for the year become taxable.

Documenting and Reporting Business Expenses

Documenting business expenses

For expenses to be allowed as deductions, you must show that you spent the money and that you spent it for a legitimate business reason. To prove that you spent the money, you generally need to provide documentary evidence that can be confirmed by a third party. Canceled checks or credit card slips are excellent evidence. To the IRS, third-party verification is important; if business expenses are paid in cash, be sure to get a receipt.

Documenting a business expense can be time-consuming. The IRS is satisfied if you note the five W's on the back of your credit card slip or other receipt:

- Why (business purpose)
- What (description, including itemized accounting of cost)
- When (date)
- Where (location)
- Who (names of those for whom the expense was incurred, e.g., meals and entertainment)

The only exception to the documentation rules is if your individual outlays for business expenses, other than for lodging, come to less than $75. The IRS does not require receipts for such expenses, although the five W's are still required. You always need a receipt for lodging expenses regardless of the amount.

Use of a church credit card can be helpful to charge church-related business expenses. However, the use of a credit card does not automatically provide substantiation without additional documentation, e.g., business purpose and business relationship.

While you are traveling out of town as an employee, your church may use a per diem for reimbursements instead of actual costs of meals (see page 106). The per diem is not subject to the 50% limitation on meal and entertainment expenses.

Remember

When a minister provides a listing of business expenses to the church or other employer—this is only a report, not documentation. Documentary evidence is much more than a report. It involves a hard-copy support of the five W's (why, what, when, where, and who).

For more detailed information, refer to IRS Publication 463, Travel, Entertainment, Gift and Car Expenses.

Forms on which expenses are reportable

Only the portion of business and professional expenses directly attributable to your Schedule C (C-EZ) income (self-employment activities) should be deducted on Schedule C (C-EZ). The portion of these expenses related to activities as an employee of the church should be deducted on Form 2106 (2106-EZ). If you receive reimbursement for any business or professional expenses and adequately account to the church under an accountable plan, you should not report the expenses on Form 2106 (2106-EZ) or Schedule C (C-EZ).

Travel and Transportation Expenses

The terms "transportation" and "travel" are often used interchangeably, but each has a distinct meaning for tax purposes. Travel is the broader category, including not only transportation expenses, but the cost of meals, lodging, and incidental expenses as well. To deduct travel expenses—including expenses you incur for meals, phone calls, cab fares, and so forth on the road—the business purpose must take you away from home overnight or require a rest stop. If you do not spend the night, you can deduct only your transportation costs.

Travel expenses

Many different expenses can add up on a business trip: air and taxi fares, costs of lodging, baggage charges, rental cars, tips, laundry and cleaning, and telephone expenses. You can deduct 100% of these expenses plus 50% of the meal and entertainment expenses you incurred while you were away, provided you meet certain guidelines:

- ▶ The trip must have a business purpose.
- ▶ The expenses cannot be "lavish and extravagant."
- ▶ You must be away from home long enough to require sleep or rest.

> **Key Issue**
>
> Travel expenses must be divided between your self-employment activities reported on Schedule C (C-EZ) and activities as an employee reported on Form 2106 (2106-EZ). Any unreimbursed travel expense that is also a meal or entertainment expense is subject to the 50% limitation for business meals and entertainment.

Deriving some personal pleasure from a trip doesn't disqualify it from being deductible. The IRS does, however, apply some important limitations to the tax treatment of foreign travel expenses.

If you are traveling within the United States, you can deduct all transportation costs, plus the costs of business-related meals (subject to the 50% limit) and lodging, if business was the primary reason for the trip. If you need to stay over Saturday night to get a lower airfare, the hotel and meal expenses for Saturday will generally be deductible. If the trip is primarily personal, none of your transportation costs can be deducted, but you can deduct other business-related travel expenses.

If you are reimbursed for travel expenses and adequately account to the church, you should not report your travel expenses on Form 2106 (2106-EZ). Further, you are not subject to the 50% limitation for business meals and entertainment.

International travel

Costs are deductible if you take an international trip for business reasons. If your trip is seven days or less, you can deduct your entire airfare even if you spend most of your time on personal activities. If you spend some days for personal reasons, your hotel, car rental, and meal costs are not deductible for those days. If your trip is more than seven days and you spend more than 25% of your time on personal activities, you must allocate all your expenses between business and personal time.

Trips to the Holy Land

Ministers often travel to the Holy Land to more closely identify with the area where Christ taught, preached, and ministered. In spite of all the obvious ministerial advantages of visiting the Holy Land, the applicability of tax deductions or tax-free reimbursements for such trips is not as clear.

Generally, no deduction or reimbursement is allowed for travel as a form of education. However, travel expense may be deductible or reimbursable if the travel is necessary to engage in an activity that gives rise to a business deduction relating to education.

A number of factors must be considered before the tax status of a Holy Land trip may be determined. To qualify as a deductible or reimbursable ministry-related expense, the trip must meet the general educational expense rules outlined on pages 118-19. Holy Land trips are also subject to the international travel rules as described above.

If you can answer "Yes" to the following questions, your expenses are more likely to qualify for reimbursement or as a deduction:

➤ Did the employing church require or strongly suggest that you make the trip to the Holy Land?

➤ Is this your first trip to the Holy Land? If you have a pattern of making the pilgrimage every few years, the trip is less likely to qualify as education expense.

➤ Will you be receiving college credit for the trip from a recognized educational institution? Is there a course syllabus?

➤ Is the trip organized for the purpose of study in the Holy Land and led by a Bible scholar?

➤ Did you take notes and pictures of places visited? If most of your photos include family members, the trip is less likely to qualify as education expense.

A tax deduction or reimbursement by a church for a minister's trip to the Holy Land should be made only after careful consideration of the facts and circumstances and the applicable tax rules.

Furlough travel

A missionary on furlough may qualify for travel status. The purpose of the travel must be primarily business, such as deputation reporting to constituents, or education, and the missionary's primary residence must remain in another country. Incidental costs for personal travel such as vacation, nonbusiness spousal costs, and travel costs of children are not deductible. If these expenses are paid by a church or missions organization, they should be included in compensation on Form W-2.

Travel expenses of your spouse or children

If your spouse or children accompany you on your business trip, their expenses are nonreimbursable and nondeductible unless they qualify for employee treatment and

▶ the travel of the spouse or dependent is for a bona fide business purpose; and

▶ the employee substantiates the time, place, amount, and business purpose of the travel under an accountable business expense reimbursement plan.

Remember

Spouses and children often accompany a minister to Christian conferences and other work-related meetings. Their expenses are reimbursable under an accountable plan or deductible only if you can document a business (ministry) purpose. For example, a minister's wife attends certain meetings at a conference and reports to the church on those meetings.

Per diem allowance

The IRS has provided per diem allowances under which the amount of away-from-home meals and lodging expenses may be substantiated. These rates may not be used to claim deductions for unreimbursed expenses. For more information, see IRS Publication 1542. The 2002 per diem rates for travel inside the continental United States are:

	Lodging	Meals and Incidentals	Total
Standard method	$55	$30	$85
High-low method			
35 highest cost areas	159	45	204
Other high-cost areas	90	35	125

Travel expenses for pastors with interim appointments

Many ministers accept or are appointed to temporary ministerial positions with churches. For example, a semiretired minister may own his or her own home and decide to not relocate for a temporary assignment. So, the minister drives 60 miles each week to serve a church that does not have a resident minister. Or, a minister may have secular employment in a city where he or she lives and is invited to preach each Sunday on an interim basis for a church located 30 miles from his or her home. The minister is able to maintain the secular job and fill the ministerial assignment with periodic trips to the church.

If a minister temporarily changes his or her job location, his or her tax home does not change to the new location. This means that the minister can deduct or be reimbursed for his or her travel expenses (auto or public transportation expense and meals) to and from the temporary location. If the minister stays overnight at the temporary location, food and lodging expenses at the temporary location become deductible or reimbursable.

When is a job location temporary? A minister will be treated as being temporarily away from home during any period of employment that is realistically expected to last and actually does last a year or less. Daily transportation expenses are deductible or reimbursable by the church if the minister qualifies for temporary work status. These rules may also apply to a minister serving more than one church (a circuit arrangement).

However, if employment away from home is realistically expected to last for more than one year or there is no realistic expectation that the employment will last for one year or less, the employment will be treated as indefinite, regardless of whether it actually exceeds one year. In this case, daily transportation expenses are not deductible or reimbursable by the church.

Caution

Ministers often drive significant distances each week to serve their churches. Auto expenses become a major issue. The transportation expenses are deductible or reimbursable only if the period of employment is for an indefinite period. Simply being classified as an "interim" minister by a church does not justify indefinite status.

Example 1: A minister lives in town A and accepts an interim pulpit assignment in town B, which is 60 miles away from town A. The assignment in town B is realistically expected to be completed in 18 months, but in fact it was completed in 10 months. The employment in town B is indefinite because it was realistically expected that the work in town B would last longer than one year, even though it actually lasted less than a year. Accordingly, travel expenses paid or incurred in town B are nondeductible.

If employment away from home in a single location initially is realistically expected to last for one year or less, but at some later date the employment is realistically expected to exceed one year, that employment will be treated as temporary (in the absence of facts and circumstances indicating otherwise) until the date that the minister's realistic expectation changes.

Example 2: An interim assignment began as a temporary assignment (a six-month assignment that was extended for a second six-month period) but at the 365th day of employment it was apparent that the contract would be extended for an additional period. At that time, the minister no longer has a realistic expectation that his or her employment would last for one year or less. Thus, the expenses the minister incurred after that 365th day were not deductible.

When a minister's realistic expectation changes, i.e., when the minister realistically expects the initially temporary employment to exceed one year, the employment becomes indefinite for the remaining term of employment. In other words, the employment can become indefinite before the end of the one-year period if, before the end of that period, the minister realistically expects that his or her employment will exceed one year.

Example 3: A minister accepted a temporary ministerial assignment, which the minister realistically expected would be completed in nine months.

After eight months, the minister was asked to remain for seven more months (for a total stay of 15 months). Although the minister's employment is temporary for the first eight months and travel expenses during that period are deductible, the minister's employment for the remaining seven months is indefinite, and the minister's travel expenses for that seven-month period are not deductible. If, after working on the assignment only three months, the minister was asked to extend his or her employment for 10 months, only the travel expenses incurred during the first three months would be deductible.

In effect, the IRS takes the position that part of a period of employment that is more than a year will still be treated as temporary if the taxpayer reasonably expected that the employment would last for a year or less when the employment started. The employment won't be treated as indefinite until the taxpayer's expectations change.

If a minister is not told how long an assignment is expected to last, other factors will have to be taken into account to determine whether it can reasonably be expected to last more than one year. Merely being classified as an interim minister by a church does not justify indefinite status. Also, the fewer connections that a minister keeps with his or her former work location, the less likely it is that the new assignment will be treated as merely temporary.

Auto Expense Deductions

Few ministers put only business miles on cars. When the odometer reading includes commuting from home to church or trips to the grocery store and the playground, an allocation must be made between your personal and business mileage. It is possible to use a car 100% of the time for business purposes, but it is highly unusual. It is apt to draw IRS scrutiny and perhaps an audit.

Mileage and actual expense methods

In determining your deduction for the business use of a personal car, you can use one of two methods to figure your deduction: the standard mileage rate or the actual expense method. Generally, you can choose the method that gives you the greater deduction. If you use the actual expense method and accelerated deprecation for the first year your car was placed in service, you may not use the standard mileage method in a subsequent

CHAPTER 6 ➤ BUSINESS EXPENSES

year. However, if you use the standard mileage method for the first year your car was placed in service, you may use either method in subsequent years.

Standard mileage rate method

If you are paid the maximum mileage allowance of 36 cents per mile in 2003 and you provide the time, place, and business purpose of your driving, you have made an adequate accounting of your automobile expenses.

If the church does not reimburse you for auto expenses or reimburses you under a nonaccountable plan, you may deduct business miles on Form 2106 (2106-EZ). The total from Form 2106 (2106-EZ) is carried to Schedule A, Miscellaneous Deductions.

> **Remember**
>
> The standard mileage rate may generate a lower deduction than using actual expenses in some instances. But the simplicity of the standard mileage method is a very compelling feature.

The standard mileage rate, which includes depreciation and maintenance costs, is based on the government's estimate of the average cost of operating an automobile. Depending upon the make, age, and cost of the car, the mileage rate may be more or less than your actual auto expense. If you use the mileage rate, you also may deduct parking fees and tolls and the business portion of personal property tax (and the business portion of interest if filing as self-employed for income tax purposes). All auto-related taxes must be claimed on Schedule A for employees.

Using the standard mileage rate reduces the tax basis of your car. You must reduce the basis by 15 cents a mile for 2002 and 16 cents a mile for 2003. This comprises the depreciation portion of the standard mileage allowance.

The standard mileage rate may also be used for leased autos (see page 112 for additional information, "Leasing your car").

➤ **Conditions on Use of Mileage Rate.** You may not use the mileage rate if

- you have claimed depreciation under MACRS, ACRS, or another accelerated method, or

- you have claimed first-year expenses under Section 179.

➤ **Use of Mileage Rate in First Year.** If you choose the standard mileage rate for the first year the car is in service, you may use the standard mileage rate or actual expense method in later years. If you do not choose the standard mileage rate in the first year, you may not use it for that car in any year.

By choosing to use the mileage rate in the first year your car is in service, you may not use the MACRS method of depreciation for the car in a later year. Also, you may not claim a deduction under Section 179. If you switch to the actual expense method in a later year before your automobile is fully depreciated, you must use the straight-line method of depreciation.

Actual expense method

If you have kept accurate records, determining your deduction for most expenses should be straightforward. Generally, the amount of depreciation you may claim and the method you use to calculate it depends on when you purchased your auto and began to use it for ministerial purposes.

Under the actual expense method, you can use either accelerated or straight-line depreciation. As the names imply, the accelerated method front-loads the depreciation, giving you larger deductions sooner. The straight-line method gives you the same depreciation deduction every year.

With either method, you calculate your depreciation deduction just as you would for any other asset used for business purposes. Your "depreciable basis" is the purchase price of the car multiplied by the percentage you use it for business purposes.

Allowable expenses under the actual expense method include

Warning

You have an important decision to make the first year you put a car into service. You will generally want to use the standard mileage rate in that first year. If you do not use the standard mileage rate in the first year, you may not use it for that car in any year.

gas and oil	interest on auto loan
repairs	lease payments
tires	automobile club membership
batteries	car washes and waxes
insurance	supplies, such as antifreeze
license plates	parking fees and tolls

Depreciating your car

Depreciation is an allowance for wear and tear on your car. To compensate for this loss of value, the tax law allows you to recover the cost of your car over a period of five years.

Typical vehicle depreciation is computed using the 200% declining balance method. You take only half a year's depreciation in the first year, no matter when actual use began, and half a year when the car is sold or traded in. This is the half-year convention. This rule spreads the depreciation deduction over six years.

The following percentages represent the allowed depreciation by year:

1st year	20.00%
2nd year	32.00%
3rd year	19.20%
4th year	11.52%
5th year	11.52%
6th year	5.76%
	100.00%

The so-called "luxury auto limit" places a ceiling on the annual depreciation deduction you can claim for a passenger automobile based on the date you place the automobile in service (see page 7 for information on electing bonus depreciation). Some large vehicles are not classified as passenger vehicles and are not subject to the luxury auto limits, but are still covered by the business-use substantiation rules. Examples of vehicles that do not meet the passenger vehicle definition include minivans or sport utility vehicles, with a gross weight rating, when loaded to capacity, above 6,000 pounds. For luxury vehicles, the depreciation deduction cannot exceed the dollar limits indicated based on the year a car is placed in service:

Placed in service	2000	2001	2002
Year one	$3,060	$3,060	$3,060
Year two	5,000	4,900	4,900
Year three	2,950	2,950	2,950
Each subsequent year	1,775	1,775	1,775

The luxury car limitations do not permanently deprive you from recovering the cost of your car. They merely postpone a portion of depreciation deductions to later years by placing a cap on the amount of depreciation that may be claimed in any year. The part of an otherwise allowable deduction may be taken after the normal recovery period.

If your car is used for both business and personal driving, depreciation is computed only on the business portion of the car's basis. Because depreciation is computed on the business portion of your car, your basis can change each year if your percentage of business use varies.

Tip

While the actual method is one of your options for obtaining a reimbursement or taking a deduction for auto expenses, it requires significantly more record-keeping than the mileage method. For example, you still need to maintain a mileage log so you can prorate costs between business and personal miles.

Example: You purchased a new car on May 15, 2002, for $15,900. During 2002, you drove the car a total of 10,000 miles. Ministerial miles were 6,000. Your depreciation deduction is $1,908 using the 200% declining balance method. Bonus depreciation was not elected.

➤ Percentage of business use

Business miles	6,000
Total miles	10,000 = 60%

➤ Business portion of basis

Purchase price	$15,900
Business percentage	60%
	$ 9,540

➤ Depreciation deduction

    Business portion of basis $ 9,540
    Depreciation percentage/1st year   20%
                                                                $ 1,908

➤ Maximum allowable depreciation

    $3,060 x 60% business   = $ 1,836

Driving an employer-owned vehicle

When an employer provides a car to a minister, the church must report the personal use of the car as income on Form W-2 or 1099-MISC. However, when a minister pays the church the fair market value of the personal use of the car, no income results to the minister. Partial payment to the church reduces the minister's income by the amount of the payment.

When a car is used for both business and personal purposes, an allocation between the two types of use must be made on the basis of the number of miles driven. The amount included in the minister's compensation is based on one of the valuation rules described in the 2003 edition of *The Zondervan Church and Nonprofit Tax & Financial Guide*.

Caution

One of the best fringe benefits for a minister is when the church or other employer provides a vehicle. However, unless the car is parked at the church when not in use, it still requires maintaining a mileage log. Personal (including commuting) miles driven must either be reimbursed to the employer or the tax-value must be placed on Form W-2.

Leasing your car

A minister who leases a car and uses it in connection with the work of the church is generally able to deduct part or all of lease payments as a rental deduction. However, business use is typically less than 100%. Therefore, the rental deduction is scaled down in proportion to the personal use. For example, a minister who uses a leased car 80% for business may deduct only 80% of the lease payments.

Additionally, the tax law is designed to bring lease payments in line with the "luxury auto" limits placed on depreciation deductions for purchased cars. For cars first leased in 2002, a "luxury auto" is one that costs more than $15,500. So, leasing a "luxury" car may not give you a tax break over buying one. However, nontax considerations may be important in the lease vs. buy decision.

The mileage method may also be used for the deduction or reimbursement of expenses for a leased car.

Commuting

Personal mileage is never deductible. Commuting expenses are nondeductible personal expenses.

Unless your home-office qualifies as a home-office (see pages 115-17), travel from home to church (a regular work location) and return for church services and other work at the church is commuting and not deductible or reimbursable. The same rule applies to multiple trips made in the same day. The cost of traveling between your home and a temporary work location is generally deductible or reimbursable. Once you arrive at the first work location, temporary or regular, you may deduct trips between work locations.

A regular place of business is any location at which you work or perform services on a regular basis. These services may be performed every week, for example, or merely on a set schedule. A temporary place of business is any location at which you perform services on an irregular or short-term (i.e., generally a matter of days or weeks) basis.

> **Key Issue**
>
> Churches (and other employers) and ministers often struggle to define commuting miles. It is a very important issue because commuting miles should not be reimbursed by an employer or deducted by a minister. The key to understanding commuting miles is defining regular and temporary work locations.

If you make calls in a certain nursing home nearly every day, it would qualify as a regular work location. However, if you only visit the nursing home a few days each month, it would generally qualify as a temporary work location.

> **Example 1:** A minister, not qualifying for an office at home, drives from home to the church. This trip is commuting and treated as personal mileage.
>
> The minister leaves the church and drives to a hospital to call on a member. From the hospital, the minister drives to the home of a prospect to make a call. These trips qualify for business mileage regardless if the hospital qualifies as a regular or a temporary work location.
>
> From the prospect's house, the minister drives home. This trip is also deductible since the minister is driving from a temporary work location.
>
> **Example 2:** A minister, not qualifying for an office at home, drives from home to a hospital to call on a member. The hospital is typically a temporary work location. This trip is deductible.
>
> The minister then drives to a member's office to make a call and then returns to the minister's office at the church. The trips to this point are deductible as business expenses because they are all trips between work

locations. The minister then drives to his home. This trip is commuting and is not deductible because the minister is driving from a regular work location to a nonwork location.

Documentation of auto expenses

To support your automobile expense deduction or reimbursement, automobile expenses must be substantiated by adequate records. A weekly or monthly mileage log that identifies dates, destinations, business purposes, and odometer readings in order to allocate total mileage between business and personal use is a basic necessity if you use the mileage method. If you use the actual expense method, a mileage log and supporting documentation on expenses is required.

Reporting auto expenses

If you are reimbursed for automobile expenses under an accountable expense plan, you should not report your travel expenses on Form 2106 (2106-EZ). This type of reimbursement eliminates the need for income or social security tax reporting by the church or the minister. If you do not have an accountable expense reimbursement plan, automobile expenses are reported on Form 2106 (2106-EZ) for minister-employees.

> **Remember**
>
> For your records to withstand an IRS audit, use a daily mileage log to document business vs. personal mileage. Whether you keep a notepad in the car and summarize the data manually or convert the data in a computer program, a log is the best approach to submitting data for reimbursement from your employer or taking a tax deduction.

Business Miles Do Not Start at Home If:

- ☐ You have a PC in your home-office and you or another member of your family occasionally uses the PC for personal use.

- ☐ Your home-office is in your bedroom, your living room, or any other room where the space is shared for church work and family living.

- ☐ The church has an adequate office. You do most of your work there but work at home once in a while.

- ☐ The church expects you to use the church office for your work but you prefer to work at home because it is convenient to you.

Home-Office Rules

Rarely is it advantageous or even appropriate for a minister to claim office-in-the-home deductions (Form 8829). A home-office provided by a minister does not generate any deductible or reimbursable expenses if all the housing expenses are already treated as tax-free via a housing allowance. Even if there is no home-office expense deduction or reimbursement available to a minister, qualifying the home-office rules will permit a minister to treat otherwise personal commuting mileage as business mileage.

Ministers generally cannot take a home-office deduction because all housing dollars should have been excluded under the housing allowance rules. However, the home-office rules are very significant to ministers because of the relationship to auto expenses (also see IRS Publication 587, Business Use of Your Home).

If a minister qualifies for home-office status, the starting (first business trip of the day) and ending (last business trip of the day) point for business miles can be the home. But ministers not qualifying under the home-office rules can only deduct or be reimbursed for miles from the minister's home to a temporary work location (a hospital, nursing home, member's home, etc.) and/or miles from a temporary work location to the minister's home. The miles between the minister's residence and the church (home to a permanent work location) are personal commuting miles—nondeductible, nonreimbursable—regardless of the number of trips made each day unless home-office status applies. Even without home-office status, when a minister has reached a work location (either permanent or temporary), trips between work locations are deductible or reimbursable.

> **Idea**
>
> The tax law provides for a home-office deduction. However, with housing expenses excluded from income by the housing allowance, ministers generally do not qualify for the home-office deduction. The home-office rules may still benefit some ministers by allowing them to start claiming business miles from their home instead of first requiring them to reach the church or other business location.

What is the value of making more travel expenses deductible or reimbursable? Let's look at an example. You qualify for home-office status and live five miles from the church. You drive to the church Monday through Friday to work each day. You make three extra trips for evening meetings each week and you make two trips to the church on Sunday. This makes 10 trips at 10 miles for each round trip or 100 miles per week times 50 weeks (allowing two weeks for your vacation). If the 5,000 miles are reimbursed by the church at the maximum IRS business mileage rate of 36.5 cents (2002 rate) per mile, the reimbursement would be $1,725 (if the church does not reimburse the minister, the minister's tax deduction is only worth $1,725 times the minister's marginal tax rate). If you do not qualify for home-office status, you do not qualify for any reimbursement (or deduction). You are $1,725 poorer (reimbursement based on home-office status vs. no reimbursement when not qualifying for home-office status).

Another advantage of home-office status for ministers relates to home computers. Without qualifying for a home-office, detailed computer use records must be maintained that busy ministers find especially bothersome. However, the home-office rules eliminate these detailed recordkeeping rules.

Under the home-office rules, a minister must meet the following qualifications to achieve home-office status:

- A specific portion of the taxpayer's home must be used *exclusively* and on a *regular basis* for business activity.

- The home office is used for the convenience of the employer (the church) or is necessary for the business of the church. Use of the home that is merely appropriate and helpful to the church is not sufficient to meet the convenience test. Similarly, use of the home for the minister's convenience or because the minister can get more work done at home also will not suffice.

- The home-office must be the minister's principal place of business. Under the new rules, conducting administrative or management activities of the church in the home-office are examples of qualifying work. Under the old standard, the principal place of business had to be demonstrated under the relative importance or time tests.

- The home-office is used for the convenience of the church and the church has no other fixed location where the minister conducts *substantial* administrative or management activities. *Note:* Insubstantial administrative or management activities that take place outside the home-office will not necessarily preclude the minister from qualifying.

For many ministers, the key is to determine if they are performing work that is so substantial that they fail the last test (see above). Based on examples provided by the House committee, a minister may do minimal paperwork at another fixed location, like the church, and meet the insubstantial test. Also, ministers conducting substantial nonadministrative or nonmanagement business activities at fixed locations other than their home-offices will not be prevented from qualifying for a home-office. For example, counseling sessions with individuals at the church will not preclude home-office status. However, extensive board and committee meetings held at the church may cause the minister to fail the insubstantial administrative and management test.

The new rules do not define if sermon preparation time qualifies as administrative or management activities. However, it seems that sermon preparation is a program activity of the church and is not administrative or management. The following activities would likely qualify as administrative or management: communication with church vendors; time spent in planning and communication with church staff or congregational leaders regarding issues such as project assignments, personnel

> **Caution**
>
> To qualify for home-office status, there are rigorous tests the minister must pass. One of the toughest is the test that requires a specific portion of the taxpayer's home to be used exclusively and on a regular basis for business activity. This is tough for many ministers when a computer in the office area is not used exclusively for business purposes.

issues, financial matters, planning for annual or quarterly congregational meetings, planning for periodic meetings of the top governing body or committees of the church.

If a minister does not perform substantially all of his or her administrative and management activities in the home-office, he or she must qualify under the relative importance or time tests:

- The relative importance test considers the importance of the activities undertaken at each place of business. The activities are compared to determine which location serves as a base for the most important functions.

- The time test considers the actual time spent at respective business locations. A minister would meet this test if he or she spent more than half of his or her time working in the home-office.

A portion of a room can qualify as a home-office. Furnish it with a desk, files, and other furniture that you use only for business, so that a portion of the room is used exclusively for business.

Ministers should keep proper records to document the required regular and exclusive business use of the home-office. They should keep a daily log of meetings with clients or customers at the home-office. They should also make videotapes or photographs to show there are no personal items in that part of the home. They also need to ensure that no personal or family activities occur in the home-office. It will also be helpful if the church has a written policy explaining the need for the minister to have a home-office.

There is no need to file Form 8829, Expenses for Business Use of Your Home, to document home-office status since you are not claiming a deduction for your home-office since all of your housing expenses have presumably already been excluded under the housing allowance rules.

Other Business and Professional Expenses

In addition to travel and transportation expenses, there are other business and professional expenses that may be deductible if unreimbursed or submitted to the church for reimbursement under an accountable plan:

- **Business gifts.** You can deduct up to $25 per donee for business gifts to any number of individuals every year. Incidental costs, such as for engraving, gift wrapping, insurance, and mailing do not need to be included in determining whether the $25 limit has been exceeded.

  The gifts must be related to your ministry. Gifts to church staff or board members would generally be deductible. Wedding and graduation gifts may qualify as business expenses based on the nature of the relationship.

- **Charitable contributions which reduce compensation.** Denominations or local churches may impose a tithing requirement on ministers. In some instances, the requirement is rigidly enforced based on periodic reviews. Ministers are dismissed for noncompliance. At other times, a more cursory review, such as the completion of an annual report form, is made to enforce the policy. Tithing records are not checked and ministers are rarely if ever dismissed for noncompliance.

Reducing compensation by withholding tithes is rarely appropriate unless there is a strict contractual requirement for the minister to tithe to the church and the minister is not legally entitled to keep required contribution amounts. If so, the Form W-2 reporting should reflect compensation net of the tithe deductions.

Warning

Some ministers ask their church or other employer to reduce the compensation reported on Form W-2 by the amount of their tithes. While this plan saves social security taxes (and income taxes for ministers using the standard deduction), it is not appropriate unless a minister is legally required to tithe to the church or other employer.

Tithes *paid* by the minister to the church are only deductible as charitable contributions. The Tax Court directly addressed this issue relating to the charitable contributions of a lay church member. But the principles of the court case generally apply to ministers.

In summary, unless a minister is not legally entitled to keep required contributions, a minister must be content with Schedule A charitable contribution deductions.

▶ **Clothing.** The cost of your clothing is deductible or reimbursable if the church requires the clothes and they are not suitable as normal wearing apparel. For example, a regular suit worn into the pulpit on Sunday is not deductible or reimbursable, but vestments are deductible or reimbursable.

▶ **Education.** The cost of educational expenses incurred may be deductible or reimbursable if the education

- meets the requirements of your church to keep your present position, or

- maintains or improves skills in your present employment.

Idea

A new $3,000 deduction starts in 2002 for college costs by itemizers and non-itemizers alike. For 2004, the limit on the deduction will be $4,000. To take this deduction, the education need not be necessary for you to keep your position. The education can even qualify you for a new occupation.

But no deduction or reimbursement is allowed, even though these requirements are met, if the education

- is required for you to meet the minimum educational requirements of your occupation, or

- is part of a program of study that will qualify you for a new occupation.

Deductible educational expenses include the cost of tuition, books, supplies, laboratory fees, correspondence courses, and travel and transportation expenses. Expenses under a written "qualified educational assistance program" are discussed on pages 56-57.

➤ **Entertainment.** Meal and entertainment expenses are deductible or reimbursable if they are ordinary and necessary and are either directly related to or associated with your ministerial responsibilities.

Do personal meals qualify when you are entertaining? Personal expenses are not deductible or reimbursable since you would be eating anyway. Granted, you might not be spending $10 for your lunch, but you would be eating. Only the amount over what you normally spend for breakfast, lunch, or dinner is deductible or reimbursable. But the IRS has decided not to enforce this part of the tax law. Unless a taxpayer is deducting outrageous amounts of personal expenses, 50% of the cost of the meals while entertaining will be allowed.

Certain entertainment expenses incurred in your home may be deductible or reimbursable if you can show a ministry relationship. Since it is difficult to precisely document the cost of meals served in the home, a reasonable cost per meal is generally allowable (for you and your guests). Keep a log including date(s), names of guests, ministry purpose, and estimated cost. Some ministers claim deductions or reimbursements for providing overnight lodging for church-related guests based on the value of motel lodging. Such deductions or reimbursements are not allowable.

➤ **Interest expense.** For a minister-employee, all auto-related interest expense is personal interest, which is not deductible.

➤ **Moving expenses.** Certain moving expenses reimbursed by a church to a minister-employee are excludable from gross income.

For minister-employees, when moving expense reimbursements have been excluded from income, there is no requirement to add these amounts to determine a minister's net earnings from self-employment, and therefore they are not subject to self-employment tax.

Moving expense reimbursements or payments are excludable only to the extent that they would qualify for a moving expense deduction if they had been paid by the minister and not reimbursed. The definition of deductible moving expenses is very restrictive. For example, meals while traveling and living in temporary quarters near the new workplace are not deductible. If a minister is reimbursed for nondeductible moving expenses, the amounts paid are additional taxable compensation.

➤ **Personal computers.** Personal computers you own and use more than 50% for ministry may be depreciated (or reimbursed) as five-year recovery property or deducted (but not reimbursed) under Section 179 up to the annual limit of $24,000 ($25,000 for 2003 and later years) on a joint return. The business portion of depreciation may be reimbursed under an accountable expense reimbursement plan if the 50% business, "convenience of the church," and "condition of employment" tests are met (see the discussion of these topics under "Telephones/cellular" on pages 120-21).

If a computer is provided by the church in the church office but you prefer to work at home on your personal computer, it is not being used for the church's convenience. If you meet the "convenience of employer" and "condition of employment" tests but do not use your computer (and related equipment) more than 50% of the time for your work, you must depreciate these items using the straight-line method. If you qualify under the office-in-the-home rules (see pages 115-17), the 50% test does not apply to you.

Warning

If a minister purchases a computer and uses it primarily for church work and meets the "condition" and "convenience" tests, only the depreciation on the business portion of the computer can be reimbursed by the church, not the entire cost of business portion of the cost, based on the Section 179 first-year write-off rules.

Adequate records of the business use of your computer or cellular telephone should be maintained to substantiate your deductions (see pages 102-3).

▶ **Section 179 deductions.** In the year of purchase, you may choose to deduct up to $24,000 ($25,000 for 2003 and later years) on a joint return of the cost of tangible personal property used for business. Section 179 generally has limited use for automobiles because of the $3,060 (2002 rate) luxury auto limit on annual auto depreciation (see page 7 for the bonus depreciation election). While Section 179 may be used by ministers to deduct expenses, the deduction is not includable under an accountable expense reimbursement plan.

▶ **Subscriptions and books.** Subscriptions to ministry-related periodicals are deductible or reimbursable. If the information in a periodical relates to your ministerial preparation, news magazines may even qualify.

Books related to your ministry with a useful life of one year or less may be deducted. The cost of books (such as commentaries) with a useful life of more than one year may be depreciated over the useful life. Books with a useful life of more than one year may generally be deducted in the year of purchase under Section 179, but they are not eligible for reimbursement by your church (also see page 53).

▶ **Telephone.** You may not deduct, as a business expense, any of the basic local service charge (including taxes) for the first telephone line into your home. Long-distance calls, a second line, special equipment, and services such as call-waiting used for business are deductible. If you are out of town on a business trip, the IRS will not challenge a reasonable number of telephone calls home.

Although your basic local telephone service is not deductible for tax purposes, it is includable as housing expense for housing allowance purposes.

▶ **Telephones/cellular.** Cellular telephones you own and use more than 50% for ministry may be depreciated (or reimbursed) as five-year recovery property or deducted under Section 179 up to the annual limit of $24,000 ($25,000 for 2003 and later years) on a joint return. The business portion of depreciation may be reimbursed under an accountable expense reimbursement plan if the 50% business, "convenience of the church," and "condition of employment" tests are met.

Remember

For monthly cellular phone user fees to qualify for reimbursement or deduction the phone must be required for the minister to perform duties properly and the business usage must exceed 50%. Written records are required to prove that the 50% level of usage has been attained.

As a minister-employee, your use of the cellular telephone must be for the "convenience of the church," and required as a "condition of employment." The "convenience of the church" test will generally be met if the cellular telephone is furnished for substantial "noncompensatory business reasons." Whether a minister (or other church employee) passes the "condition of employment" test is based on all the facts and circumstances and is not determined merely by a statement by the employer that the use of the cellular telephone is a condition of employment.

If you meet the "convenience of employer" and "condition of employment" tests but do not use your cellular telephone more than 50% of the time for your work, you must depreciate it using the straight-line method and you may be reimbursed (or deduct as unreimbursed business expense on Schedule A) the business-related telephone call charges and the business-related portion of the monthly fees. If you qualify under the office-in-the-home rules (see pages 115-17), the 50% test does not apply to you.

A log or similar documentation of the business use of your cellular telephone should be maintained to substantiate your deduction (see pages 102-3).

Allocation of Business Expenses

The IRS is becoming aggressive in limiting the deduction of excluded unreimbursed business expenses to the extent that they are "allocable" to an excluded housing allowance or the fair rental value of church-provided housing. Tax Court cases clearly document their position. IRS Publication 517 (Social Security and Other Information for Members of the Clergy and Religious Workers) explains this topic in detail and includes the concept in a completed tax return example. The *Tax Guide for Churches and Other Religious Organizations* and the *MSSP Audit Guide for Ministers' Returns,* both issued by the IRS, clearly apply the expense allocation concept.

Under these guidelines, if you exclude a parsonage allowance or are provided housing by your church, you cannot deduct expenses that are allocable to your excluded rental or parsonage allowance. This rule, called the Deason rule, does not apply to your deductions for home mortgage interest or real estate taxes.

A statement containing all the following information must be attached to your tax return:

- A list of each item of taxable ministerial income by source (such as wages, salary, honoraria from weddings, baptisms, etc.) plus the amount;
- The amount of your excluded housing allowance or the fair rental value of church-provided housing;
- A list of each item of unreimbursed ministerial expense plus the amount;
- A statement that the other deductions on your tax return are not allocable to your excluded housing allowance.

This limitation requires the following calculation:

1. Amount of tax-exempt income (the fair rental value of a church-provided parsonage and the housing allowance excluded from gross income; this may be less than the church-designated housing allowance) $ _____

2. Total income from ministry:
   Salary (including the fair rental value of a church-provided parsonage and the housing allowance excluded from gross income) $ _____
   Fees _____
   Allowances (nonaccountable plan) _____
   $ _____

3. Divide line 1 amount by line 2 amount = nontaxable income % _____ %

4. Total unreimbursed business and professional expenses less 50% of meals and entertainment expenses $ _____

5. Multiply line 4 total by line 3 percentage (these are nondeductible expenses allowable to tax-exempt income) $ _____

6. Subtract line 5 amount from line 4 amount (these are deductible expenses for federal income tax purposes on Form 2106 [2106-EZ]) $ _____

 **Action Steps**

- Request that your church adopt an accountable expense reimbursement plan.
- Fully document all business expenses. Keep a log of auto miles driven for business purposes.
- Supply full substantiation for business expenses when submitting data to the church under an accountable reimbursement plan. The mere reporting of your expenses to the church does not constitute substantiation.
- If you are claiming unreimbursed business expenses, review the discussion in IRS Publication 517 on allocating expenses to tax-free income.

Social Security Tax

In This Chapter

- The two social security systems
- Computing the self-employment tax
- Both spouses are ministers
- Self-employment tax deductions
- Use of voluntary withholding agreement to pay social security taxes
- Opting out of social security
- Working after you retire
- Canada Pension Plan

Calculating the portion of your income that is subject to social security is a complex process. For example, the housing allowance is taxable for social security purposes although potentially tax-exempt for income tax purposes. The IRS forms provide little help for ministers with this calculation.

The Two Social Security Systems

Social security taxes are collected under two systems. Under the Federal Insurance Contributions Act (FICA), the employer pays one-half of the tax and the employee pays the other half. Under the Self-Employment Contributions Act (SECA), the self-employed person pays all the tax (self-employment tax) as calculated on the taxpayer's Schedule SE. IRS Publications 517 and 1828 provide information on social security taxes.

Ministers are always self-employed for social security purposes under the tax law with respect to services performed in the exercise of their ministry, whether employed by a church, integral agency of a church, or a parachurch organization. Ministers are self-employed for social security purposes regardless of how their employer categorizes them for income tax purposes. Ministers are not subject to FICA-type social security taxes, even through they report their income taxes as employees and receive a Form W-2 from their employer.

When FICA is inappropriately withheld (7.65%) from a minister's pay and matched (7.65%) by the employer, it subjects the minister and the employer to possible action by the IRS because:

▶ the minister has often underpaid his or her income taxes. The 7.65% match that was withheld from the church is really compensation that is avoiding income tax because it is not being reported in Box 1 of the Form W-2. Additionally, the minister is paying FICA instead of SECA and the IRS could require that this be corrected retroactively.

▶ the employer is underreporting the employee's income by the 7.65% FICA match. Also, the employer is reporting FICA social security taxes when it should not. The IRS could require the employer to retroactively correct Form 941s and W-2s.

Warning

Churches and other employers commonly subject ministers to the wrong type of social security. If a minister qualifies for a housing allowance, he or she is not subject to FICA-type social security. The inappropriate use of FICA instead of SECA may result in the underpayment of a minister's income taxes.

Example: A church hires and pays you to perform ministerial services for it, subject to its control. Under the common law rules (pages 33-36), you are an employee of the church while performing those services. The church reports your wages on Form W-2 for income tax purposes, but no social security taxes are withheld. You are self-employed for social security purposes. You must pay self-employment tax (SECA) on those wages yourself unless you request and receive an exemption from self-employment tax. On Form W-2, Boxes 3-6 are left blank.

Many churches reimburse ministers for a portion or all of their SECA liability. SECA reimbursements represent additional taxable compensation in the year paid to the minister for both income and social security tax purposes.

SOCIAL SECURITY SYSTEMS

FICA (Federal Insurance Contributions Act)	SECA (Self-Employment Contributions Act)
Nonminister employees of a church are all subject to FICA.	All qualified ministers are subject to SECA (unless they have opted out of social security).
Employee pays 7.65% Employer pays 7.65% 15.30%	Self-employed individuals pay the full 15.3%.
The 15.3% is paid on a wage base of up to $84,900 for 2002.	The 15.3% is paid on a wage base of up to $84,900 for 2002.
Both the employer and employee pay a 1.45% tax rate on all wages above $84,900.	The individual pays a 2.9% tax rate on all wages above $84,900.

Because of the SECA deductions (see page 126), a full SECA reimbursement is effectively less than the gross 15.3% rate.

Example: A church provides a cash salary of $35,000 and provides a parsonage that has an annual fair rental value of $15,000. Even though a full reimbursement of the minister's SECA is slightly less than 15.3%, the church decides to reimburse at the 15.3% rate for simplicity. Since the minister has entered into a voluntary withholding arrangement with the church for federal income taxes, the church grosses up the monthly pay by $637.50 (15.3 times $50,000, or $7,650 divided by 12) and withholds federal income tax of $637.50 plus a sufficient amount to cover the minister's estimated federal income tax.

Computing the Self-Employment Tax

When computing the self-employment tax, your net earnings include the gross income earned from performing qualified services minus the deductions related to that income.

This includes church compensation reported in Box 1 of Form W-2 (the designated housing allowance should not be shown in this box), the net profit or loss from Schedule C or C-EZ, any housing allowance excluded from Box 1 of Form W-2, the fair rental value of church-provided housing, and amounts that should have been included in Box 1 of Form W-2, such as: business expense reimbursements made under a nonaccountable plan, a self-employment social security tax reimbursement or allowance, love offerings, etc.

> **Key Issue**
>
> Unless a minister has opted out of social security, the net ministerial income plus the excluded housing allowance and the fair rental value of church provided housing is subject to self-employment social security tax. This is true even if the minister is retired and receiving social security benefits. There is no age limit on paying social security tax.

The following tax rates apply to net earnings from self-employment of $400 or more each year:

	Tax Rate		Earnings Base	
Year	OASDI	Medicare	OASDI	Medicare
2000	12.4%	2.9%	76,200	no limit
2001	12.4%	2.9%	80,400	no limit
2002	12.4%	2.9%	84,900	no limit
2003	12.4%	2.9%	87,000 est.	no limit
2004	12.4%	2.9%	90,300 est.	no limit

OASDI = Old-age, survivors, and disability insurance, or social security

Only business expenses are deductible in determining income subject to SECA. The minister may deduct unreimbursed business expenses for the SECA computation even if deductions are not itemized on Schedule A.

Self-Employment Social Security Tax Worksheet

Inclusions:

Salary paid by church as reflected on Form W-2, Box 1 $ _____

Net profit or loss as reflected on Schedule C or C-EZ
(includes speaking honoraria, offerings you receive for
marriages, baptisms, funerals, and other fees)   _____

Housing allowance excluded from salary on Form W-2   _____

Fair rental value of church-provided housing (including paid utilities)   _____

Nonaccountable business expense reimbursements
(if not included on Form W-2)   _____

Reimbursement of self-employment taxes (if not included
on Form W-2)   _____

Other amounts that should have been included on Form W-2, Box 1,
such as love offerings   _____

Total inclusions   _____

Deductions:

Unreimbursed ministerial business (disregarding the Deason rule — see
pages 121-22) and professional expenses (included on Form W-2) or reimbursed
expenses paid under a nonaccountable plan (included on Form W-2)

    A. Deductible on Schedule A before the 2% of AGI limitation
        whether or not you itemized[1] or   _____

    B. Not deductible on Form 2106/2106 EZ or Schedule C/C-EZ
        because expenses were allocated to taxable/nontaxable income   _____

Total deductions   _____

Net earnings from self-employment (to Schedule SE) $ _____

[1]The 50% unreimbursed meal and entertainment expense limitation applies to amounts subject to social security tax. In other words, if some of your meal and entertainment expenses were subject to the 50% limit, the remainder cannot be deducted here.

Note 1: Your net earnings from self-employment are not affected by the foreign earned income exclusion or the foreign housing exclusion or deduction if you are a U.S. citizen or resident alien who is serving abroad and living in a foreign country.

Note 2: Amounts received as pension payments or annuity payments related to a church-sponsored tax-sheltered annuity by a retired minister are generally considered to be excluded from the social security calculation.

Moving expenses do not qualify as business expenses. Therefore, moving expenses are not deductible in computing self-employment tax. However, for minister-employees, reimbursed moving expenses are excludable from Form W-2. Therefore, the reimbursements are not included for income or social security tax purposes.

Example: You have the following ministerial income and expenses: church salary $30,000 (of which the housing allowance is $12,000); net Schedule C (C-EZ) income related to special speaking engagements, weddings, funerals, etc. $1,350; Schedule A employee business expenses (after offsetting 50% of nondeductible meal and entertainment) $1,800. You do not itemize your deductions on Schedule A since the standard deduction is more beneficial.

Your self-employment income is

Salary from church	$18,000
Church-designated housing allowance	12,000
Schedule C (C-EZ) net earnings	1,350
Schedule A employee business expenses	(1,800)
Total	**$29,550**

Use the worksheet on page 126 to calculate net earnings from self-employment. Net earnings are transferred to Form SE, page 1, line 2, to calculate the SECA.

Both Spouses Are Ministers

If a husband and wife who are both duly ordained, commissioned, or licensed ministers have an agreement with a church that each will perform specific services for which they will receive pay, jointly or separately, they must divide the compensation according to the agreement. Such a division of income would have no impact on their income tax if they filed a joint return. But each of them could obtain social security coverage by dividing the compensation and subjecting the compensation to social security tax.

If the agreement for services is with one spouse only and the other spouse receives no pay for any specific duties, amounts paid for services are included only in the income of the spouse having the agreement.

If you have already filed a return and incorrectly divided, or failed to divide, the income for self-employment tax purposes, you may file an amended return showing the corrected amount as self-employment income for each spouse.

If one spouse is ordained, commissioned, or licensed and the other is not, the "qualified" minister under

> **Caution**
>
> A minister's spouse who is not duly ordained, commissioned, or licensed as a minister of a church but who receives pay for performing services for the organization should not include the earnings with the minister's self-employment income. The nonminister spouse is generally an employee of the church for federal income tax and social security (FICA) tax purposes.

the tax law generally receives 100% of the compensation from the church, and the spouse is considered a volunteer. This is true even though they may have been hired as a team and each spouse provides significant services to the church.

However, it may be legitimate to split the compensation from the church based on the duties of each spouse. Pay should never be split merely for the purpose of allowing a spouse to qualify for social security or to avoid exceeding the social security earnings limit for one spouse.

Self-Employment Tax Deductions

You can take an income tax deduction equal to one-half of your self-employment tax liability. The deduction is claimed against gross income on line 29 of Form 1040, page 1.

You also may deduct a portion of your self-employment tax liability in calculating your self-employment tax. This deduction is made on Schedule SE, Section A, line 4 or Section B, line 4a, by multiplying self-employment income by .9235.

The purpose of these deductions is to equalize the social security (and income) taxes paid by (and for) employees and self-employed persons with equivalent income.

Idea

Because of the deductibility of the self-employment tax in both the income tax and self-employment tax computations, if your church desires to reimburse your entire social security tax obligation, it is effectively less than the gross 15.3% rate. See pages 65-66 for the effective rate at various marginal income tax rates.

Use of Voluntary Withholding Agreement to Pay Social Security Taxes

Under a voluntary withholding agreement, a minister-employee may ask the church to withhold a sufficient amount to cover federal income taxes plus enough for the self-employment taxes (SECA). The church must report all amounts withheld under such an arrangement as federal income taxes. The other option for the payment of income and social security taxes is to use the Form 1040-ES in paying quarterly estimated taxes.

Key Issue

Take advantage of opportunities to enter into a voluntary withholding arrangement with your employer to withhold enough federal income tax to cover both their federal income tax and self-employment social security tax obligation. Withholding the proper amount each week of payday is a very efficient way to pay your taxes. You do not run the risk of filing Forms 1040-ES late and incurring underpayment penalties.

Example: A minister projected that he will owe $1,000 of federal income tax for 2003 and $3,000 of self-employment social security tax for a total tax obligation of $4,000. The minister and his spouse will not have withholding from nonchurch employment. He will not qualify for the earned income tax credit. The minister could enter into a voluntary withholding agreement whereby the church would withhold federal income tax from each paycheck so that by the end of 2003, $4,000 was withheld (this would be reported on Form W-2, Box 2). No FICA-type social security tax is withheld from the minister's pay since he is not subject to that type of social security. Alternately, the minister could file Forms 1040-ES on April 15, 2002, June 15, 2002, September 15, 2002, and January 15, 2002, and submit payments of $1,000 per filing.

Opting Out of Social Security

All ministers are automatically covered by social security (SECA) for services in the exercise of ministry unless an exemption has been received based on the filing with and approval by the IRS of Form 4361. You must certify that you oppose, either conscientiously or because of religious principles, the acceptance of any public insurance (with respect to services performed as a minister), including social security coverage. Either opposition must be based on religious belief. This includes an opposition to insurance that helps pay for or provide services for medical care (such as Medicare) and social security benefits.

Warning

Opting out of social security is relatively simple. Form 4361 must be filed by the due date of the minister's tax return for the second year with $400 or more of ministerial income. But the simplicity of opting out should not be confused with the significant difficulty of complying with the reasons for opting out.

To claim the exemption from self-employment tax, you must

➤ file Form 4361,

➤ be conscientiously opposed to public insurance (which includes insurance systems established by the Social Security Act) because of your individual religious considerations (not because of your general conscience), or because of the principles of your religious denomination,

➤ file for *other than* economic reasons,

➤ inform the ordaining, commissioning, or licensing body of your church or order that you are opposed to public insurance if you are a minister,

➤ establish that the religious organization that ordained, commissioned, or licensed you or your religious order is a tax-exempt religious organization,

➤ establish that the organization is a church or a convention or association of churches, and

➤ sign and return the statement the IRS mails to you to verify that you are requesting an exemption based on the grounds listed on the statement.

Deadline for filing for an exemption

The application for exemption from self-employment tax must be filed by the date your tax return is due, including extensions, for the second year in which you had net ministerial income of $400 or more. These do not have to be consecutive tax years.

Caution

Even though a minister signs Form 4361 and certifies that he or she is opposed to accepting public insurance benefits which is based on earnings services performed in his or her capacity as a minister, the minister can still purchase life insurance or participate in retirement programs administered by non-governmental institutions.

Example 1: A minister ordained in 2001 has net earnings of $400 in 2001 and $500 in 2002. An application for exemption must be filed by April 15, 2003. If the minister does not receive the approved exemption by April 15, 2001, the self-employment tax for 2001 is due by that date.

Example 2: A minister has $300 in net clergy earnings in 2001 but earned $400 in both 2000 and 2002. An application for exemption must be filed by April 15, 2003. If the minister does not receive the approved exemption by April 16, 2001, the self-employment tax for 2000 is due by that date.

Example 3: A minister, ordained in 1999, earned $700 net for that year. In 2000, ministerial compensation was $1,000 and related expenses were over $1,000. Therefore, the 2000 net earnings were zero. Also in 2000, $7,000 in net self-employment earnings was received from nonministerial sources. In 2001, net ministerial earnings were $1,500 and $12,000 from nonministerial sources.

Because the minister had ministerial net earnings in 1999 and 2001 that were more than $400 each year, the application for exemption must be filed by April 15, 2002. If the minister does not receive the approved exemption by April 16, 2000, the self-employment tax for 1999 is due by that date.

Tip

If the exemption is approved, it does not apply to nonministerial wages or to any other self-employment income. For example, a bivocational pastor who is employed part-time in a secular job is subject to FICA on the wages from the secular job. If a minister performs independent contractor services unrelated to his ministry, this net profit is subject to social security.

CHAPTER 7 ► SOCIAL SECURITY TAX

Form 4361 (Rev. December 1999)
Department of the Treasury
Internal Revenue Service

Application for Exemption From Self-Employment Tax for Use by Ministers, Members of Religious Orders and Christian Science Practitioners

OMB No. 1545-0168

File Original and Two Copies

File original and two copies and attach supporting documents. This exemption is granted only if the IRS returns a copy to you marked "approved."

1 Name of taxpayer applying for exemption (as shown on Form 1040)
Harold T. Baldwin

Social security number: 603 : 42 : 8941

Number and street (including apt. no.)
P.O. Box 183

Telephone number (optional)
(   )

City or town, state, and ZIP code
Milton, PA 17647

2 Check ONE box: ☐ Christian Science practitioner ☑ Ordained minister, priest, rabbi
☐ Member of religious order not under a vow of poverty ☐ Commissioned or licensed minister (see line 6)

3 Date ordained, licensed, etc. (Attach supporting document. See instructions.)

4 Legal name of ordaining, licensing, or commissioning body or religious order
Christian General Conference

07 / 01 / 00

Number, street, and room or suite no.
P.O. Box 5002

Employer identification number
48-9017682

City or town, state, and ZIP code
Nashville, AR 71852

5 Enter the first 2 years, after the date shown on line 3, that you had net self-employment earnings of $400 or more, any of which came from services as a minister, priest, rabbi, etc.; member of a religious order; or Christian Science practitioner ▶   00   01

6 If you apply for the exemption as a licensed or commissioned minister, and your denomination also ordains ministers, please indicate how your ecclesiastical powers differ from those of an ordained minister of your denomination. Attach a copy of your denomination's bylaws relating to the powers of ordained, commissioned, or licensed ministers.

7 I certify that I am conscientiously opposed to, or because of my religious principles I am opposed to, the acceptance (for services I perform as a minister, member of a religious order not under a vow of poverty, or a Christian Science practitioner) of any public insurance that makes payments in the event of death, disability, old age, or retirement; or that makes payments toward the cost of, or provides services for, medical care. (Public insurance includes insurance systems established by the Social Security Act.)

I certify that as a duly ordained, commissioned, or licensed minister of a church or a member of a religious order not under a vow of poverty, I have informed the ordaining, commissioning, or licensing body of my church or order that I am conscientiously opposed to, or because of religious principles, I am opposed to the acceptance (for services I perform as a minister or as a member of a religious order) of any public insurance that makes payments in the event of death, disability, old age, or retirement; or that makes payments toward the cost of, or provides services for, medical care, including the benefits of any insurance system established by the Social Security Act.

I certify that I did not file an effective waiver certificate (Form 2031) electing social security coverage on earnings as a minister, member of a religious order not under a vow of poverty, or a Christian Science practitioner.

I request to be exempted from paying self-employment tax on my earnings from services as a minister, member of a religious order not under a vow of poverty, or a Christian Science practitioner, under section 1402(e) of the Internal Revenue Code. I understand that the exemption, if granted, will apply only to these earnings. Under penalties of perjury, I declare that I have examined this application and to the best of my knowledge and belief, it is true and correct.

Signature ▶ *Harold T. Baldwin*   Date ▶ 04-15-03

Caution: Form 4361 is **not proof** of the right to an exemption from Federal income tax withholding or social security tax, the right to a parsonage allowance exclusion (section 107 of the Internal Revenue Code), assignment by your religious superiors to a particular job, or the exemption or church status of the ordaining, licensing, or commissioning body, or religious order.

For Internal Revenue Service Use

☐ Approved for exemption from self-employment tax on ministerial earnings
☐ Disapproved for exemption from self-employment tax on ministerial earnings

By ....
       (Director's signature)   (Date)

General Instructions

Section references are to the Internal Revenue Code.

Purpose of form. File Form 4361 to apply for an exemption from self-employment tax if you are:

• An ordained, commissioned, or licensed minister of a church;

• A member of a religious order who has not taken a vow of poverty;

• A Christian Science practitioner; or

• A commissioned or licensed minister of a church or church denomination that ordains ministers, if you have authority to perform substantially all religious duties of your church or denomination.

This application must be based on your religious or conscientious opposition to the acceptance (for services performed as a minister, member of a religious order not under a vow of poverty, or Christian Science practitioner) of any public insurance that makes payments for death, disability, old age, or retirement; or that makes payments for the cost of, or provides services for, medical care, including any insurance benefits established by the Social Security Act.

If you are a duly ordained, commissioned, or licensed minister of a church or a member of a religious order not under a vow of poverty, prior to filing this form you must inform the ordaining, commissioning, or licensing body of your church or order that you are opposed to the acceptance of public insurance benefits based on ministerial service on religious or conscientious grounds.

Do not file Form 4361 if:

• You ever filed a waiver certificate (Form 2031); or

• You belong to a religious order and took a vow of poverty. You are automatically exempt from self-employment tax on earnings for services you perform for your church or its agencies. No tax exemption applies to earnings for services you perform for any other organization.

Additional information. See Pub. 517, Social Security and Other Information for Members of the Clergy and Religious Workers.

When to file. File Form 4361 by the due date, including extensions, of your tax return for the 2nd tax year in which you had at least $400 of net earnings from self-employment, any of which came from services performed as a minister, member of a religious order, or Christian Science practitioner.

Effective date of exemption. An exemption from self-employment tax is effective for all tax years ending after 1967 in which you have net self-employment earnings of $400 or more, if you receive any of it from ministerial services.

(continued on page 2)

For Privacy Act and Paperwork Reduction Act Notice, See page 2   Cat. No. 41586H   Form **4361** (Rev. 12-99)

Caution: Very few ministers qualify to file Form 4361. The filing must be based on the minister's conscience or religious principles, not because of a preference to invest retirement funds elsewhere.

Example 4: A minister was ordained in 2001 with $1,000 and $2,000 of net ministerial earnings for 2001 and 2002, respectively. The minister filed Form 4361 in 2002 (this was a timely filing since the last day to file without extensions was April 15, 2003) and the application was approved by the IRS. The minister paid self-employment social security tax on the $1,000 of net ministerial earnings for 2001 since the Form 4361 had not yet been filed. Based on the approval of Form 4361, the minister can file an amended income tax return for 2001 using Form 1040X (see pages 144 and 148) and receive a refund of the social security tax paid on the net ministerial earnings for that year.

A minister must include with Form 4361 a statement that he has informed the ordaining body of his church of his opposition to the coverage.

A second ordination with a second church generally does not provide a second opportunity for a minister to opt out by filing Form 4361.

Securing another copy of approved Form 4361

If a minister has lost the approved copy of the Form 4361, Application for Exemption from Self-Employment Tax, he or she may write the Internal Revenue Service Center where the form was filed and request a copy.

A copy of the Form 4361 also may be requested from the Social Security Administration, Office of Central Records Operations, Metro West Building, 300 North Green Street, Baltimore, MD 21201. In either case, include your name and social security number and the approximate date the form was filed.

Caution

When the IRS approved your application to opt out of social security, they will return a copy of Form 4361 to you marked "approved." It is very important to keep this copy of Form 4361 for your permanent records. If you do not have an approved copy and do not pay your social security taxes, the IRS could assess the tax and penalties for the last three tax years.

Basis of filing for exemption

Neither economics nor any other nonreligious reason is a valid basis for the exemption. Many ministers are improperly counseled to opt out of social security because it may not be a "good investment." Your view of the soundness of the social security program has absolutely no relationship to the application for exemption.

Your first consideration is your ability to sign Form 4361 with a clear conscience. Key words in qualifying for exemption from social security coverage on ministerial earnings are "religious principles" and "conscientiously opposed to the acceptance of any public insurance." Religious principles do not simply consist of the conviction that perhaps social security will not be there when you retire or that a better retirement can be purchased through an annuity or other retirement program. The belief must be an integral part of your religious system of beliefs, your theology.

Further, this religious principle must be one that would prevent you from ever asking for the benefits from such a plan based on your church salary. No basis exists for an objection related to paying the taxes or to the level of the taxes to be paid.

If you opt out and do not have sufficient credits from prior employment or from future nonministerial employment, neither you nor your dependents will be covered under social security benefits, survivors' benefits, or Medicare. If you opt out of social security, you should make alternate plans to provide for catastrophic illness, disability, or death as well as for retirement.

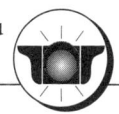

Caution

Opting out of social security is one of the most abused provisions of the tax law that applies to ministers. Too often ministers have opted out because they are concerned about long-term safety of the program or they feel they have a better way to invest the funds. These reasons do not provide a basis to sign Form 4361.

This is not a decision to be taken lightly. First, you must act on religious convictions. Second, you must be prepared financially with alternatives to the benefits of social security coverage.

Although a minister may opt out of social security with respect to ministerial income, the minister may still receive social security benefits related to nonministerial wages or other self-employment income.

Opting back into social security

Until April 15, 2002, ministers could opt back into social security by filing Form 2031. This was a special two-year window based on a law passed in 1999. With the window to opt back into social security closed, there is currently no formal method available for ministers to opt back into social security.

Working After You Retire

If you continue to work after you retire, your social security benefits are reduced if you earn over certain levels if you are between ages 62 and 64. When you reach retirement age (currently 65), your social security benefits are not reduced regardless of your earnings.

The 2002 penalty levels are as follows:

Age	Social Security Benefits Will Be Reduced If Your Earnings Are Over
62-64	$11,280
Retirement age (currently 65)	No reduction (2000 and later)

For beneficiaries reaching age 65 in 2002, the earnings limit is $30,000 until the individual turns age 65.

If you are receiving social security benefits in the age 62 to 65 range and you are receiving a cash housing allowance or living in a parsonage, the Social Security Administration will generally include the housing allowance or value of the housing provided in your earnings to determine if your benefits will be reduced.

Tip

Even though your social security benefits are not reduced because of working after you retire, you may be subject to income tax on some of the social security benefits. Generally, your adjusted gross income must exceed $32,000, if married filing jointly, before the taxation of social security benefits becomes effective.

Canada Pension Plan

Under an agreement between the U.S. and Canada, a minister is subject to the laws of the country in which the services are performed for the purposes of U.S. social security and Canada Pension Plan, respectively. In other words, a Canadian citizen who moves to the U.S. to pastor a church generally must pay U.S. social security (SECA) tax.

There is one exception to the general rule: If the minister is required by a Canadian employer to transfer to a related organization in the U.S. on a temporary basis for a period not exceeding 60 months, with the intention of returning to the employment with the Canadian employer at the end of the temporary assignment. In this case, the Canadian employer must complete Form CPT 56. Canada Customs and Revenue Agency (CCRA) has issued Information Circular No. 84-6 explaining these provisions. Copies may be obtained by writing CCRA, Customs, Excise and Taxation, Ottawa, Ontario K1A 0L8.

Action Steps

- Encourage your church board to perform an annual review of the entire pay package.
- If you qualify for special tax treatment as a minister, be sure the church is not withholding or paying FICA tax for you.
- Take advantage of all your allowable exclusions and deductions in computing income subject to SECA.
- You may cover your SECA liability through a voluntary withholding arrangement by having the church withhold additional federal income tax.
- Take your self-employment tax deduction on line 29 of Form 1040, page 1.
- Do not opt out of social security because you do not think it is a good investment or you just prefer to handle the money yourself.

Paying Your Taxes

In This Chapter

- Tax withholding
- Estimated tax
- Excess social security withheld (FICA)
- Earned income credit
- Extension of time to file
- Extension of time to pay
- Offers in compromise
- Filing an amended tax return

The federal income tax is a pay-as-you-go tax. You must pay the tax as you earn or receive income during the year. Employees usually have income tax withheld from their pay. However, the pay of qualified ministers is not subject to federal income tax withholding. Ministers who are employees for income tax purposes may enter into a voluntary withholding agreement with the church to cover any income and self-employment social security taxes that are due. IRS Publication 505 provides additional information on tax withholding and estimated taxes.

Tax Withholding

Federal income tax withheld from earnings as an employee should be reported to you on your Form W-2. The total amount withheld from all sources should be entered on line 62, Form 1040.

Churches are *not required* to withhold income taxes from wages paid to ministers for services performed in the exercise of their ministry. The exemption does not apply to nonministerial church employees such as a secretary, organist, or custodian.

A minister-employee may have a *voluntary* withholding agreement with the employing church to cover income taxes (the amount may be set high enough to also cover the self-employment social security tax liability). An agreement to withhold income taxes from wages must be in writing. There is no required form for the agreement. It may be as simple as a letter from the minister to the church requesting that a specified amount be withheld as federal income taxes, or a minister may request voluntary withholding by submitting Form W-4 (Employee's Withholding Allowance Certificate) to the church and indicate an additional amount to be withheld in excess of the tax table amount.

If federal income taxes are withheld sufficient to cover both the minister's income and self-employment social security (SECA) taxes, it is very important that the amounts be reported as "federal income taxes withheld" when the church completes quarterly Form 941 and annual forms W-2 and W-3. FICA social security taxes should never be withheld or remitted relating to qualified ministers.

Idea

Though not required, churches should offer to withhold federal (and state and local, where applicable) income taxes (never FICA taxes!) from a minister's pay. Filing Forms 1040-ES often means saving up money for the 4/15, 6/15, 9/15, and 1/15 deadlines. Withholding the proper amount each week or payday is so much more efficient.

For personal budgeting purposes, a minister may request the church to withhold amounts from compensation. Coinciding with the Form 1040-ES due dates (April 15, June 15, September 15, and January 15), the church pays the withheld amounts directly to the minister and then the minister uses the funds to make the appropriate estimated tax payments to the IRS. The withholding is not reflected on Form W-2.

Estimated Tax

Estimated tax is the method used to pay income and self-employment taxes for income that is not subject to withholding. Your estimated tax is your expected tax for the year minus your expected withholding and credits.

If you are filing a declaration of estimated tax, complete the quarterly Forms 1040-ES. If your 2003 estimated taxes are $1,000 or less, no declaration of estimated tax is required.

If your estimated tax payments for 2003 equal 90% of your 2002 tax liability, you will avoid underpayment penalties. An option is to make the 2003 estimated tax payments equal 100% of your 2002 federal and social security taxes (Form 1040, page 2, line 61). This method generally avoids underpayment penalties and is easier to calculate. The estimated tax payments for certain higher income taxpayers must be 110% of the prior year tax.

Ministers with an adjusted gross income of over $150,000 ($75,000 for married individuals filing

Filing Tip

When using the estimated tax method of submitting income and social security tax money to the IRS, pay at least as much as your previous year total taxes (before offsetting withholding, estimated tax payments, etc.). Spread the payments equally over the four Forms 1040-ES. This will generally avoid underpayment penalties.

Three Ways To Pay Your Taxes

1

Estimated Taxes

The minister pays federal income taxes and social security taxes (SECA) directly to the IRS.

2

Voluntary Withholding

Church withholds federal income tax and pays quarterly to the IRS. Additional federal income tax may be withheld to cover the minister's social security tax (SECA) liability.

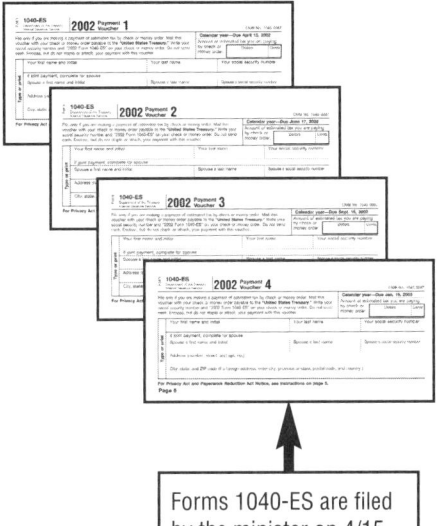

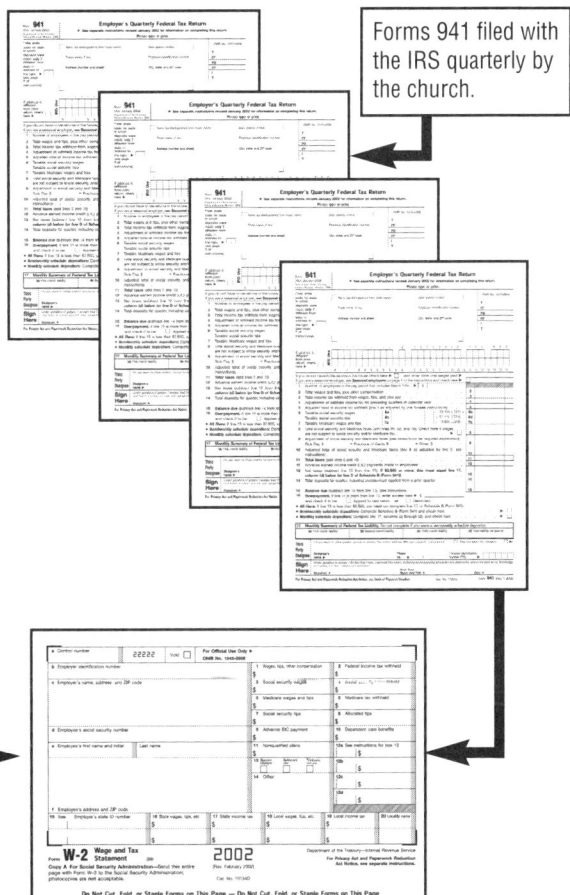

Forms 941 filed with the IRS quarterly by the church.

Forms 1040-ES are filed by the minister on 4/15, 6/15, 9/15, and 1/15.

Form 941 data are annually summarized on Form W-2. The W-2 is provided to the minister and the IRS.

3

Payroll withholding from the minister's pay. The church does not remit the amounts withheld to the IRS. The amounts are paid directly to the minister on or before 4/15, 6/15, 9/15, and 1/15. The minister then files Form 1040-ES and remits the money to the IRS.

Calculate Your Most Important Tax Planning Number of 2003

You only have to pay by December 31 (January 15 if you are paying estimates) the smallest of the "safe harbor" amounts. Use this worksheet to calculate them so you will know how much to withhold or pay in estimated taxes.

100% of your 2002 tax liability
(the number on line 58 on your Form 1040): _____ *

90% of your estimated 2003 tax (federal income tax
and self-employment social security tax) liability.
Recalculate this number at least three times before
October to update changes in your tax circumstances.
(The October date gives you enough time to make
changes in withholdings or your final estimated payment.):

Estimated 2003 tax liability: _____ x 90% =   _____ *

You can also avoid a penalty if you owe less than $1,000 on April 15 after considering withholdings. But be careful using this loophole—if you miscalculate just a little bit, you could be facing a penalty. So recalculate this at least three times a year as well.

Estimated 2003 tax liability: _____

Minus Projected 2003 Federal Income Tax
Withholdings: _____

Equals: (must be less than $1,000) _____ *

Fill in the smallest of these numbers: _____

You only have to pay this amount by the end of the year.

A special rule applies to individuals with adjusted gross income for the previous year in excess of $150,000.

separately) may fall under special rules requiring larger estimated tax payments. At this income level, if your estimated tax payments for 2003 equal 110% of your 2002 tax liability, you will avoid underpayment penalties.

In estimating 2003 taxes, net earnings from self-employment should be reduced by 7.65% before calculating the self-employment tax of 15.3%. There also is an income tax deduction for one-half of your self-employment tax (Form 1040, page 1, line 29).

You pay one-fourth of your total estimated taxes in installments as follows:

For the Period	Due Date
January 1 - March 31	April 15
April 1 - May 31	June 15
June 1 - August 31	September 15
September 1 - December 31	January 15

Estimated tax payments are counted as paid when the IRS receives them. Thus, paying more later does not offset shortfalls from prior installments. Withheld tax is considered as paid evenly throughout the year. Therefore, increasing withholding late in a year offsets earlier underpayments.

Excess Social Security Withheld (FICA)

If you worked for two or more employers during 2002 and together they paid you more than $84,900 in wages, too much FICA tax was probably withheld from your wages. You can claim the extra amount as a credit on line 65 of Form 1040, page 2, to reduce your income tax when you file your return. If the social security tax withholding shown in Box 4 of all your Forms W-2 exceeds $5,263.80 for 2002, you are entitled to a refund of the excess.

If you are filing a joint return, you cannot add any social security withheld from your spouse's income to the amount withheld from your income. You must figure the excess separately for both you and your spouse to determine if either of you has excess withholding.

Earned Income Credit

Many ministers qualify for the earned income credit (EIC). The program currently furnishes a basic benefit for families even when there are no dependent children. There are three supplemental benefits to adjust for families with two or more children, those with a newborn child, and those that incur certain health insurance costs for their children.

> **Remember**
>
> Prior to 2002 tax returns, the amount excluded from income as a housing allowance, the annual rental value of a parsonage, and contributions by salary reduction to either a cafeteria plan or 403(b) annuity was included in the definition of earned income for earned income credit purposes. Starting with 2002, these items are not included in earned income.

Employees may be eligible for the EIC if their 2002 taxable and nontaxable earned income was less than $11,060 if there is no qualifying child; less than $29,201 if there is one qualifying child; and less than $33,178 if there are two or more children. You cannot claim the EIC unless your investment income is $2,450 or less.

Your child is a qualifying child if your child meets three tests: relationship, age, and residency:

- **Relationship.** Your child must be either your son, daughter, adopted child, grandchild, stepchild, or eligible foster child.

- **Age.** Your child must be under age 19 at the end of 2002, a full-time student under age 24 at the end of 2002, or permanently and totally disabled at any time during 2001, regardless of age.

- **Residency.** Your child must have lived with you in the U.S. for more than half of 2002 (all of 2002 if an eligible foster child).

If you can claim the EIC, you can either have the IRS figure the amount of your credit, or you can figure it yourself (you must complete and attach Schedule EIC to your return if you have at least one qualifying child). If you calculate it, complete a worksheet found in the IRS instructions that determines whether your earned income credit is based on your earned income or modified adjusted gross income (generally equal to your adjusted gross income after disregarding certain losses). Then look up the amount of your credit in an IRS table.

Advance EIC payments

Do you expect to be eligible for the EIC in 2003 and to have a qualifying child? If so, you can choose to get payments of the EIC in your paycheck instead of waiting to get your EIC all at once in 2004 when you file your tax return for the year 2003. These payments are called advance EIC payments. If you qualify for advance EIC payments, complete Form W-5 and give it to your church or other employer.

Extension of Time to File

Your 2002 return should be filed with the IRS service center and payment made by April 15, 2003, to avoid penalties and interest.

If you have obtained an extension of time to file your return, remember that your final payment is still due by April 15, 2003, with the extension application. *The extension of time to file is not an extension of your time to pay.*

Remember

Obtaining a four-month extension is easy. No reason for late filing is needed. The IRS will automatically grant the extension. However, this is not an extension of time to pay—only an extension of time to file. If the amount you owe on your return will generate an underpayment penalty, Filing 4868 will not help you.

Four-month extension

To receive a four-month extension of time, you should file Form 4868, Application for Automatic Extension of Time to File U.S. Individual Income Tax Return. The form must be filed by April 15, 2003.

As an option to filing a paper Form 4868, you can file Form 4868 by telephone (1-888-796-1074) from March 1 through April 15 by making a direct debit to your checking account or sending a paper check. Filing by telephone is advantageous because you get a confirmation number. You can also file for an extension by using your personal tax software or through a tax professional.

Two-month extension

If you have reached the end of the four-month automatic extension period and still need more time to file, you can request two additional months by filing Form 2688, Application for Additional Extension of Time to File (see page 146). Except for undue hardship, the IRS will not accept Form 2688 unless a Form 4868 has been filed. Be sure to file Form 2688 at least a few weeks before the end of the four-month automatic extension period. If you do not give the IRS adequate time to consider your request, it is less likely to be approved.

> **Warning**
>
> Obtaining an extra two-month extension is not automatic. You must furnish a valid reason. If you have not yet received information from an outside party that is necessary for the completion of your return, this will generally be a valid reason. Other reasons that might be accepted by the IRS include illness in your family or destruction or loss of your records.

You may qualify to file Form 2350 for a special two-month extension of time to file in certain instances when you are out of the country.

Penalties

An elaborate system of penalties exists to make sure that tax returns are filed correctly and tax liabilities are paid on time. In addition, interest is charged on many penalties, including the late filing penalty, substantial understatement penalty, overvaluation penalty, negligence penalty, and fraud penalty.

➤ **Failure to pay penalty.** Even if the IRS grants an extension of time to file, if 90% of your tax is not paid on time, you will be subject to a penalty of one-half of 1% of the unpaid tax for each month or part of a month that the tax is not paid, to a maximum of 25% of the tax. You can avoid the penalty only if you can show that your failure to pay is due to reasonable cause and not willful neglect.

> **Tip**
>
> Ask a professional to look over tax due notices from the IRS. It is not unusual for the IRS to send a penalty notice when no penalty is actually due. Demonstrating that you do not owe a penalty may be as simple as completing Form 2210.

➤ **Penalty computed by the IRS.** If you do not want to figure your penalty and pay it when you file your tax return, you do not have to. The IRS will figure it for you and send you a bill. In certain situations you must complete Form 2210 and attach it to your return.

➤ **Form 2210.** If you want to figure your penalty, complete Part I and either Part II or Part III of Form 2210, Underpayment of Estimated Tax by Individuals and Fiduciaries.

You will not generally have to pay a penalty if any of the following situations applies to you:

- ☐ The total of your withholding and estimated tax payments was at least as much as your 2001 tax, you are not subject to the special rule limiting use of prior year's tax, and all required estimated tax payments were on time.

- ☐ The tax balance on your return is no more than 10% of your total 2002 tax, and all required estimated tax payments were on time.

- ☐ Your total 2002 tax minus withholding is less than $1,000.

- ☐ You did not owe tax for 2002.

Interest

If you have not paid the entire tax due by April 15, 2003, you must pay interest from then until the date you pay your tax liability. Receiving an automatic extension of time to file your tax return will not relieve you of the burden of interest.

State extensions

For states that have a state income tax, check the instruction forms that come with your return to determine how to file an extension. In some states, if you owe no additional tax, you need not file a separate state extension. Instead, the state will allow the same extensions that the IRS grants, and you just attach a copy of your federal extension to your state return for filing. Other states may require their own forms.

Extension of Time to Pay

File your return on time even if it is impossible to pay the tax. Filing on time will avoid late filing penalties which are one-half of 1% per month based on the balance of tax due, up to a maximum penalty of 25%. Filing stops the penalties, not the interest.

If you can't pay the full amount due, pay as much as possible when filing the return. Generally, you should not charge your taxes directly to a credit unless it's a small amount that can be paid off shortly. While you might earn frequent flyer miles, you'll pay interest charges to the credit card company plus a credit card cost to the IRS of up to 3% and none of that is deductible.

Installment payments

The IRS may permit you to pay your taxes on the installment plan. When you file your tax return, include Form 9465, Installment Agreement Request (see page 147). Within a month, the IRS will notify you whether the installment payment plan has been approved. But the IRS requires you to start paying within a month. If approved, you will have up to 60 months to pay and will still owe the IRS the late-payment penalty plus interest including interest on the penalty. To limit interest and penalty charges, file your return on time and pay as much of the tax as possible with your return. The IRS charges a user fee of $43 for an installment agreement.

> **Tip**
>
> If you want to pay your taxes on the installment plan, ask for a six-month extension of time to pay, or make the IRS an offer in compromise, consider obtaining professional assistance. These are very specialized forms.

Six-month extension

Don't confuse the six-month extension with the four-month filing extension, which you can obtain automatically by submitting Form 4868. Even if you do get an extension to file your return by August 15, 2003 (by filing Form 4868), you must pay your taxes by April 15, 2003.

You may be able to put off paying your taxes for six months without a penalty by using Form 1127, Application for Extension of Time for Payment of Tax. Getting this extension is not easy. You will have to prove to the IRS that you do not have the money to pay the taxes, cannot borrow, and, if forced to pay up, you and your family will suffer "undue hardship."

Hardship means more than inconvenience. You must show that you will have substantial financial loss if you pay your tax on the date it is due. This loss could be caused by selling property at a sacrifice price.

If you file for this extension, you must include a complete statement of all your assets and liabilities and an itemized list of money you received and spent for three months before you request the extension. Plus, the IRS may require security such as a notice of lien, mortgage, pledge, deed of trust of specific property, or personal surety.

Offers in Compromise

Ask the IRS for an offer in compromise if additional time won't enable you to fully satisfy your tax liability. The IRS agent will negotiate with you and may well settle on the theory that collecting something is better than collecting nothing.

The IRS may legally compromise for one of the following reasons:

- Doubt as to liability—doubt exists that the assessed tax is correct.
- Doubt as to collectibility—doubt exists that you could ever pay the full amount of tax owed.
- Effective tax administration—there is no doubt the tax is correct and no doubt the amount owed could be collected, but an exceptional circumstance exists that allows the IRS to consider the offer. To be eligible for compromise on this basis, you must demonstrate that collection of the tax would create an economic hardship or would be unfair and inequitable.

To work out an offer in compromise, you must show that paying the whole tax would cause a severe or unusual economic hardship. Examples of economic hardship include:

- Incapability of earning a living because of long-term medical condition.
- Liquidation of assets would render the taxpayer unable to pay his or her basic living expenses.

File Form 656, Offer in Compromise, with the district director's office where the liability is pending.

Filing an Amended Tax Return

There is probably still time to revise your 1999 and 2000 and 2001 income tax returns by filing Form 1040X (see page 148). Review these tax returns to determine if you missed out on any tax savings. Or if you find you owe more money, you can pay before the IRS catches up with you and the interest due has increased. Do not include any interest or penalties on Form 1040X; the IRS will adjust them.

File Form 1040X only after you have filed your original return. Generally, Form 1040X must be filed within three years, plus extensions, after the date you filed the original return or within two years after the date you paid the tax, whichever is later. A return filed early is considered filed on the due date. If you are correcting your wages or other employee compensation, attach a copy of all additional or corrected Form W-2s you received after you filed your original return.

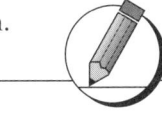

Tip

You may need to amend your tax return to pay more taxes or to get a refund from the IRS. Your tax returns can generally be amended if you file Form 1040X within three years of the due date, plus extensions, of the year you are amending.

Don't forget to amend your state return, too, especially if you owe additional tax. The IRS and the state tax authorities exchange information. If you file an amended federal return and forget to file one for the state, the state is likely to find out about the additional tax from the IRS.

Action Steps

- Carefully estimate your tax liability with a goal of owing very little tax or receiving a small refund.
- Pay your taxes through either Form 1040-ES or a voluntary withholding arrangement with your church.
- Include your social security taxes (SECA) in either the estimated tax payments or the withholding arrangement.
- To avoid underpayment penalties, pay in an amount equal to 100% of your previous year's tax liability.
- If you are afraid you will not be able to mail your return on time, just fill out Form 4868 and mail it to the IRS by midnight of April 15, 2003, for a four-month extension. If you owe income or social security tax, estimate the amount due and include your check.
- If you file Form 4868 for a four-month extension, try to file your return before the August 15, 2003, deadline. Obtaining an additional extension of time to file (Form 2688) is relatively difficult.
- Paying your taxes on the installment plan (Form 9465) or getting a six-month extension of time to pay are options of the last resort.
- Seek professional assistance if you are considering an offer in compromise (Form 656).
- If you have a sound basis, do not be afraid to file an amended return.

2003 MINISTER'S TAX AND FINANCIAL GUIDE

Form **2688**	**Application for Additional Extension of Time To File U.S. Individual Income Tax Return**	OMB No. 1545-0066
Department of the Treasury Internal Revenue Service	▶ See instructions on back. ▶ You must complete all items that apply to you.	2001

Please type or print.

Your first name and initial: Milton L.
Last name: Brown
Your social security number: 541 16 8194

If a joint return, spouses first name and initial: Alessia S.
Last name: Brown
Spouse's social security number: 238 49 7209

File by the due date for filing your return.

Home address (number and street): 418 Trenton Street

City, town or post office, state, and ZIP code: Springfield, OH 45504

Please fill in the Return Label at the bottom of this page.

1. I request an extension of time until .....10-15-02....., to file Form 1040EZ, Form 1040A, Form 1040, Form 1040NR-EZ, or Form 1040NR for the calendar year 2001, or other tax year ending ....

2. Explain why you need an extension. You must give an adequate explanation ▶ Our residence was damaged by tornadic winds in June 2000. Some of our 1999 tax records were destroyed. Additional time to file is needed to secure microfilm copies of bank statements and canceled checks.

3. Have you filed Form 4868 to request an automatic extension of time to file for this tax year? ☑ Yes ☐ No
   If you checked "No," we will grant your extension only for undue hardship. Fully explain the hardship in item 2. Attach any information you have that helps explain the hardship.

If you expect to file a gift or generation-skipping transfer (GST) tax return, complete line 4.

4. If you or your spouse plan to file a gift or GST tax return (Form 709 or 709-A) for 2000, generally due by April 16, 2001, see the instructions and check here .... } Yourself ▶ ☐ Spouse ▶ ☐

Signature and Verification

Under penalties of perjury, I declare that I have examined this form, including accompanying schedules and statements, and to the best of my knowledge and belief, it is true, correct, and complete; and, if prepared by someone other than the taxpayer, that I am authorized to prepare this form.

Signature of taxpayer ▶ *Milton L. Brown*   Date ▶ 04-15-02

Signature of spouse ▶ *Alessia S. Brown*   Date ▶ 04-15-02
(If filing jointly, **both** must sign even if only one had income.)

Signature of preparer other than taxpayer ▶ _____   Date ▶ _____

Please fill in the **Return Label** below with your name, address, and social security number. The IRS will complete the **Notice to Applicant** and return it to you. If you want it sent to another address or to an agent acting for you, enter the other address and add the agent's name.

(Do not detach)

Notice to Applicant To Be Completed by the IRS

☐ We **have** approved your application.
☐ We **Have Not** approved your application.
However, we have granted a 10-day grace period to .... This grace period is considered a valid extension of time for elections otherwise required to be made on a timely return.
☐ We **Have Not** approved your application. After considering the information you provided in item 2 above, we cannot grant your request for an extension of time to file. We are not granting a 10-day grace period.
☐ We cannot consider your application because it was filed after the due date of your return.
☐ Other ....

Director _____   Date _____

Return Label (Please type or print)

Taxpayer's name (and agents name, if applicable). If a joint return, also give spouses name.
Taxpayers social security number

Number and street (include suite, room, or apt. no.) or P.O. box number
Spouses social security number

City, town or post office, state, and ZIP code
Agents:
Always include taxpayers name on Return Label.

For Privacy Act and Paperwork Reduction Act Notice, see back of form.   Cat. No. 11958F   Form **2688** (2000)

Without a compelling reason for an additional extension, a request for further time will often be denied (see page 141).

CHAPTER 8 ▸ PAYING YOUR TAXES

Form 9465 (Rev. November 2000)
Department of the Treasury
Internal Revenue Service (99)

Installment Agreement Request

▸ If you are filing this form with your tax return, attach it to the front of the return. Otherwise, see instructions.

OMB No. 1545-1350

Caution: *Do not file this form if you are currently making payments on an installment agreement. You must pay your other Federal tax liabilities in full or you will be in default on your agreement.*

1. Your first name and initial: **Milton L.** Last name: **Brown** Your social security number: **541 16 8194**
   If a joint return, spouse's first name and initial: **Alessia S.** Last name: **Brown** Spouse's social security number: **238 49 7209**
   Your current address (number and street). If you have a P.O. box and no home delivery, enter your box number.: **418 Trenton Street** Apt. number:
   City, town or post office, state, and ZIP code. If a foreign address, enter city, province or state, and country. Follow the country's practice for entering the postal code.: **Springfield, OH 45504**

2. If this address is new since you filed your last tax return, check here ▸ ☐

3. (**513**) **831-8742** **7-9 p.m.**
   Your home phone number / Best time for us to call

4. (**513**) **831-6873** Ext. **9-5**
   Your work phone number / Best time for us to call

5. Name of your bank or other financial institution:
   Springfield Credit Union
   Address: **489 High Drive**
   City, state, and ZIP code: **Springfield, OH 45504**

6. Your employer's name:
   Magnolia Springs Church
   Address: **4867 Douglas Road**
   City, state, and ZIP code: **Springfield, OH 45504**

TIP *If you are filing this form in response to a notice, do not complete lines 7 through 9. Instead, attach the bottom section of the notice to this form and go to line 10.*

7. Enter the tax return for which you are making this request (for example, Form 1040) ▸ **7** | **Form 1040**
8. Enter the tax year for which you are making this request (for example, 2000) ▸ **8** | **2000**
9. Enter the total amount you owe as shown on your tax return . . . . | **9** | **8,642**
10. Enter the amount of any payment you are making with your tax return (or notice). See instructions | **10** | **1,000**
11. Enter the amount you can pay each month. **Make your payments as large as possible to limit interest and penalty charges.** The charges will continue until you pay in full . . . | **11** | **500**
12. Enter the date you want to make your payment each month. **Do not** enter a date later than the 28th. ▸ **12** | **1st**
13. If you want to make your payments by direct debit, see the instructions and fill in lines 13a, 13b, and 13c.
    ▸ a Routing number ☐☐☐☐☐☐☐☐☐ ▸ c Type: ☐ Checking ☐ Savings
    ▸ b Account number ☐☐☐☐☐☐☐☐☐

I authorize the U.S. Treasury and its designated Financial Agent to initiate a monthly ACH debit (electronic withdrawal) entry to the financial institution account indicated for payments of my Federal taxes owed, and the financial institution to debit the entry to this account. This authorization is to remain in full force and effect until I notify the U.S. Treasury Financial Agent to terminate the authorization. To revoke payment, I must contact the U.S. Treasury Financial Agent at **1-800-829-8815** no later than 7 business days prior to the payment (settlement) date. I also authorize the financial institutions involved in the processing of the electronic payments of taxes to receive confidential information necessary to answer inquiries and resolve issues related to the payments.

Your signature: *Milton L. Brown* Date: **08-15-02**
Spouse's signature. If a joint return, **both** must sign. *Alessia S. Brown* Date: **08-15-02**

General Instructions

Section references are to the Internal Revenue Code.

Purpose of Form

Use Form 9465 to request a monthly installment plan if you cannot pay the full amount you owe shown on your tax return (or on a notice we sent you). But before requesting an installment agreement, you should consider other less costly alternatives, such as a bank loan. If you have any questions about this request, call 1-800-829-1040.

Your request for an installment agreement cannot be turned down if the tax you owe is not more than $10,000 and **all three** of the following apply.

1. During the past 5 tax years, you (and your spouse if you are making a request for a joint return) have timely filed all income tax returns and paid any income tax due, and have not entered into an installment agreement for payment of income tax.

2. The IRS determines that you cannot pay the tax owed in full when it is due and you give the IRS any information needed to make that determination.

3. You agree to pay the full amount you owe within 3 years and to comply with the tax laws while the agreement is in effect.

⚠ *A Notice of Federal Tax Lien may be filed to protect the government's interest until you pay in full.*

Bankruptcy or Offer-in-Compromise. If you are in bankruptcy or we have accepted your offer-in-compromise, **do not** file this form. Instead, call 1-800-829-1040 to get the number of your local IRS Insolvency function for bankruptcy or Technical Support function for offer-in-compromise.

For Privacy Act and Paperwork Reduction Act Notice, see back of form. Cat. No. 14842Y Form **9465** (Rev. 11-2000)

This form must be filed with your tax return to request installment payment of your taxes (see page 143).

Form 1040X — Amended U.S. Individual Income Tax Return

Form 1040X (Rev. November 2002)
Department of the Treasury—Internal Revenue Service
Amended U.S. Individual Income Tax Return
▶ See separate instructions.
OMB No. 1545-0091

This return is for calendar year ▶ _____ , or fiscal year ended ▶ _____ , _____ .

Your first name and initial	Last name	Your social security number
Milton L.	Brown	541 : 16 : 8194

If a joint return, spouse's first name and initial	Last name	Spouse's social security number
Alessia S.	Brown	238 : 49 : 7209

Home address (no. and street) or P.O. box if mail is not delivered to your home: **418 Trenton Street**   Apt. no.   Phone number ( )

City, town or post office, state, and ZIP code. If you have a foreign address, see page 2 of the instructions.
Springfield, OH 45504

For Paperwork Reduction Act Notice, see page 6.

A If the name or address shown above is different from that shown on the original return, check here ▶ ☐

B Has the original return been changed or audited by the IRS or have you been notified that it will be? ☐ Yes ☒ No

C Filing status. Be sure to complete this line. **Note.** You cannot change from joint to separate returns after the due date.
On original return ▶ ☐ Single ☒ Married filing joint return ☐ Married filing separate return ☐ Head of household* ☐ Qualifying widow(er)
On this return ▶ ☐ Single ☒ Married filing joint return ☐ Married filing separate return ☐ Head of household* ☐ Qualifying widow(er)
* If the qualifying person is a child but not your dependent, see page 2.

Use Part II on the back to explain any changes

	Income and Deductions (see pages 2–6)		A. Original amount or as previously adjusted (see page 2)	B. Net change—amount of increase or (decrease)—explain in Part II	C. Correct amount
1	Adjusted gross income (see page 3)	1	32,000	(3,000)	29,000
2	Itemized deductions or standard deduction (see page 3)	2	7,100	300	7,400
3	Subtract line 2 from line 1	3	24,900	(3,300)	21,600
4	Exemptions. If changing, fill in Parts I and II on the back	4	10,200		10,200
5	Taxable income. Subtract line 4 from line 3	5	14,700	(3,300)	11,400
Tax Liability					
6	Tax (see page 4). Method used in col. C _____	6	2,209	(495)	1,714
7	Credits (see page 4)	7			
8	Subtract line 7 from line 6. Enter the result but not less than zero	8			
9	Other taxes (see page 4)	9	5,500		5,500
10	Total tax. Add lines 8 and 9	10	7,709	495	7,214
Payments					
11	Federal income tax withheld and excess social security and tier 1 RRTA tax withheld. If changing, see page 4	11	8,000		8,000
12	Estimated tax payments, including amount applied from prior year's return	12			
13	Earned income credit (EIC)	13			
14	Additional child tax credit from Form 8812	14			
15	Credits from Form 2439 or Form 4136	15			
16	Amount paid with request for extension of time to file (see page 4)	16			
17	Amount of tax paid with original return plus additional tax paid after it was filed	17			
18	Total payments. Add lines 11 through 17 in column C	18			8,000
Refund or Amount You Owe					
19	Overpayment, if any, as shown on original return or as previously adjusted by the IRS	19			291
20	Subtract line 19 from line 18 (see page 5)	20			7,709
21	**Amount you owe.** If line 10, column C, is more than line 20, enter the difference and see page 5	21			
22	If line 10, column C, is less than line 20, enter the difference	22			495
23	Amount of line 22 you want **refunded to you**	23			495
24	Amount of line 22 you want **applied to your** estimated tax	24			

Sign Here
Joint return? See page 2. Keep a copy for your records.
Under penalties of perjury, I declare that I have filed an original return and that I have examined this amended return, including accompanying schedules and statements, and to the best of my knowledge and belief, this amended return is true, correct, and complete. Declaration of preparer (other than taxpayer) is based on all information of which the preparer has any knowledge.

Milton L. Brown 6-18-03   *Alessia S. Brown* 6-18-03
Your signature Date   Spouse's signature. If a joint return, **both** must sign. Date

Paid Preparer's Use Only
Preparer's signature _____ Date _____ Check if self-employed ☐ Preparer's SSN or PTIN _____
Firm's name (or yours if self-employed), address, and ZIP code ▶ _____ EIN _____ Phone no. ( )

Cat. No. 11360L   Form **1040X** (Rev. 11-2002)

Amended returns must be filed within three years of the return due date plus approved extensions (see pages 144–45).

➤ SAMPLE RETURNS

Example No. 1

- Accountable expense reimbursement plan
- Own their own residence
- Pays federal taxes through voluntary withholding
- Church reimbursed nonqualifying moving expenses
- Fair rental value test applied
- New saver's tax credit
- New education deduction
- New educator expense deduction

Minister considered to be an employee for income tax purposes with an accountable business expense plan.

The Browns live in a home they are personally purchasing. Pastor Brown has entered into a voluntary withholding agreement with the church and $15,500 of federal income taxes are withheld.

Income, Benefits, and Reimbursements:

Church salary	$69,150
Christmas and other special occasion gifts paid by the church based on designated member-gifts to the church	750
Honoraria for performing weddings, funerals, and baptisms	650
Honorarium for speaking as an evangelist at another church	1,000
Mutual fund dividend income:	
Capital gain distributions	150
Ordinary	954
Interest income:	
Taxable	675
Tax-exempt	1,200
Reimbursement of self-employment tax	12,000

Business Expenses, Itemized Deductions, Housing, and Other Data:

100% of church-related expenses paid personally ($7,593) were reimbursed by the church under an accountable expense plan, based on timely substantiation of the expenses.

Expenses related to honoraria income:	
Parking	$25
Travel — 1,250 miles	456
Meals and entertainment	50
Other	200
Potential itemized deductions:	
Unreimbursed doctors, dentists, and drugs	1,500
State and local income taxes:	
2001 taxes paid in 2002	400
Withheld from salary	1,600
Real estate taxes on home	1,000
Home mortgage interest	15,000
Cash contributions	8,200
Noncash contributions — fair market value	266
Student loan interest (paid during first 60 months in which interest payments are allowed):	2,125
Housing data:	
Designation	26,000
Actual expenses	25,625
Fair rental value	25,000
Expenses relating to deductions new for 2002:	
Educator expenses (Form 1040, line 23)	200
(Pastor Brown taught over the required 900 hours in an elementary school operated by the church)	
Education expenses (Form 1040, line 26)	800

2003 MINISTER'S TAX AND FINANCIAL GUIDE

Form 1040 Department of the Treasury—Internal Revenue Service
U.S. Individual Income Tax Return 2002 (99) OMB No. 1545-0074

For the year Jan. 1–Dec. 31, 2002, or other tax year beginning , 2002, ending , 20

Label (See instructions on page 19.) Use the IRS label. Otherwise, please print or type.

Your first name and initial: Milton L.
Last name: Brown
Your social security number: 541 16 8194

If a joint return, spouse's first name and initial: Alessia S.
Last name: Brown
Spouse's social security number: 238 49 7209

Home address (number and street). If you have a P.O. box, see page 19.: 418 Trenton Road

City, town or post office, state, and ZIP code. If you have a foreign address, see page 19.: Springfield, OH 45504

Important! You **must** enter your SSN(s) above.

Presidential Election Campaign (See page 19.)
Note. Checking "Yes" will not change your tax or reduce your refund.
Do you, or your spouse if filing a joint return, want $3 to go to this fund? . . . ▶ You: [X] Yes [ ] No Spouse: [X] Yes [ ] No

Filing Status
Check only one box.
1. [ ] Single
2. [X] Married filing jointly (even if only one had income)
3. [ ] Married filing separately. Enter spouse's SSN above and full name here. ▶
4. [ ] Head of household (with qualifying person). (See page 19.) If the qualifying person is a child but not your dependent, enter this child's name here. ▶
5. [ ] Qualifying widow(er) with dependent child (year spouse died ▶). (See page 19.)

Exemptions
6a [X] **Yourself.** If your parent (or someone else) can claim you as a dependent on his or her tax return, **do not** check box 6a
b [X] **Spouse**
c Dependents:
 (1) First name / Last name
 (2) Dependent's social security number
 (3) Dependent's relationship to you
 (4) ✓ if qualifying child for child tax credit (see page 20)

If more than five dependents, see page 20.

No. of boxes checked on 6a and 6b: 2
No. of children on 6c who:
• lived with you
• did not live with you due to divorce or separation (see page 20)
Dependents on 6c not entered above
Add numbers on lines above ▶ 2

d Total number of exemptions claimed

Income
Attach Forms W-2 and W-2G here. Also attach Form(s) 1099-R if tax was withheld.

If you did not get a W-2, see page 21.
Enclose, but do not attach, any payment. Also, please use Form 1040-V.

7 Wages, salaries, tips, etc. Attach Form(s) W-2 . . . . | 7 | 62,650
8a Taxable interest. Attach Schedule B if required . . . . | 8a | 675
b Tax-exempt interest. **Do not** include on line 8a . . . | 8b | 1,200
9 Ordinary dividends. Attach Schedule B if required . . . . | 9 | 954
10 Taxable refunds, credits, or offsets of state and local income taxes (see page 22) . . | 10 |
11 Alimony received . . . . | 11 |
12 Business income or (loss). Attach Schedule C or C-EZ . . . . | 12 | 944
13 Capital gain or (loss). Attach Schedule D if required. If not required, check here ▶ [ ] | 13 | 250
14 Other gains or (losses). Attach Form 4797 . . . . | 14 |
15a IRA distributions . | 15a | b Taxable amount (see page 23) | 15b |
16a Pensions and annuities | 16a | b Taxable amount (see page 23) | 16b |
17 Rental real estate, royalties, partnerships, S corporations, trusts, etc. Attach Schedule E | 17 |
18 Farm income or (loss). Attach Schedule F . . . . | 18 |
19 Unemployment compensation . . . . | 19 |
20a Social security benefits . | 20a | b Taxable amount (see page 25) | 20b |
21 Other income. List type and amount (see page 27) | 21 | 1,000
22 Add the amounts in the far right column for lines 7 through 21. This is your **total income** ▶ | 22 | 66,373

Adjusted Gross Income
23 Educator expenses (see page xx) . . . . | 23 | 200
24 IRA deduction (see page 27) . . . . | 24 |
25 Student loan interest deduction (see page 28) . . . | 25 | 2,125
26 Tuition and fees deduction (see page XX) . . . . . | 26 | 800
27 Archer MSA deduction. Attach Form 8853 . . . . . | 27 |
28 Moving expenses. Attach Form 3903 . . . . | 28 |
29 One-half of self-employment tax. Attach Schedule SE | 29 | 6,184
30 Self-employed health insurance deduction (see page 30) | 30 |
31 Self-employed SEP, SIMPLE, and qualified plans . . | 31 |
32 Penalty on early withdrawal of savings . . . . . . | 32 |
33a Alimony paid b Recipient's SSN ▶ | 33a |
34 Add lines 23 through 33a . . . . | 34 | 9,309
35 Subtract line 34 from line 22. This is your **adjusted gross income** . . . . ▶ | 35 | 57,064

For Disclosure, Privacy Act, and Paperwork Reduction Act Notice, see page 72. Cat. No. 11320B Form **1040** (2002)

Line 21 - See page 156 for calculation of the excess housing allowance.
Line 29 - See page 128 for explanation of the self-employment tax deduction.

EXAMPLE NO. 1 ▶ MINISTER-EMPLOYEE FOR INCOME TAX PURPOSES (ACCOUNTABLE PLAN)

Form 1040 (2002)   Milton L. & Alessia S. Brown   Page **2**

Tax and Credits	36	Amount from line 35 (adjusted gross income)	57,064
	37a	Check if: ☐ **You** were 65 or older, ☐ Blind; ☐ **Spouse** was 65 or older, ☐ Blind. Add the number of boxes checked above and enter the total here ▶ 37a	
Standard Deduction for—	b	If you are married filing separately and your spouse itemizes deductions, or you were a dual-status alien, see page 31 and check here ▶ 37b ☐	
• People who checked any box on line 37a or 37b **or** who can be claimed as a dependent, see page 31.	38	**Itemized deductions** (from Schedule A) **or** your **standard deduction** (see left margin)	26,466
	39	Subtract line 38 from line 36	30,598
	40	If line 36 is $103,000 or less, multiply $3,000 by the total number of exemptions claimed on line 6d. If line 36 is over $103,000, see the worksheet on page 32	6,000
• All others: Single, $4,700	41	**Taxable income.** Subtract line 40 from line 39. If line 40 is more than line 39, enter -0-	24,598
	42	**Tax** (see page 33). Check if any tax is from: a ☐ Form(s) 8814 b ☐ Form 4972	3,086
Head of household, $6,900	43	**Alternative minimum tax** (see page 34). Attach Form 6251	
Married filing jointly or Qualifying widow(er), $7,850	44	Add lines 42 and 43 ▶	3,086
	45	Foreign tax credit. Attach Form 1116 if required 45	
	46	Credit for child and dependent care expenses. Attach Form 2441 46	
	47	Credit for the elderly or the disabled. Attach Schedule R 47	
Married filing separately, $3,925	48	Education credits. Attach Form 8863 48	
	49	Retirement savings contributions credit. Attach Form 8880 49	
	50	Child tax credit (see page XX) 50	
	51	Adoption credit. Attach Form 8839 51	
	52	Credits from: a ☐ Form 8396 b ☐ Form 8859 52	
	53	Other credits. Check applicable box(es): a ☐ Form 3800 b ☐ Form 8801 c ☐ Specify 53	
	54	Add lines 45 through 53. These are your **total credits**	3,086
	55	Subtract line 54 from line 44. If line 54 is more than line 44, enter -0- ▶	12,369
Other Taxes	56	Self-employment tax. Attach Schedule SE	
	57	Social security and Medicare tax on tip income not reported to employer. Attach Form 4137	
	58	Tax on qualified plans, including IRAs, and other tax-favored accounts. Attach Form 5329 if required	
	59	Advance earned income credit payments from Form(s) W-2	
	60	Household employment taxes. Attach Schedule H	
	61	Add lines 55 through 60. This is your **total tax** ▶	15,455
Payments	62	Federal income tax withheld from Forms W-2 and 1099 62 15,500	
	63	2002 estimated tax payments and amount applied from 2001 return 63	
If you have a qualifying child, attach Schedule EIC.	64	**Earned income credit (EIC)** 64	
	65	Excess social security and tier 1 RRTA tax withheld (see page 51) 65	
	66	Additional child tax credit. Attach Form 8812 66	
	67	Amount paid with request for extension to file (see page 51) 67	
	68	Other payments from: a ☐ Form 2439 b ☐ Form 4136 c ☐ Form 8885 68	
	69	Add lines 62 through 68. These are your **total payments** ▶	15,500
Refund	70	If line 69 is more than line 61, subtract line 61 from line 69. This is the amount you **overpaid**	45
Direct deposit? See page 51 and fill in 71b, 71c, and 71d.	71a	Amount of line 70 you want **refunded to you** ▶	45
	b	Routing number ▶ c Type: ☐ Checking ☐ Savings	
	d	Account number	
	72	Amount of line 70 you want **applied to your 2003 estimated tax** ▶ 72	
Amount You Owe	73	**Amount you owe.** Subtract line 69 from line 61. For details on how to pay, see page 52 ▶	
	74	Estimated tax penalty (see page 52) 74	
Third Party Designee	Do you want to allow another person to discuss this return with the IRS (see page 53)? ☐ **Yes.** Complete the following. ☐ **No**		
	Designee's name ▶ Phone no. ▶ ( ) Personal identification number (PIN) ▶		
Sign Here Joint return? See page 19. Keep a copy for your records.	Under penalties of perjury, I declare that I have examined this return and accompanying schedules and statements, and to the best of my knowledge and belief, they are true, correct, and complete. Declaration of preparer (other than taxpayer) is based on all information of which preparer has any knowledge.		
	Your signature *Milton L. Brown* Date 4-15-03 Your occupation Minister Daytime phone number ( )		
	Spouse's signature. If a joint return, **both** must sign. *Alessia S. Brown* Date 4-15-03 Spouse's occupation Housewife		
Paid Preparer's Use Only	Preparer's signature Date Check if self-employed ☐ Preparer's SSN or PTIN		
	Firm's name (or yours if self-employed), address, and ZIP code ▶ EIN Phone no. ( )		

Form **1040** (2002)

Line 57 - The minister had income tax withheld under a voluntary withholding agreement with the church. Notice that income tax was withheld relating to both the income and social security tax liability.

SCHEDULES A&B (Form 1040)	**Schedule A—Itemized Deductions**	OMB No. 1545-0074
Department of the Treasury Internal Revenue Service (99)	(Schedule B is on back) ▶ Attach to Form 1040. ▶ See Instructions for Schedules A and B (Form 1040).	2002 Attachment Sequence No. 07
Name(s) shown on Form 1040 Milton L. Brown		Your social security number 541 16 8194

Medical and Dental Expenses	1	Caution. Do not include expenses reimbursed or paid by others. Medical and dental expenses (see page A-2)	1	1,500
	2	Enter amount from Form 1040, line 36 [2]		
	3	Multiply line 2 above by 7.5% (.075)	3	4,279
	4	Subtract line 3 from line 1. If line 3 is more than line 1, enter -0-	4	0
Taxes You Paid (See page A-2.)	5	State and local income taxes	5	2,000
	6	Real estate taxes (see page A-2)	6	1,000
	7	Personal property taxes	7	
	8	Other taxes. List type and amount ▶	8	
	9	Add lines 5 through 8	9	3,000
Interest You Paid (See page A-3.) Note. Personal interest is not deductible.	10	Home mortgage interest and points reported to you on Form 1098	10	15,000
	11	Home mortgage interest not reported to you on Form 1098. If paid to the person from whom you bought the home, see page A-3 and show that person's name, identifying no., and address ▶	11	
	12	Points not reported to you on Form 1098. See page A-3 for special rules	12	
	13	Investment interest. Attach Form 4952 if required. (See page A-3.)	13	
	14	Add lines 10 through 13	14	15,000
Gifts to Charity If you made a gift and got a benefit for it, see page A-4.	15	Gifts by cash or check. If you made any gift of $250 or more, see page A-4	15	8,200
	16	Other than by cash or check. If any gift of $250 or more, see page A-4. You **must** attach Form 8283 if over $500	16	
	17	Carryover from prior year	17	266
	18	Add lines 15 through 17	18	8,466
Casualty and Theft Losses	19	Casualty or theft loss(es). Attach Form 4684. (See page A-5.)	19	
Job Expenses and Most Other Miscellaneous Deductions (See page A-5 for expenses to deduct here.)	20	Unreimbursed employee expenses—job travel, union dues, job education, etc. You **must** attach Form 2106 or 2106-EZ if required. (See page A-5.) ▶	20	
	21	Tax preparation fees	21	200
	22	Other expenses—investment, safe deposit box, etc. List type and amount ▶	22	
	23	Add lines 20 through 22	23	200
	24	Enter amount from Form 1040, line 36 [24]		
	25	Multiply line 24 above by 2% (.02)	25	1,141
	26	Subtract line 25 from line 23. If line 25 is more than line 23, enter -0-	26	0
Other Miscellaneous Deductions	27	Other—from list on page A-6. List type and amount ▶	27	
Total Itemized Deductions	28	Is Form 1040, line 36, over $137,300 (over $68,650 if married filing separately)? ☐ **No.** Your deduction is not limited. Add the amounts in the far right column for lines 4 through 27. Also, enter this amount on Form 1040, line 38. ☐ **Yes.** Your deduction may be limited. See page A-6 for the amount to enter. ▶	28	26,466

For Paperwork Reduction Act Notice, see Form 1040 instructions. Cat. No. 11330X Schedule A (Form 1040) 2002

Lines 6 and 10 - The real estate taxes and home mortgage interest are deducted on this form plus excluded from income on line 7, Form 1040, page 1 as a housing allowance.

Line 20 - There are no unreimbursed employee expenses to deduct since the church reimbursed all the professional expenses under an accountable expense reimbursement plan.

EXAMPLE NO. 1 ▶ MINISTER-EMPLOYEE FOR INCOME TAX PURPOSES (ACCOUNTABLE PLAN)

Schedules A&B (Form 1040) 2002   OMB No. 1545-0074   Page **2**

Name(s) shown on Form 1040. Do not enter name and social security number if shown on other side.
Milton L. and Alessia S. Brown

Your social security number: 541 16 8194

Schedule B—Interest and Ordinary Dividends

Attachment Sequence No. **08**

Part I — Interest

(See page B-1 and the instructions for Form 1040, line 8a.)

1 List name of payer. If any interest is from a seller-financed mortgage and the buyer used the property as a personal residence, see page B-1 and list this interest first. Also, show that buyer's social security number and address ▶

	Amount
	1,200
	675
Subtotal	1,875
Less: Tax-Exempt Interest	-1,200

Note. If you received a Form 1099-INT, Form 1099-OID, or substitute statement from a brokerage firm, list the firm's name as the payer and enter the total interest shown on that form.

2 Add the amounts on line 1 . . . . **2** 675

3 Excludable interest on series EE and I U.S. savings bonds issued after 1989 from Form 8815, line 14. You **must** attach Form 8815 . . . . **3**

4 Subtract line 3 from line 2. Enter the result here and on Form 1040, line 8a ▶ **4** 675

Note. If line 4 is over $400, you must complete Part III.

Part II — Ordinary Dividends

(See page B-1 and the instructions for Form 1040, line 9.)

5 List name of payer. Include only ordinary dividends. If you received any capital gain distributions, see the instructions for Form 1040, line 13 ▶

	Amount
	954

Note. If you received a Form 1099-DIV or substitute statement from a brokerage firm, list the firm's name as the payer and enter the ordinary dividends shown on that form.

6 Add the amounts on line 5. Enter the total here and on Form 1040, line 9 . ▶ **6** 954

Note. If line 6 is over $400, you must complete Part III.

Part III — Foreign Accounts and Trusts

(See page B-2.)

You must complete this part if you **(a)** had over $400 of taxable interest or ordinary dividends; **(b)** had a foreign account; or **(c)** received a distribution from, or were a grantor of, or a transferor to, a foreign trust.

	Yes	No
7a At any time during 2002, did you have an interest in or a signature or other authority over a financial account in a foreign country, such as a bank account, securities account, or other financial account? See page B-2 for exceptions and filing requirements for Form TD F 90-22.1 . . .		X
b If "Yes," enter the name of the foreign country ▶		
8 During 2002, did you receive a distribution from, or were you the grantor of, or transferor to, a foreign trust? If "Yes," you may have to file Form 3520. See page B-2		X

For Paperwork Reduction Act Notice, see Form 1040 instructions.   Schedule B (Form 1040) 2002

2003 MINISTER'S TAX AND FINANCIAL GUIDE

SCHEDULE C-EZ (Form 1040)
Department of the Treasury
Internal Revenue Service (99)

Net Profit From Business
(Sole Proprietorship)
▶ Partnerships, joint ventures, etc., must file Form 1065 or 1065-B.
▶ Attach to Form 1040 or 1041. ▶ See instructions on back.

OMB No. 1545-0074

2002

Attachment Sequence No. **09A**

Name of proprietor: Milton L. Brown
Social security number (SSN): 541 : 16 : 8194

Part I — General Information

You May Use Schedule C-EZ Instead of Schedule C Only If You:
- Had business expenses of $2,500 or less.
- Use the cash method of accounting.
- Did not have an inventory at any time during the year.
- Did not have a net loss from your business.
- Had only one business as a sole proprietor.

And You:
- Had no employees during the year.
- Are not required to file **Form 4562**, Depreciation and Amortization, for this business. See the instructions for Schedule C, line 13, on page C-3 to find out if you must file.
- Do not deduct expenses for business use of your home.
- Do not have prior year unallowed passive activity losses from this business.

A Principal business or profession, including product or service

B Enter code from pages C-7 & 8 ▶ 8 1 3 0 0 0

C Business name. If no separate business name, leave blank.

D Employer ID number (EIN), if any

E Business address (including suite or room no.). Address not required if same as on Form 1040, page 1.

City, town or post office, state, and ZIP code

Part II — Figure Your Net Profit

1. Gross receipts. Caution. If this income was reported to you on Form W-2 and the "Statutory employee" box on that form was checked, see **Statutory Employees** in the instructions for Schedule C, line 1, on page C-2 and check here ▶ ☐ .... **1** | 1,650

2. Total expenses. If more than $2,500, you **must** use Schedule C (see instructions) .... **2** | 706

3. Net profit. Subtract line 2 from line 1. If less than zero, you **must** use Schedule C. Enter on Form 1040, line 12, and **also** on Schedule SE, line 2. (Statutory employees **do not** report this amount on Schedule SE, line 2. Estates and trusts, enter on Form 1041, line 3.) ..... **3** | 944

Part III — Information on Your Vehicle. Complete this part **only** if you are claiming car or truck expenses on line 2.

4. When did you place your vehicle in service for business purposes? (month, day, year) ▶ ...... / ...... / ......

5. Of the total number of miles you drove your vehicle during 2002, enter the number of miles you used your vehicle for:
   Schedule C   1,250
   a Business ...... 9,412 ...... **b** Commuting ...... 2,480 ...... **c** Other ......

6. Do you (or your spouse) have another vehicle available for personal use? .... ☒ Yes ☐ No

7. Was your vehicle available for personal use during off-duty hours? .... ☒ Yes ☐ No

8a. Do you have evidence to support your deduction? .... ☒ Yes ☐ No

   b If "Yes," is the evidence written? .... ☒ Yes ☐ No

Gross receipts:		Expenses:	
Honoraria (weddings, etc.)	$650	Parking	$ 25
Speaking honorarium	1,000	Miles (1,250 x 36.5)	456
	$1,650	Meals & entertainment ($50 x 50%)	25
		Other	200
			$ 706

Most ministers considered to be employees for income tax purposes (with that income reported on line 7, Form 1040, page 1) also have honoraria and fee income and related expenses that are reportable on Schedule C (C-EZ).

EXAMPLE NO. 1 ▶ MINISTER-EMPLOYEE FOR INCOME TAX PURPOSES (ACCOUNTABLE PLAN)

Schedule SE (Form 1040) 2002 — Attachment Sequence No. 17 — Page 2

Name of person with **self-employment** income (as shown on Form 1040): Milton L. Brown
Social security number of person with **self-employment** income ▶ 541 16 8194

Section B—Long Schedule SE

Part I Self-Employment Tax

Note. If your only income subject to self-employment tax is **church employee income**, skip lines 1 through 4b. Enter -0- on line 4c and go to line 5a. Income from services you performed as a minister or a member of a religious order **is not** church employee income. See page SE-1.

A If you are a minister, member of a religious order, or Christian Science practitioner **and** you filed Form 4361, but you had $400 or more of **other** net earnings from self-employment, check here and continue with Part I . . . . . ▶ ☐

Line	Description	Amount
1	Net farm profit or (loss) from Schedule F, line 36, and farm partnerships, Schedule K-1 (Form 1065), line 15a. **Note.** Skip this line if you use the farm optional method. See page SE-3	
2	Net profit or (loss) from Schedule C, line 31; Schedule C-EZ, line 3; Schedule K-1 (Form 1065), line 15a (other than farming); and Schedule K-1 (Form 1065-B), box 9. Ministers and members of religious orders, see page SE-1 for amounts to report on this line. See page SE-2 for other income to report. **Note.** Skip this line if you use the nonfarm optional method. See page SE-3	89,594
3	Combine lines 1 and 2	89,594
4a	If line 3 is more than zero, multiply line 3 by 92.35% (.9235). Otherwise, enter amount from line 3	82,740
4b	If you elect one or both of the optional methods, enter the total of lines 15 and 17 here	
4c	Combine lines 4a and 4b. If less than $400, **do not** file this schedule; you do not owe self-employment tax. **Exception.** If less than $400 and you had **church employee income,** enter -0- and continue ▶	82,740
5a	Enter your **church employee income** from Form W-2. **Caution.** See page SE-1 for definition of church employee income	
5b	Multiply line 5a by 92.35% (.9235). If less than $100, enter -0-	
6	**Net earnings from self-employment.** Add lines 4c and 5b	82,740
7	Maximum amount of combined wages and self-employment earnings subject to social security tax or the 6.2% portion of the 7.65% railroad retirement (tier 1) tax for 2002	84,900 00
8a	Total social security wages and tips (total of boxes 3 and 7 on Form(s) W-2) and railroad retirement (tier 1) compensation	
8b	Unreported tips subject to social security tax (from Form 4137, line 9)	
8c	Add lines 8a and 8b	
9	Subtract line 8c from line 7. If zero or less, enter -0- here and on line 10 and go to line 11 ▶	80,400
10	Multiply the **smaller** of line 6 or line 9 by 12.4% (.124)	9,970
11	Multiply line 6 by 2.9% (.029)	2,399
12	**Self-employment tax.** Add lines 10 and 11. Enter here and on **Form 1040, line 56**	12,369
13	**Deduction for one-half of self-employment tax.** Multiply line 12 by 50% (.5). Enter the result here and on **Form 1040, line 29** . . . 13 6,184	

Part II Optional Methods To Figure Net Earnings (See page SE-3.)

Farm Optional Method. You may use this method **only** if:
- Your gross farm income[1] was not more than $2,400 **or**
- Your net farm profits[2] were less than $1,733.

14	Maximum income for optional methods	1,600 00
15	Enter the **smaller** of: two-thirds (⅔) of gross farm income[1] (not less than zero) **or** $1,600. Also include this amount on line 4b above	

Nonfarm Optional Method. You may use this method **only** if:
- Your net nonfarm profits[3] were less than $1,733 and also less than 72.189% of your gross nonfarm income[4] **and**
- You had net earnings from self-employment of at least $400 in 2 of the prior 3 years.

Caution. You may use this method no more than five times.

| 16 | Subtract line 15 from line 14 | |
| 17 | Enter the **smaller** of: two-thirds (⅔) of gross nonfarm income[4] (not less than zero) **or** the amount on line 16. Also include this amount on line 4b above | |

[1] From Sch. F, line 11, and Sch. K-1 (Form 1065), line 15b.
[2] From Sch. F, line 36, and Sch. K-1 (Form 1065), line 15a.
[3] From Sch. C, line 31; Sch. C-EZ, line 3; Sch. K-1 (Form 1065), line 15a; and Sch. K-1 (Form 1065-B), box 9.
[4] From Sch. C, line 7; Sch. C-EZ, line 1; Sch. K-1 (Form 1065), line 15c; and Sch. K-1 (Form 1065-B), box 9.

Line 2 - See the worksheet on page 157 for the calculation of this amount.

Line 4 - This line results in the deduction of a portion of the self-employment tax liability.

A minister must use Section B-Long Schedule if he or she received nonministerial wages (subject to FICA) and the total of these wages and net ministerial self-employment earnings (W-2 and Schedule C [C-EZ]-related) is more than $84,900.

Housing Allowance Worksheet
Minister Living in Home
Minister Owns or Is Buying

Minister's Name: __Milton L. Brown__

For the period __January 1__, 200_2_ to __December 31__, 200_2_

Date designation approved __December 20__, 200_1_

Allowable Housing Expenses *(expenses paid by minister from current income)*

	Estimated Expenses	Actual
Down payment on purchase of housing	$	$
Housing loan principal and interest payments	18,117	18,875
Real estate commission, escrow fees		
Real property taxes	900	1,000
Personal property taxes on contents		
Homeowner's insurance	500	550
Personal property insurance on contents	150	200
Umbrella liability insurance	100	
Structural maintenance and repair		550
Landscaping, gardening, and pest control		200
Furnishings *(purchase, repair, replacement)*		400
Decoration and redecoration		
Utilities *(gas, electricity, water)* and trash collection	3,500	3,500
Local telephone expense *(base charge)*	150	150
Homeowner's association dues/condominium fees	219	200
Subtotal	23,636	
10% allowance for unexpected expenses	2,364	
TOTAL	$ 26,000	$ 25,625 (A)
Properly designated housing allowance		$ 26,000 (B)
Fair rental value of home		$ 25,000 (C)

Note: The amount excludable from income for federal income tax purposes is the *lowest* of A, B, or C.

The $1,000 difference between the designation ($26,000) and the fair rental value ($25,000) is reported as additional income on Form 1040, line 21.

EXAMPLE NO. 1 ➤ MINISTER-EMPLOYEE FOR INCOME TAX PURPOSES (ACCOUNTABLE PLAN)

Self-Employment Social Security Tax Worksheet

Inclusions:

Salary paid by church as reflected on Form W-2	$ 62,650
Net profit or loss as reflected on Schedule C or C-EZ (includes speaking honoraria, offerings you receive for marriages, baptisms, funerals, and other fees)	944
Housing allowance excluded from salary on Form W-2	26,000
Fair rental value of parsonage provided (including paid utilities)	
Nonaccountable business expense reimbursements (if not included on Form W-2)	
Reimbursement of self-employment taxes (if not included on Form W-2)	
Value of meals provided to you, your spouse, and your dependents whether or not provided for your employer's convenience (these amounts may have been excluded from gross income)	
Total inclusions	89,594

Deductions:

Unreimbursed ministerial business and professional expenses (included on Form W-2) or reimbursed expenses paid under a nonaccountable plan (included on Form W-2) A. Deductible on Schedule A before the 2% of AGI limitation whether or not you itemized[1] or B. Not deductible on Form 2106/2106 EZ because expenses were allocated to taxable/nontaxable income	
Total deductions	
Net earnings from self-employment (to Schedule SE)	$ 89,594

[1] The 50% unreimbursed meal and entertainment expense limitation applies to amounts subject to social security tax. In other words, if some of your meal and entertainment expenses were subjected to the 50% limit, the remainder cannot be deducted here.

Note 1: Your net earnings from self-employment are not affected by the foreign earned income exclusion or the foreign housing exclusion or deduction if you are a U.S. citizen or resident alien who is serving abroad and living in a foreign country.

Note 2: Amounts received as pension payments or annuity payments related to a church-sponsored tax-sheltered annuity by a retired minister are generally considered to be excluded from the social security calculation.

Net earnings from self-employment are entered on Schedule SE, line 2 (see page 155). While the W-2 portion of the self-employment income could be shown on Schedule SE, line 5a, the example shows the simpler approach of transferring the total self-employment income to line 2.

Form W-2 Wage and Tax Statement (2002)

Box	Field	Value
a	Control number	22222
b	Employer identification number	38-9418217
c	Employer's name, address, and ZIP code	Magnolia Springs Church, 4865 Douglas Road, Springfield, OH 45504
d	Employee's social security number	541-16-8194
e	Employee's first name and initial	Milton L.
	Last name	Brown
	Employee's address	418 Trenton Street, Springfield, OH 45504
1	Wages, tips, other compensation	62650.00
2	Federal income tax withheld	15500.00
13	Retirement plan	X
15	State	OH
	Employer's state ID number	627803
16	State wages, tips, etc.	62650.00
17	State income tax	3000.00

Explanation of compensation reported on Form W-2, Box 1:

Salary ($69,150 less $26,000 housing allowance)	$43,150
Special occasion gifts	750
Reimbursement of self-employment tax	12,000
Moving expense reimbursement of nonqualified expenses	6,750
	$62,650

Pastor Brown received reimbursements of $7,593 under an accountable expense reimbursement plan. The reimbursements are not included on Form W-2 or deductible on Form 1040. There is no requirement to add the reimbursements to income taxable for social security purposes on Schedule SE.

Pastor Brown was also reimbursed for $6,000 of nonqualified moving expenses. He failed the distance test in that his new principal place of work was less than 50 miles farther from his old residence than the old residence was from his old place of work.

> SAMPLE RETURNS

Example No. 2

- Nonaccountable expense reimbursements
- Occupies a church-provided parsonage
- Pays federal taxes using Form 1040-ES
- Qualifies for the Earned Income Credit
- 403(b) contribution by salary reduction and employer contributions
- Church did not reimburse moving expenses

Minister considered to be an employee for income tax purposes with a nonaccountable business expense plan.

The Halls live in church-provided housing. Pastor Hall files Form 1040-ES to pay income and social security (SECA) taxes and paid $300 each quarter.

Income, Benefits, and Reimbursements:

Church salary – Donald	$6,700
Salary – Julie (W-2 not shown)	12,150
Christmas and other special occasion gifts paid by the church based on designated member-gifts to the church	500
Honoraria for performing weddings, funerals, baptisms, and outside speaking engagements	5,000
Interest income (taxable)	3,000
Reimbursement of self-employment tax	2,100
Business expense allowance (no accounting provided to church)	3,700

Business Expenses, Itemized Deductions, 403(b) Contributions, Housing Data, and Moving Expense Data:

Church-related expenses paid personally:

Business use of personally-owned auto (W-2 related)	11,901 miles
Personal nondeductible commuting	2,432 miles
Seminar expenses:	
Airfare	$675 (1)
Meals	233 (1)
Lodging	167 (1)
Subscriptions	200 (1)
Books (less than one-year lives)	100 (1)
Supplies	250 (1)
Entertainment expenses	1,207 (1)
Continuing education tuition (related to church employment)	500 (1)
Travel expense related to honoraria:	
Airfare	2,042 (1)
Business use of personally-owned auto	3,660 miles
Lodging	400 (1)
Supplies	200 (1)

Potential itemized deductions:

Unreimbursed doctors, dentists, and drugs	1,200
State and local income taxes	750
Personal property taxes	300
Cash contributions	2,600

403(b) pretax contributions for Pastor Hall:

Voluntary employee contributions made under a salary reduction agreement	500
Nonvoluntary employer contributions	2,000

Housing data:

Designation	2,000
Actual expenses	1,000
Fair rental value, including utilities	11,150
Moving expenses	1,000

(1) 5% of these expenses are unallowable (see page 171).

159

2003 MINISTER'S TAX AND FINANCIAL GUIDE

Form 1040 Department of the Treasury—Internal Revenue Service
U.S. Individual Income Tax Return 2002 (99) IRS Use Only—Do not write or staple in this space.

For the year Jan. 1–Dec. 31, 2002, or other tax year beginning , 2002, ending , 20 OMB No. 1545-0074

Label (See instructions on page 19.)
Use the IRS label. Otherwise, please print or type.

Your first name and initial: Donald L.   Last name: Hall
Your social security number: 482 11 6043

If a joint return, spouse's first name and initial: Julie M.   Last name: Hall
Spouse's social security number: 720 92 1327

Home address (number and street). If you have a P.O. box, see page 19.   Apt. no.
604 Linden Avenue

City, town or post office, state, and ZIP code. If you have a foreign address, see page 19.
Wabash, IN 46992

▲ **Important!** ▲
You **must** enter your SSN(s) above.

Presidential Election Campaign (See page 19.)
Note. Checking "Yes" will not change your tax or reduce your refund.
Do you, or your spouse if filing a joint return, want $3 to go to this fund? ▶
You: ☐ Yes ☒ No   Spouse: ☐ Yes ☒ No

Filing Status
Check only one box.
1. ☐ Single
2. ☒ Married filing jointly (even if only one had income)
3. ☐ Married filing separately. Enter spouse's SSN above and full name here. ▶ _____
4. ☐ Head of household (with qualifying person). (See page 19.) If the qualifying person is a child but not your dependent, enter this child's name here. ▶
5. ☐ Qualifying widow(er) with dependent child (year spouse died ▶). (See page 19.)

Exemptions
6a ☒ **Yourself.** If your parent (or someone else) can claim you as a dependent on his or her tax return, **do not** check box 6a
b ☒ **Spouse**

No. of boxes checked on 6a and 6b: **2**

c Dependents:
(1) First name Last name	(2) Dependent's social security number	(3) Dependent's relationship to you	(4) ✓ if qualifying child for child tax credit (see page 20)
David K. Hall	514 42 7465	Son	☒
Sarah E. Hall	516 49 0125	Daughter	☒
			☐
			☐

If more than five dependents, see page 20.

No. of children on 6c who:
• lived with you
• did not live with you due to divorce or separation (see page 20)
Dependents on 6c not entered above
Add numbers on lines above ▶ **4**

d Total number of exemptions claimed

Income
Attach Forms W-2 and W-2G here. Also attach Form(s) 1099-R if tax was withheld.

If you did not get a W-2, see page 21.

Enclose, but do not attach, any payment. Also, please use Form 1040-V.

7	Wages, salaries, tips, etc. Attach Form(s) W-2	7	22,650
8a	Taxable interest. Attach Schedule B if required	8a	3,000
b	Tax-exempt interest. **Do not** include on line 8a	8b	
9	Ordinary dividends. Attach Schedule B if required	9	
10	Taxable refunds, credits, or offsets of state and local income taxes (see page 22)	10	
11	Alimony received	11	
12	Business income or (loss). Attach Schedule C or C-EZ	12	1,221
13	Capital gain or (loss). Attach Schedule D if required. If not required, check here ▶ ☐	13	
14	Other gains or (losses). Attach Form 4797	14	
15a	IRA distributions 15a	b Taxable amount (see page 23)	15b	
16a	Pensions and annuities 16a	b Taxable amount (see page 23)	16b	
17	Rental real estate, royalties, partnerships, S corporations, trusts, etc. Attach Schedule E	17	
18	Farm income or (loss). Attach Schedule F	18	
19	Unemployment compensation	19	
20a	Social security benefits 20a	b Taxable amount (see page 25)	20b	
21	Other income. List type and amount (see page 27) Excess housing allowance	21	1,000
22	Add the amounts in the far right column for lines 7 through 21. This is your **total income** ▶	22	27,871

Adjusted Gross Income

23	Educator expenses (see page xx)	23	
24	IRA deduction (see page 27)	24	
25	Student loan interest deduction (see page 28)	25	
26	Tuition and fees deduction (see page XX)	26	
27	Archer MSA deduction. Attach Form 8853	27	
28	Moving expenses. Attach Form 3903	28	1,000
29	One-half of self-employment tax. Attach Schedule SE	29	1,252
30	Self-employed health insurance deduction (see page 30)	30	
31	Self-employed SEP, SIMPLE, and qualified plans	31	
32	Penalty on early withdrawal of savings	32	
33a	Alimony paid b Recipient's SSN ▶	33a	
34	Add lines 23 through 33a	34	2,252
35	Subtract line 34 from line 22. This is your **adjusted gross income** ▶	35	25,619

For Disclosure, Privacy Act, and Paperwork Reduction Act Notice, see page 72.   Cat. No. 11320B   Form **1040** (2002)

Line 7 - Julie's W-2, $12,150, plus Donald's W-2, $10,500.

Line 21 - See page 172 for the calculation of the excess housing allowance.

Line 27 - See page 128 for explanation of the self-employment tax deduction.

EXAMPLE NO. 2 ➤ MINISTER-EMPLOYEE FOR INCOME TAX PURPOSES (NONACCOUNTABLE PLAN)

Form 1040 (2002) Donald L. & Julie M. Hall — Page **2**

Line	Description	Amount
Tax and Credits		
36	Amount from line 35 (adjusted gross income)	25,619
37a	Check if: ☐ You were 65 or older, ☐ Blind; ☐ Spouse was 65 or older, ☐ Blind. Add the number of boxes checked above and enter the total here ▶ 37a	
b	If you are married filing separately and your spouse itemizes deductions, or you were a dual-status alien, see page 31 and check here ▶ 37b ☐	
38	Itemized deductions (from Schedule A) or your standard deduction (see left margin)	9,747
39	Subtract line 38 from line 36	15,872
40	If line 36 is $103,000 or less, multiply $3,000 by the total number of exemptions claimed on line 6d. If line 36 is over $103,000, see the worksheet on page 32	12,000
41	**Taxable income.** Subtract line 40 from line 39. If line 40 is more than line 39, enter -0-	3,872
42	Tax (see page 33). Check if any tax is from: a ☐ Form(s) 8814 b ☐ Form 4972	388
43	**Alternative minimum tax** (see page 34). Attach Form 6251	
44	Add lines 42 and 43 ▶	388
45	Foreign tax credit. Attach Form 1116 if required	
46	Credit for child and dependent care expenses. Attach Form 2441	
47	Credit for the elderly or the disabled. Attach Schedule R	
48	Education credits. Attach Form 8863	
49	Retirement savings contributions credit. Attach Form 8880	250
50	Child tax credit (see page XX)	138
51	Adoption credit. Attach Form 8839	
52	Credits from: a ☐ Form 8396 b ☐ Form 8859	
53	Other credits. Check applicable box(es): a ☐ Form 3800 b ☐ Form 8801 c ☐ Specify	
54	Add lines 45 through 53. These are your **total credits**	388
55	Subtract line 54 from line 44. If line 54 is more than line 44, enter -0- ▶	0
Other Taxes		
56	Self-employment tax. Attach Schedule SE	2,503
57	Social security and Medicare tax on tip income not reported to employer. Attach Form 4137	
58	Tax on qualified plans, including IRAs, and other tax-favored accounts. Attach Form 5329 if required	
59	Advance earned income credit payments from Form(s) W-2	
60	Household employment taxes. Attach Schedule H	
61	Add lines 55 through 60. This is your **total tax** ▶	2,503
Payments		
62	Federal income tax withheld from Forms W-2 and 1099	
63	2002 estimated tax payments and amount applied from 2001 return	1,200
64	**Earned income credit (EIC)**	1,591
65	Excess social security and tier 1 RRTA tax withheld (see page 51)	
66	Additional child tax credit. Attach Form 8812	
67	Amount paid with request for extension to file (see page 51)	
68	Other payments from: a ☐ Form 2439 b ☐ Form 4136 c ☐ Form 8885	
69	Add lines 62 through 68. These are your **total payments** ▶	2,791
Refund		
70	If line 69 is more than line 61, subtract line 61 from line 69. This is the amount you **overpaid**	288
71a	Amount of line 70 you want **refunded to you** ▶	288
b	Routing number	
c	Type: ☐ Checking ☐ Savings	
d	Account number	
72	Amount of line 70 you want **applied to your 2003 estimated tax** ▶ 72	
Amount You Owe		
73	**Amount you owe.** Subtract line 69 from line 61. For details on how to pay, see page 52 ▶	
74	Estimated tax penalty (see page 52)	

Standard Deduction for—
- People who checked any box on line 37a or 37b **or** who can be claimed as a dependent, see page 31.
- All others:
  Single, $4,700
  Head of household, $6,900
  Married filing jointly or Qualifying widow(er), $7,850
  Married filing separately, $3,925

Third Party Designee — Do you want to allow another person to discuss this return with the IRS (see page 53)? ☐ Yes. Complete the following. ☒ No

Sign Here — Under penalties of perjury, I declare that I have examined this return and accompanying schedules and statements, and to the best of my knowledge and belief, they are true, correct, and complete. Declaration of preparer (other than taxpayer) is based on all information of which preparer has any knowledge.

Your signature: Donald L. Hall — Date: 04-15-03 — Your occupation: Minister
Spouse's signature: Julie M. Hall — Date: 04-15-03 — Spouse's occupation: Housewife

Paid Preparer's Use Only

Form **1040** (2002)

Line 58 - The minister pays federal taxes (income and social security) by quarterly filing Form 1040-ES.

161

Schedule A—Itemized Deductions

(Schedule B is on back)

► Attach to Form 1040. ► See Instructions for Schedules A and B (Form 1040).

OMB No. 1545-0074
2002
Attachment Sequence No. 07

SCHEDULES A&B (Form 1040)
Department of the Treasury
Internal Revenue Service (99)

Name(s) shown on Form 1040: Donald L. and Julie M. Hall
Your social security number: 482 11 6043

Medical and Dental Expenses
1. Medical and dental expenses (see page A-2) — Caution. Do not include expenses reimbursed or paid by others. ... **1** 1,200
2. Enter amount from Form 1040, line 36 [2] 25,619
3. Multiply line 2 above by 7.5% (.075) ... **3** 1,921
4. Subtract line 3 from line 1. If line 3 is more than line 1, enter -0- ... **4** 0

Taxes You Paid (See page A-2.)
5. State and local income taxes ... **5** 750
6. Real estate taxes (see page A-2) ... **6**
7. Personal property taxes ... **7** 300
8. Other taxes. List type and amount ► ... **8**
9. Add lines 5 through 8 ... **9** 1,050

Interest You Paid (See page A-3.)
Note. Personal interest is not deductible.
10. Home mortgage interest and points reported to you on Form 1098 ... **10**
11. Home mortgage interest not reported to you on Form 1098. If paid to the person from whom you bought the home, see page A-3 and show that person's name, identifying no., and address ► ... **11**
12. Points not reported to you on Form 1098. See page A-3 for special rules ... **12**
13. Investment interest. Attach Form 4952 if required. (See page A-3.) ... **13**
14. Add lines 10 through 13 ... **14**

Gifts to Charity
If you made a gift and got a benefit for it, see page A-4.
15. Gifts by cash or check. If you made any gift of $250 or more, see page A-4 ... **15** 2,600
16. Other than by cash or check. If any gift of $250 or more, see page A-4. You **must** attach Form 8283 if over $500 ... **16**
17. Carryover from prior year ... **17**
18. Add lines 15 through 17 ... **18** 2,600

Casualty and Theft Losses
19. Casualty or theft loss(es). Attach Form 4684. (See page A-5.) ... **19**

Job Expenses and Most Other Miscellaneous Deductions (See page A-5 for expenses to deduct here.)
20. Unreimbursed employee expenses—job travel, union dues, job education, etc. You **must** attach Form 2106 or 2106-EZ if required. (See page A-5.) ► See Form 2106-EZ ... **20** 6,609
21. Tax preparation fees ... **21**
22. Other expenses—investment, safe deposit box, etc. List type and amount ► ... **22**
23. Add lines 20 through 22 ... **23** 6,609
24. Enter amount from Form 1040, line 36 [24] 25,619
25. Multiply line 24 above by 2% (.02) ... **25** 512
26. Subtract line 25 from line 23. If line 25 is more than line 23, enter -0- ... **26** 6,097

Other Miscellaneous Deductions
27. Other—from list on page A-6. List type and amount ► ... **27**

Total Itemized Deductions
28. Is Form 1040, line 36, over $137,300 (over $68,650 if married filing separately)?
☐ **No.** Your deduction is not limited. Add the amounts in the far right column for lines 4 through 27. Also, enter this amount on Form 1040, line 38.
☐ **Yes.** Your deduction may be limited. See page A-6 for the amount to enter. ► **28** 9,747

For Paperwork Reduction Act Notice, see Form 1040 instructions. Cat. No. 11330X Schedule A (Form 1040) 2002

Line 20 - Because the minister did not have an accountable expense reimbursement plan, the unreimbursed expenses appear on this line. One of the disadvantages of this approach is the 2% deduction (line 25), which costs the minister $512 of deductions.

EXAMPLE NO. 2 ▶ MINISTER-EMPLOYEE FOR INCOME TAX PURPOSES (NONACCOUNTABLE PLAN)

SCHEDULE C (Form 1040)
Department of the Treasury
Internal Revenue Service (99)

Profit or Loss From Business
(Sole Proprietorship)
▶ Partnerships, joint ventures, etc., must file Form 1065 or 1065-B.
▶ Attach to Form 1040 or 1041. ▶ See Instructions for Schedule C (Form 1040).

OMB No. 1545-0074
2002
Attachment Sequence No. 09

Name of proprietor: Donald L. Hall
Social security number (SSN): 482 : 11 : 6043

A Principal business or profession, including product or service (see page C-1 of the instructions): Minister
B Enter code from pages C-7 & 8: ▶ 8 1 3 0 0 0

C Business name. If no separate business name, leave blank.
D Employer ID number (EIN), if any

E Business address (including suite or room no.) ▶ 604 Linden Avenue, Wabash, IN 46992
City, town or post office, state, and ZIP code

F Accounting method: (1) [X] Cash (2) ☐ Accrual (3) ☐ Other (specify) ▶
G Did you "materially participate" in the operation of this business during 2002? If "No," see page C-2 for limit on losses ☐ Yes ☐ No
H If you started or acquired this business during 2002, check here ▶ ☐

Part I Income

1 Gross receipts or sales. Caution. If this income was reported to you on Form W-2 and the "Statutory employee" box on that form was checked, see page C-2 and check here ▶ ☐	1	5,000
2 Returns and allowances	2	
3 Subtract line 2 from line 1	3	5,000
4 Cost of goods sold (from line 42 on page 2)	4	
5 Gross profit. Subtract line 4 from line 3	5	5,000
6 Other income, including Federal and state gasoline or fuel tax credit or refund (see page C-3)	6	
7 Gross income. Add lines 5 and 6 ▶	7	5,000

Part II Expenses. Enter expenses for business use of your home **only** on line 30.

8 Advertising	8		19 Pension and profit-sharing plans	19	
9 Bad debts from sales or services (see page C-3)	9		20 Rent or lease (see page C-4):		
			a Vehicles, machinery, and equipment	20a	
10 Car and truck expenses (see page C-3)	10	1,269	b Other business property	20b	
			21 Repairs and maintenance	21	
11 Commissions and fees	11		22 Supplies (not included in Part III)	22	190
12 Depletion	12		23 Taxes and licenses	23	
13 Depreciation and section 179 expense deduction (not included in Part III) (see page C-3)	13		24 Travel, meals, and entertainment:		
			a Travel	24a	2,320
14 Employee benefit programs (other than on line 19)	14		b Meals and entertainment		
15 Insurance (other than health)	15		c Enter nondeductible amount included on line 24b (see page C-5)		
16 Interest:					
a Mortgage (paid to banks, etc.)	16a		d Subtract line 24c from line 24b	24d	
b Other	16b		25 Utilities	25	
17 Legal and professional services	17		26 Wages (less employment credits)	26	
18 Office expense	18		27 Other expenses (from line 48 on page 2)	27	

28 Total expenses before expenses for business use of home. Add lines 8 through 27 in columns ▶ | 28 | 3,779
29 Tentative profit (loss). Subtract line 28 from line 7 | 29 | 1,221
30 Expenses for business use of your home. Attach Form 8829 | 30 |
31 Net profit or (loss). Subtract line 30 from line 29.
• If a profit, enter on Form 1040, line 12, and also on Schedule SE, line 2 (statutory employees, see page C-5). Estates and trusts, enter on Form 1041, line 3.
• If a loss, you must go to line 32. | 31 | 1,221

32 If you have a loss, check the box that describes your investment in this activity (see page C-6).
• If you checked 32a, enter the loss on Form 1040, line 12, and also on Schedule SE, line 2 (statutory employees, see page C-5). Estates and trusts, enter on Form 1041, line 3.
• If you checked 32b, you must attach Form 6198.

32a ☐ All investment is at risk.
32b ☐ Some investment is not at risk.

For Paperwork Reduction Act Notice, see Form 1040 instructions. Cat. No. 11334P Schedule C (Form 1040) 2002

Expenses have been reduced by 5% as allocable to tax-free income (see calculation on page 171).

Most ministers who consider themselves employees for income tax purposes (with that income reported on line 7, Form 1040, page 1) also have honoraria and fee income and related expenses that are reportable on Schedule C (C-EZ).

163

Schedule C (Form 1040) 2002 — Page 2

Part III Cost of Goods Sold (see page C-6)

33 Method(s) used to value closing inventory: **a** ☐ Cost **b** ☐ Lower of cost or market **c** ☐ Other (attach explanation)

34 Was there any change in determining quantities, costs, or valuations between opening and closing inventory? If "Yes," attach explanation . . . . ☐ Yes ☐ No

35 Inventory at beginning of year. If different from last year's closing inventory, attach explanation . . . | 35 |

36 Purchases less cost of items withdrawn for personal use . . . . | 36 |

37 Cost of labor. Do not include any amounts paid to yourself . . . . | 37 |

38 Materials and supplies . . . . | 38 |

39 Other costs . . . . | 39 |

40 Add lines 35 through 39 . . . . | 40 |

41 Inventory at end of year . . . . | 41 |

42 **Cost of goods sold.** Subtract line 41 from line 40. Enter the result here and on page 1, line 4 . . . | 42 |

Part IV Information on Your Vehicle. Complete this part **only** if you are claiming car or truck expenses on line 10 and are not required to file Form 4562 for this business. See the instructions for line 13 on page C-3 to find out if you must file.

43 When did you place your vehicle in service for business purposes? (month, day, year) ▶ 05 / 01 / 98

44 Of the total number of miles you drove your vehicle during 2002, enter the number of miles you used your vehicle for:

    a Business 3,660   **b** Commuting 2,432   **c** Other 11,901 (W-2-related)

45 Do you (or your spouse) have another vehicle available for personal use? . . . . ☒ Yes ☐ No

46 Was your vehicle available for personal use during off-duty hours? . . . . ☒ Yes ☐ No

47a Do you have evidence to support your deduction? . . . . ☒ Yes ☐ No

    b If "Yes," is the evidence written? . . . . ☒ Yes ☐ No

Part V Other Expenses. List below business expenses not included on lines 8–26 or line 30.

48 Total other expenses. Enter here and on page 1, line 27 . . . . | 48 |

Schedule C (Form 1040) 2002

EXAMPLE NO. 2 ▶ MINISTER-EMPLOYEE FOR INCOME TAX PURPOSES (NONACCOUNTABLE PLAN)

SCHEDULE SE (Form 1040)
Department of the Treasury
Internal Revenue Service (99)

Self-Employment Tax

▶ Attach to Form 1040. ▶ See Instructions for Schedule SE (Form 1040).

OMB No. 1545-0074
2002
Attachment Sequence No. **17**

Name of person with **self-employment** income (as shown on Form 1040): Donald L. Hall
Social security number of person with **self-employment** income ▶ 482 : 11 : 6043

Who Must File Schedule SE

You must file Schedule SE if:

- You had net earnings from self-employment from **other than** church employee income (line 4 of Short Schedule SE or line 4c of Long Schedule SE) of $400 or more **or**
- You had church employee income of $108.28 or more. Income from services you performed as a minister or a member of a religious order **is not** church employee income. See page SE-1.

Note. Even if you had a loss or a small amount of income from self-employment, it may be to your benefit to file Schedule SE and use either optional method in Part II of Long Schedule SE. See page SE-3.

Exception. If your only self-employment income was from services as a minister, member of a religious order, or Christian Science practitioner **and** you filed Form 4361 and received IRS approval not to be taxed on those earnings, **do not** file Schedule SE. Instead, write Exempt Form 4361 on Form 1040, line 56.

May I Use Short Schedule SE or Must I Use Long Schedule SE?

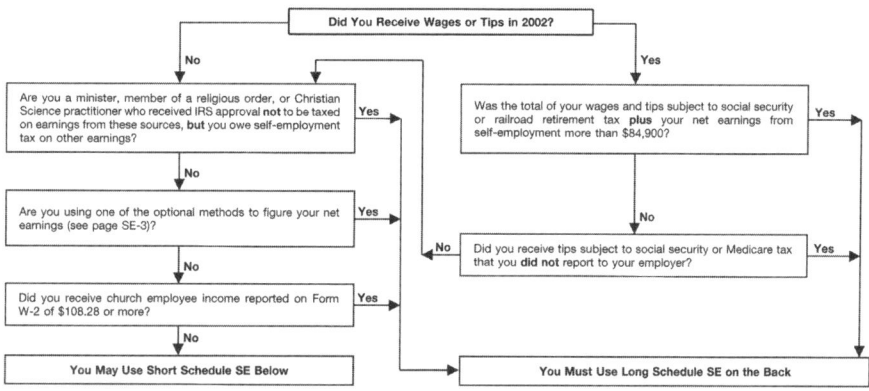

Section A—Short Schedule SE. Caution. Read above to see if you can use Short Schedule SE.

1	Net farm profit or (loss) from Schedule F, line 36, and farm partnerships, Schedule K-1 (Form 1065), line 15a **1**	
2	Net profit or (loss) from Schedule C, line 31; Schedule C-EZ, line 3; Schedule K-1 (Form 1065), line 15a (other than farming); and Schedule K-1 (Form 1065-B), box 9. Ministers and members of religious orders, see page SE-1 for amounts to report on this line. See page SE-2 for other income to report **2**	17,716
3	Combine lines 1 and 2 . . . . **3**	17,716
4	**Net earnings from self-employment.** Multiply line 3 by 92.35% (.9235). If less than $400, **do not** file this schedule; you do not owe self-employment tax . . . . ▶ **4**	16,361
5	**Self-employment tax.** If the amount on line 4 is: • $84,900 or less, multiply line 4 by 15.3% (.153). Enter the result here and on **Form 1040, line 56.** • More than $84,900, multiply line 4 by 2.9% (.029). Then, add $10,527.60 to the result. Enter the total here and on **Form 1040, line 56.** **5**	2,503
6	**Deduction for one-half of self-employment tax.** Multiply line 5 by 50% (.5). Enter the result here and on **Form 1040, line 29** **6**	1,252	

Line 2 - See the schedule on page 173 for the calculation of this amount.

Line 4 - This line results in the deduction of a portion of the self-employment tax liability.

A minister may use Section A-Short Schedule unless he received nonministerial wages (subject to FICA) and the total of these wages and net ministerial self-employment earnings (W-2 and Schedule C-related) is more than $84,900.

SCHEDULE EIC (Form 1040A or 1040) Department of the Treasury Internal Revenue Service (99)	**Earned Income Credit** Qualifying Child Information Complete and attach to Form 1040A or 1040 only if you have a qualifying child. 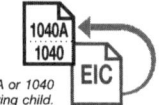	OMB No. 1545-0074 20**02** Attachment Sequence No. **43**
Name(s) shown on return Donald L. and Julie M. Hall		Your social security number 482 : 11 : 6043

Before you begin: See the instructions for Form 1040A, line 41, or Form 1040, line 64, to make sure that **(a)** you can take the EIC and **(b)** you have a qualifying child.

- If you take the EIC even though you are not eligible, you may not be allowed to take the credit for up to 10 years. See back of schedule for details.
- It will take us longer to process your return and issue your refund if you do not fill in all lines that apply for each qualifying child.
- Be sure the child's name on line 1 and social security number (SSN) on line 2 agree with the child's social security card. Otherwise, at the time we process your return, we may reduce or disallow your EIC. If the name or SSN on the child's social security card is not correct, call the Social Security Administration at 1-800-772-1213.

Qualifying Child Information	Child 1	Child 2
1 Child's name If you have more than two qualifying children, you only have to list two to get the maximum credit.	First name: David K. Last name: Hall	First name: Sarah E. Last name: Hall
2 Child's SSN The child must have an SSN as defined on page 42 of the Form 1040A instructions or page 44 of the Form 1040 instructions unless the child was born and died in 2002. If your child was born and died in 2002 and did not have an SSN, enter "Died" on this line and attach a copy of the child's birth certificate.	514 : 42 : 7465	516 : 49 : 0125
3 Child's year of birth	Year 1996 ___ ___ If born after 1983, skip lines 4a and 4b; go to line 5.	Year 2001 ___ ___ If born after 1983, skip lines 4a and 4b; go to line 5.
4 If the child was born before 1984— a Was the child under age 24 at the end of 2002 and a student?	☐ Yes. ☐ No. Go to line 5. Continue	☐ Yes. ☐ No. Go to line 5. Continue
b Was the child permanently and totally disabled during any part of 2002?	☐ Yes. ☐ No. Continue The child is not a qualifying child.	☐ Yes. ☐ No. Continue The child is not a qualifying child.
5 Child's relationship to you (for example, son, daughter, grandchild, foster child, etc.)	Son	Daughter
6 Number of months child lived with you in the United States during 2002 • If the child lived with you for more than half of 2002 but less than 7 months, enter "7". • If the child was born or died in 2002 and your home was the child's home for the entire time he or she was alive during 2002, enter "12".	12 months Do not enter more than 12 months.	12 months Do not enter more than 12 months.

 You may also be able to take the additional child tax credit if your child **(a)** was under age 17 at the end of 2002, **(b)** is claimed as your dependent on line 6c of Form 1040A or Form 1040, **and (c)** is a U.S. citizen or resident alien. For more details, see the instructions for line 42 of Form 1040A or line 66 of Form 1040.

If you are eligible for the Earned Income Credit, you must file page 1 of Schedule EIC if you have a qualifying child. Compute your credit on the worksheet in the IRS instruction booklet.

There could have been a much larger Earned Income Credit if Pastor Hall's business expenses had been reimbursed and a lower salary prospectively established. The expenses claimed on Form 2106-EZ do not offset earned income for the EIC calculation.

EXAMPLE NO. 2 ► MINISTER-EMPLOYEE FOR INCOME TAX PURPOSES (NONACCOUNTABLE PLAN)

EIC Worksheet B—Earned Income Credit (EIC)

Keep for Your Records

Use this worksheet if you were self-employed, or you are filing Schedule SE because you had church employee income, or you are filing Schedule C or C-EZ as a statutory employee.

TIP: You can tear this worksheet from the booklet before you begin

✓ Complete the parts below (Parts 1–3) that apply to you. Then, go to Part 4.
✓ If you are married filing a joint return, include your spouse's amounts, if any, with yours to figure the amounts to enter in Parts 1 through 3.

Part 1 — Self-Employed and People With Church Employee Income Filing Schedule SE

1a. Enter the amount from Schedule SE, Section A, line 3, or Section B, line 3, whichever applies. — **1a** 17,716 (1)
b. Enter any amount from Schedule SE, Section B, line 4b and line 5a. + **1b**
c. Add lines 1a and 1b. = **1c** 17,716
d. Enter the amount from Schedule SE, Section A, line 6, or Section B, line 13, whichever applies. − **1d** 1,252
e. Subtract line 1d from 1c. = **1e** 16,464

Part 2 — Self-Employed NOT Filing Schedule SE

For example, your net earnings from self-employment were less than $400.

2. Do not include on these lines any statutory employee income or any amount exempt from self-employment tax as the result of the filing and approval of Form 4029 or Form 4361.
a. Enter any net farm profit (or loss) from Schedule F, line 36, and from farm partnerships, Schedule K-1 (Form 1065), line 15a.* — **2a**
b. Enter any net profit (or loss) from Schedule C, line 31; Schedule C-EZ, line 3; Schedule K-1 (Form 1065), line 15a (other than farming); and Schedule K-1 (Form 1065-B), box 9.* — **2b**
c. Combine lines 2a and 2b. = **2c**

*Also enter any Schedule K-1 amounts on the appropriate line(s) of Schedule SE, Section A. Put your name and social security number on Schedule SE and attach it to your return.

Part 3 — Statutory Employees Filing Schedule C or C-EZ

3. Enter the amount from Schedule C, line 1, or Schedule C-EZ, line 1, that you are filing as a statutory employee. — **3**

Part 4 — All Filers Using EIC Worksheet B

If line 4b includes income on which you should have paid self-employment tax but did not, the IRS may reduce your credit by the amount of self-employment tax not paid.

4a. Enter your earned income from Worksheet 2, line 8. + **4a**
b. Combine lines 1e, 2c, 3, and 4a. **This is your total earned income.** = **4b** 17,464

5. Is the amount on line 4b less than:
- $11,060 ($12,060 for married filing jointly) if you do not have a qualifying child,
- $29,201 ($30,201 for married filing jointly) if you have one qualifying child, **or**
- $33,178 ($34,178 for married filing jointly) if you have two or more qualifying children?

☐ **Yes.** If you want the IRS to figure your credit, see page 25. *If you want to figure the credit yourself, enter the amount from line 4b on line 6 (page 31).*

☐ **No.** (STOP) You cannot take the credit. *Put "No" directly to the right of line 64 (Form 1040); or line 41 (Form 1040A); or on line 8 (Form 1040EZ).*

(1) Included on Line 1a:

Julie Hall's salary	$12,150
Schedule SE income	17,716
Less: Parsonage fair rental value	(11,150)
Less: Excluded housing allowance	(1,000)
	$17,716

Worksheet B is found in the IRS instruction booklet. Complete this worksheet whether or not you have a qualifying child.

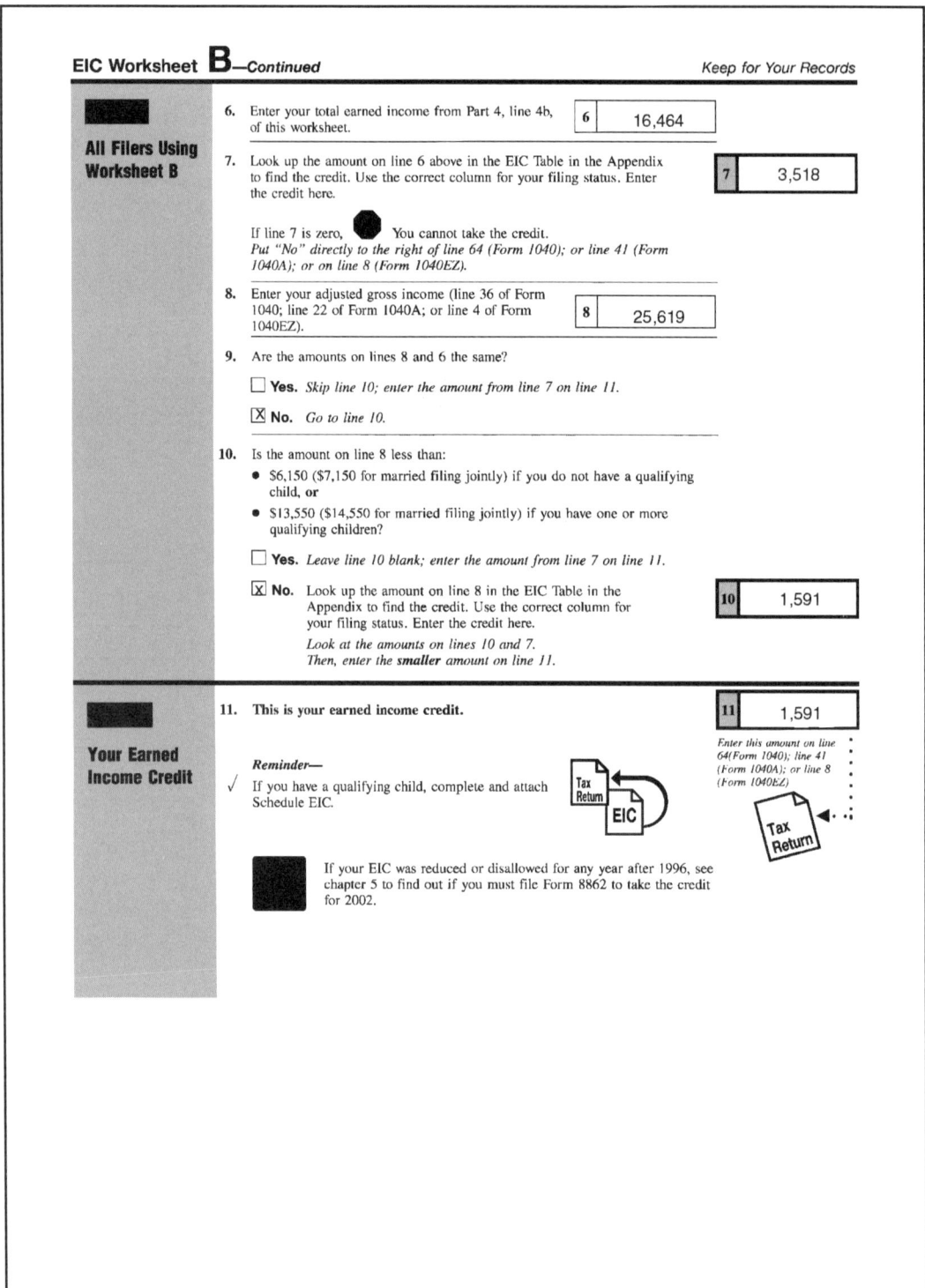

EXAMPLE NO. 2 ▶ MINISTER-EMPLOYEE FOR INCOME TAX PURPOSES (NONACCOUNTABLE PLAN)

Form 2106-EZ
Department of the Treasury
Internal Revenue Service (99)

Unreimbursed Employee Business Expenses
▶ Attach to Form 1040.

OMB No. 1545-1441
2002
Attachment Sequence No. **54A**

Your name: Donald L. Hall
Occupation in which you incurred expenses: Minister
Social security number: 482 11 6043

You May Use This Form Only if All of the Following Apply.

- You are an employee deducting expenses attributable to your job.
- You **do not** get reimbursed by your employer for any expenses (amounts your employer included in box 1 of your Form W-2 are not considered reimbursements.)
- If you are claiming vehicle expense, you are using the standard mileage rate for 2002.

Caution: *You can use the standard mileage rate for 2002 only if: (a) you owned the vehicle and used the standard mileage rate for the first year you placed the vehicle in service or (b) you leased the vehicle and used the standard mileage rate for the portion of the lease period after 1997.*

Part I — Figure Your Expenses

1	Vehicle expense using the standard mileage rate. Complete Part II and multiply line 8a by 36½¢ (.365)	4,127
2	Parking fees, tolls, and transportation, including train, bus, etc., that **did not** involve overnight travel or commuting to and from work	
3	Travel expense while away from home overnight, including lodging, airplane, car rental, etc. **Do not** include meals and entertainment	800
4	Business expenses not included on lines 1 through 3. **Do not** include meals and entertainment	998
5	Meals and entertainment expenses: $ __1,368__ x 50% (.50) (Employees subject to Department of Transportation (DOT) hours of service limits: Multiply meal expenses by 65% (.65) instead of 50%. For details, see instructions.)	684
6	**Total expenses.** Add lines 1 through 5. Enter here and **on line 20 of Schedule A (Form 1040).** (Fee-basis state or local government officials, qualified performing artists, and individuals with disabilities: See the instructions for special rules on where to enter this amount.)	6,609

Part II — Information on Your Vehicle. Complete this part **only** if you are claiming vehicle expense on line 1.

7 When did you place your vehicle in service for business use? (month, day, year) ▶ 05 / 01 / 98

8 Of the total number of miles you drove your vehicle during 2002, enter the number of miles you used your vehicle for:
   a Business 11,901 (W-2 related) **b** Commuting 2,432 **c** Other 3,660 (Schedule C-related)

9   Do you (or your spouse) have another vehicle available for personal use? . . . . ☒ Yes ☐ No
10 Was your vehicle available for personal use during off-duty hours? . . . . ☒ Yes ☐ No
11a Do you have evidence to support your deduction? . . . . ☒ Yes ☐ No
  b If "Yes," is the evidence written? . . . . ☒ Yes ☐ No

General Instructions

Section references are to the Internal Revenue Code.

Changes To Note

Standard mileage rate. The standard mileage rate has been increased to 36½ cents for each mile of business use in 2002.

Meal expenses. The amount of meal expenses that may be deducted by employees subject to Department of Transportation (DOT) hours of service limits has been increased to 65% for 2002.

Purpose of Form

You may use Form 2106-EZ instead of Form 2106 to claim your unreimbursed employee business expenses if you meet all the requirements listed above Part I.

Recordkeeping

You cannot deduct expenses for travel (including meals, unless you used the standard meal allowance), entertainment, gifts, or use of a car or other listed property, unless you keep records to prove the time, place, business purpose, business relationship (for entertainment and gifts), and amounts of these expenses. Generally, you must also have receipts for all lodging expenses (regardless of the amount) and any other expense of $75 or more.

Additional Information

For more details about employee business expenses, see:

Pub. 463, Travel, Entertainment, Gift, and Car Expenses
Pub. 529, Miscellaneous Deductions
Pub. 587, Business Use of Your Home (Including Use by Day-Care Providers)
Pub. 946, How To Depreciate Property

For Paperwork Reduction Act Notice, see back of form.   Cat. No. 20604Q   Form **2106-EZ** (2002)

Lines 1, 3, 4, 5 - See allocations on page 171.

Line 6 - The total expenses on this line are carried forward to Form 1040, Schedule A, line 20.

Form **8880**	**Credit for Qualified Retirement Savings Contributions**	OMB No. 1545-xxxx
Department of the Treasury Internal Revenue Service	▶ Attach to Form 1040 or Form 1040A.	2002 Attachment Sequence No. **129**

Name(s) shown on return	Your social security number
Donald L. & Julie M. Hall	482 11 6043

⚠ CAUTION You **cannot** claim this credit if any of the following apply.
- The amount on Form 1040, line 36, or Form 1040A, line 22, is more than $25,000 ($37,500 if head of household, $50,000 if married filing jointly).
- You were born after January 1, 1985.
- You are claimed as a dependent on someone's (such as your parent's) 2002 tax return.
- You were a **student** in 2002 (see instructions).

			(a) You	(b) Your spouse
1	Traditional and Roth IRA contributions for 2002	1		
2	Elective deferrals to a 401(k) or other qualified employer plan and voluntary contributions for 2002 (see instructions)	2	500	
3	Add lines 1 and 2	3	500	
4	Enter the total of all Roth IRA distributions, plus all taxable distributions from other qualified retirement plans, that were made after 1999 and before the due date (including extensions) of your 2002 tax return. If married filing jointly, include both spouses' amounts in both columns. See instructions for exceptions.	4		
5	Subtract line 4 from line 3. If zero or less, enter -0-	5		
6	In each column, enter the **smaller** of line 5 or $2,000	6	500	
7	Add the amounts on line 6. If zero, **stop**; you cannot claim the credit	7	500	
8	Enter the amount from Form 1040, line 36*, or Form 1040A, line 22	8	25,619	
9	Enter the applicable decimal amount shown below:			

If line 8 is—		And your filing status is—		
Over—	But not over—	Married filing jointly	Head of household	Single, Married filing separately, or Qualifying widow(er)
		Enter on line 9—		
---	$15,000	.5	.5	.5
$15,000	$16,250	.5	.5	.2
$16,250	$22,500	.5	.5	.1
$22,500	$24,375	.5	.2	.1
$24,375	$25,000	.5	.1	.1
$25,000	$30,000	.5	.1	.0
$30,000	$32,500	.2	.1	.0
$32,500	$37,500	.1	.1	.0
$37,500	$50,000	.1	.0	.0
$50,000	---	.0	.0	.0

9	X .5

Note: *If line 9 is zero, **stop**; you cannot claim the credit.*

10	Multiply line 7 by line 9	10	250
11	Enter the amount from Form 1040, line 44, or Form 1040A, line 28	11	388
12	Enter the total of your credits from Form 1040, lines 45 through 48, or Form 1040A, lines 29 through 31	12	
13	Subtract line 12 from line 11. If zero, **stop**; you cannot take the credit	13	
14	**Credit for qualified retirement savings contributions.** Enter the **smaller** of line 10 or line 13 here and on Form 1040, line 49, or Form 1040A, line 32	14	250

*See Pub. 590 for the amount to enter if you are filing Form 2555, 2555-EZ, or 4563 or you are excluding income from Puerto Rico.

For Paperwork Reduction Act Notice, see page 4.   Cat. No. 33394O   Form **8880** (2002)

EXAMPLE NO. 2 ➤ MINISTER-EMPLOYEE FOR INCOME TAX PURPOSES (NONACCOUNTABLE PLAN)

Computation of Unallowed Part of Business Expenses

		Taxable	Tax-Free	Total
Salary as a minister		$ 6,700		$ 6,700
Special occasion gifts		500		500
Reimbursement of self-employment tax		2,100		2,100
Expense allowance under nonaccountable plan		3,700		3,700
Housing allowance:				
Designated	$2,000			
Less expenses	1,000			
Excess	$1,000	1,000	$ 1,000	2,000
Schedule C gross income				
from ministry		5,000		5,000
Ministerial income		$19,000	$ 1,000	$20,000
		95%	5%	100%

Note: Each expense line on Schedule C (page 163) and Form 2106-EZ (page 169) has been reduced by 5% because the expenses are allocable to tax-free income.

Expenses reflected on Form 2106-EZ were allocated as follows:

		95% Deductible	5% Not Deductible
Vehicle expense			
11,901 x 36.5 cents		$ 4,127	$ 217
Travel expense:			
Airfare		641	34
Lodging		159	8
Business expenses:			
Subscriptions		190	10
Books and supplies		333	17
Continuing education tuition		475	25
Meals and entertainment expense:			
Meals	$ 233		
Entertainment	1,207		
	$1,440 (1)	684	36
		$ 6,609	$ 347

(1) 50% disallowed by meals and entertainment rules before allocating for taxable and tax-free income.

Housing Allowance Worksheet
Minister Living in a Parsonage
Owned by or Rented by the Church

Minister's Name: __Donald L. Hall__

For the period __January 1__, 200_2_ to __December 31__, 200_2_

Date designation approved __December 20__, 200_1_

Allowable Housing Expenses *(expenses paid by minister from current income)*

	Estimated Expenses	Actual
Utilities *(gas, electricity, water)* and trash collection	$ _____	$ _____
Local telephone expense *(base charge)*	250	275
Decoration and redecoration		
Structural maintenance and repair		
Landscaping, gardening, and pest control		
Furnishings *(purchase, repair, replacement)*	1,218	460
Personal property insurance on minister-owned contents	200	190
Personal property taxes on contents	150	75
Umbrella liability insurance		
Subtotal	1,818	
10% allowance for unexpected expenses	182	
TOTAL	$ 2,000	$ 1,000 (A)
Properly designated housing allowance		$ 2,000 (B)

The amount excludable from income for federal income tax purposes is the lowest of A or B.

Because actual housing expenses are less than the designated allowance, the housing exclusion is limited to $1,000. The $1,000 difference between the designation and the exclusion is reported as excess housing allowance on Form 1040, line 21 (see page 160).

EXAMPLE NO. 2 ➤ **MINISTER-EMPLOYEE FOR INCOME TAX PURPOSES (NONACCOUNTABLE PLAN)**

Self-Employment Social Security Tax Worksheet

Inclusions:

Salary paid by church as reflected on Form W-2	$ 10,500
Net profit or loss as reflected on Schedule C or C-EZ (includes speaking honoraria, offerings you receive for marriages, baptisms, funerals, and other fees)	1,221
Housing allowance excluded from salary on Form W-2	2,000
Fair rental value of parsonage provided (including paid utilities)	11,150
Nonaccountable business expense reimbursements (if not included on Form W-2)	
Reimbursement of self-employment taxes (if not included on Form W-2)	
Value of meals provided to you, your spouse, and your dependents whether or not provided for your employer's convenience (these amounts may have been excluded from gross income)	
Total inclusions	24,871

Deductions:

Unreimbursed ministerial business and professional expenses (included on Form W-2) or reimbursed expenses paid under a nonaccountable plan (included on Form W-2)

A. Deductible on Schedule A before the 2% of AGI limitation whether or not you itemized[1] or (see page 171)	6,609
B. Not deductible on Form 2106/2106 EZ or Schedule C/C-EZ because expenses were allocated to taxable/nontaxable income (see page 171)	546
Total deductions	7,155
Net earnings from self-employment (to Schedule SE)	$ 17,716

[1] The 50% unreimbursed meal and entertainment expense limitation applies to amounts subject to social security tax. In other words, if some of your meal and entertainment expenses were subject to the 50% limit, the remainder cannot be deducted here.

Your net earnings from self-employment are not affected by the foreign earned income exclusion or the foreign housing exclusion or deduction if you are a U.S. citizen or resident alien who is serving abroad and living in a foreign country.

Amounts received as pension payments or annuity payments related to a church-sponsored tax-sheltered annuity by a retired minister are generally considered to be excluded from the social security calculation.

Net earnings from self-employment are entered on Schedule SE, line 2 (see page 165).

2003 MINISTER'S TAX AND FINANCIAL GUIDE

a Control number: 22222 Void ☐ For Official Use Only ▶ OMB No. 1545-0008		
b Employer identification number: 35-7921873	**1** Wages, tips, other compensation: $10500.00	**2** Federal income tax withheld: $
c Employer's name, address, and ZIP code: Lancaster Community Church, 1425 Spencer Avenue, Wabash, IN 46992	**3** Social security wages: $	**4** Social security tax withheld: $
	5 Medicare wages and tips: $	**6** Medicare tax withheld: $
	7 Social security tips: $	**8** Allocated tips: $
d Employee's social security number: 482-11-6043	**9** Advance EIC payment: $	**10** Dependent care benefits: $
e Employee's first name and initial: Donald L. Last name: Hall	**11** Nonqualified plans: $	**12a** See instructions for box 12: $
604 Linden Avenue, Wabash, IN 46992	**13** Statutory employee ☐ Retirement plan ☐ Third-party sick pay ☐	**12b** $
	14 Other	**12c** $
		12d $
f Employee's address and ZIP code		
15 State: IN Employer's state ID number:	**16** State wages, tips, etc.: $10500.00 **17** State income tax: $	**18** Local wages, tips, etc.: $ **19** Local income tax: $ **20** Locality name

Form **W-2** Wage and Tax Statement (99) **2002** (Rev. February 2002)
Department of the Treasury—Internal Revenue Service
For Privacy Act and Paperwork Reduction Act Notice, see separate instructions.

Copy A For Social Security Administration—Send this entire page with Form W-3 to the Social Security Administration; photocopies are **not** acceptable.   Cat. No. 10134D

Do Not Cut, Fold, or Staple Forms on This Page — Do Not Cut, Fold, or Staple Forms on This Page

---

Explanation of compensation reported on Form W-2, Box 1:

Salary ($6,700 less $2,000 housing allowance and $500 403[b] contributions)	$ 4,200
Special occasion gifts	500
Reimbursement of self-employment tax	2,100
Expense allowance under nonaccountable plan	3,700
	$10,500

Form **1040-ES** Department of the Treasury Internal Revenue Service   **2002** Payment Voucher **4**   OMB No. 1545-0087

File only if you are making a payment of estimated tax by check or money order. Mail this voucher with your check or money order payable to the "**United States Treasury**." Write your social security number and "2002 Form 1040-ES" on your check or money order. Do not send cash. Enclose, but do not staple or attach, your payment with this voucher.

Calendar year—Due Jan. 15, 2003
Amount of estimated tax you are paying by check or money order. Dollars $ 300   Cents

Your first name and initial: Doanld L.	Your last name: Hall	Your social security number: 482-11-6043
If joint payment, complete for spouse		
Spouse's first name and initial: Julie M.	Spouse's last name: Hall	Spouse's social security number: 720-94-1327
Address (number, street, and apt. no.): 604 Linden Avenue		
City, state, and ZIP code (If a foreign address, enter city, province or state, postal code, and country.): Wabash, IN 46992		

For Privacy Act and Paperwork Reduction Act Notice, see instructions on page 5.

This is an example of one of the quarterly estimate forms. The taxpayer filed the other three estimates on a timely basis.

Citations

Chapter 1, Taxes for Ministers

- **Administrative and teaching positions**

    Treas. Reg. 31.3401(a)(9)-1(b)(3)-(5)

    Treas. Reg. 31.3121(b)(8)-1(c)(2)-(3)

    Treas. Reg. 1.1402(c)-5(b)(2)

    Ltr. Rul. 9126048

    T.A.M. 9033002

    Ltr. Rul. 8930038

    Ltr. Rul. 8826043

    Ltr. Rul. 8520043

    Flowers v. Commissioner, 82-1 USTC para. 9114 (N.D. Tex. 1981)

    Ltr. Rul. 8142076

    Boyer v. Commissioner, 69 T.C.M. 521 (1977)

    Rev. Rul. 70-549

    Rev. Rul. 63-90

    Rev. Rul. 57-129

- **Commissioned ministers**

    Ltr. Rul. 9221025

- **Counseling and chaplaincy positions**

    Ltr. Rul. 200002040

    Ltr. Rul. 9743037

    Ltr. Rul. 9231053

    Ltr. Rul. 9124059

    Ltr. Rul. 8825025

    Ltr. Rul. 8519004

    Ltr. Rul. 8138184

    Ltr. Rul. 8004046

    Ltr. Rul. 7809092

    Ltr. Rul. 7727019

    Rev. Rul. 71-258

- **Employees v. self-employed for income tax purposes**

    Treas. Reg. 31.3401(c)-1(b)-(c)

    Alford v. U.S., Civil 94-1074 (W. D. Ark. 1996) Reversed by 8th Cir., 96-3287 (1997)

    Greene v. Commissioner, T.C.M. 531 (1996)

    Weber v. Commissioner, 103 T.C.M. 19 (1994), Affirmed

    4th Cir., 94-2609 (1995)

    Shelley v. Commissioner, T.C.M. 432 (1994)

    Ltr. Rul. 9414022

    Cosby v. Commissioner, T.C.M. Sum. Op. 1987-141

    Rev. Rul. 87-41

    Rev. Proc. 85-18

    Rev. Rul. 80-110

- **Exempt from FICA**

    Code Sec. 3121(b)(8)(A)

- **Exempt from income tax withholding**

    Code Sec. 3121(b)(8)

    Code Sec. 3401(a)(9)

    Treas. Reg. 31.3401(a)(8)-1

- **Qualifying tests for ministerial status**

    Treas. Reg. 1.1402(c)-5

    Ltr. Rul. 199910055

    Haimowitz v. Commissioner, T.C.M. 40 (1997)

    Mosley v. Commissioner, T.C.M. 457 (1994)

    Reeder v. Commissioner, T.C.M. 287 (1993)

    Ltr. Rul. 9221025

    Eade v. U.S., Dist. Court, Western Dist., VA, Roanoke Division (1991)

    Knight v. Commissioner, 92 T.C.M. 12 (1989)

    T.A.M. 8915001

    Wingo v. Commissioner, 89 T.C.M. 922 (1987)

    Rev. Rul. 78-301

    Rev. Rul. 68-68

    Lawrence v. Commissioner, 50 T.C.M. 494 (1968)

    Salkov v. Commissioner, 46 T.C.M. 190 (1966)

    Rev. Rul. 59-270

- **Religious orders**

    Ltr. Rul. 9630011

    Ltr. Rul. 9418012

    Ltr. Rul. 9219012

    Rev. Proc. 91-20

- **Subject to income tax**

    Murdock v. Pennsylvania, 319 U.S. 105 (1943)

- **Teachers and administrator**

  Ltr. Rul. 9126048

  Ltr. Rul. 8646018

  Ltr. Rul. 7833017

  Rev. Rul. 63-90

- **Voluntary withholding of income tax for ministers**

  Treas. Reg. 31.3402(p)-1

  Treas. Reg. 31.4302(i)-1(a)

  Rev. Rul. 68-507

- **Withholding of income tax for nonministerial employees**

  Bethel Baptist Church v. U.S., 822 F.2d 1334 (3rd Cir. 1987)

  Eighth Street Baptist Church, Inc. v. U. S., 295 F. Supp. 1400 (D. Kan. 1969)

Chapter 2, Compensation Planning

- **Avoiding recharacterization of income**

  Ltr. Rul. 9325023

Chapter 3, The Pay Package

- **Deferred compensation**

  Code Sec. 457

  Rev. Proc. 92-64

- ***De Minimis* fringes**

  Code Sec. 132(e)(1)

- **Dependent care**

  Code Sec. 129

- **Disability payments**

  Code Sec. 104(a)(3)

  Reg. 1.104-1(d)

  Ltr. Rul. 9103014

  Ltr. Rul. 9103043

  Ltr. Rul. 9105032

- **Educational assistance**

  Code Sec. 127

- **Employer-paid vehicle fuel**

  Notice 91-41

- **Frequent flyer awards**

  IRS Announcement 2002-18

- **Group-term life insurance**

  Code Sec. 3401(a)(14)

- **Health reimbursement arrangements**

  Code Sec. 105(b), (e)

  IRS Policy 80,600

  Rev. Rul. 2002-41

  IRS Notice 2002-45

- **Highly compensated employees**

  Code Sec. 414(q)

  Treas. Reg. 1.132-8(f)(1)

- **Key employees**

  Code Sec. 416(i)(1)

- **Loans to employees**

  Code Sec. 7872(c)(1)(B)

  Code Sec. 7872(c)(3)(A)

  Code Sec. 7872(f)(10)

- **Meals and lodging**

  Code Sec. 119(a)

  Kalms v. Commissioner, T.C.M. 394 (1992)

  Ltr. Rul. 9129037

  Goldsboro Christian School, Inc. v. Commissioner, 436 F. Supp. 1314 (D.D.C. 1978), Affirmed 103 S. Ct. 2017 (1983)

  Ltr. Rul. 8213005

  Bob Jones University v. Commissioner, 670 F.2d 167 Ct. Cl. (1982)

  Rev. Rul. 77-80

- **Medical insurance premiums paid by the employer**

  Code Sec. 106(a)

  Code Sec. 4980B

  Treas. Reg. 1.106-1

  Rev. Rul. 70-179

  Rev. Rul. 58-90

- **Medical insurance premiums paid by employee/reimbursed by church**

  Ltr. Rul. 9022060

  Rev. Rul. 85-44

  Rev. Rul. 75-241

  Rev. Rul. 61-146

- **Medical plans, self-insured**

  Code Sec. 105(h)

- **Moving expenses**

  Code Sec. 132(g)

  Code Sec. 217

- **Nontaxable fringe benefits**

  Code Sec. 132

- **Pension plans**

  Code Sec. 83

CITATIONS

Code Sec. 401(a)

Code Sec. 414(e)

- **Property transfers**

  Treas. Reg. 1.61-2(d)(2)

  Potito v. Commissioner,
  534 F.2d 49 (5th Cir. 1976)

- **Reasonable compensation**

  Truth Tabernacle, Inc. v. Commissioner, T.C.M. (1989)-451

- **Reimbursement payments excludable from recipient's income**

  Ltr. Rul. 9112022

- **Retirement gifts**

  Code Sec. 102(c)

  Commissioner v. Duberstein, 363 U.S. 278, 285 (1960)

  Perkins v. Commissioner, 34 T.C.M. 117 (1960)

  Stanton v. U.S., 163 F.2d 727 (2nd Cir. 1959)

  Rev. Rul. 55-422

  Abernathy v. Commissioner, 211 F.2d 651 (D.C. Cir. 1954)

  Kavanagh v. Hershman, 210 F.2d 654 (6th Cir. 1954)

  Mutch v. Commissioner, 209 F.2d 390 (3rd Cir. 1954)

  Schall v. Commissioner, 174 F.2d 893 (5th Cir. 1949)

  Rev. Rul. 55-422

- **Sabbatical pay**

  Kant v. Commissioner, T.C. Memo. 1997-217

- **Social security reimbursements**

  Rev. Rul. 68-507

- **Special occasion gifts**

  Goodwin v. U.S., 94-2 U.S.T.C (S.D. Iowa 1994) Affirmed 8th Cir. Ct. of Appeals

  Banks v. Commissioner, T.C.M. 641 (1991)

- **Tax-sheltered annuities**

  Code Sec. 403(b)

  Code Sec. 415

  Code Sec. 1402(a)

  Code Sec. 3121(a)(5)(D)

  Rev. Rul. 78-6

  Rev. Rul. 68-395

  Azad v. Commissioner, 388 F.2d 74 (8th Cir. 1968)

  Rev. Rul. 66-274

- **Tuition and fee reductions**

  Code Sec. 117(d)

  Ltr. Rul. 200149030

  Rasmussen v. Commissioner, T.C. 7264-92 (1994)

Chapter 5, Housing Allowance

- **Allowed without documentation**

  Kizer v. Commissioner, T.C.M. 582 (1992)

- **Designation of housing allowance**

  Treas. Reg. 1.107-1(b)

  Whittington v. Commissioner, T.C.M. 296 (2000)

Mosley v. Commissioner, T.C.M. 457 (1994)

Kizer v. Commissioner, T.C.M. 584 (1992)

Holland v. Commissioner, 47 T.C.M. 494 (1983)

Libman v. Commissioner, 44 T.C.M. 370 (1982)

Hoelz v. Commissioner, 42 T.C.M. 1037 (1981)

Boyd v. Commissioner, 42 T.C.M. 1136 (1981)

Rev. Rul. 75-22

Rev. Rul. 62-117

Eden v. Commissioner, 41 T.C.M. 605 (1961)

- **Determination of housing exclusion amount**

  Clergy Housing Allowance Clarification Act, Public Law 107-181

  Warren v. Commissioner, 114 T.C. No. 23 (1998) Appealed by IRS to Ninth Cir. Court of Appeals (Feb. 2000) Case dismissed by Ninth Cir. Court of Appeals (Aug. 2002)

  Rasmussen v. Commissioner, T.C.M. 311 (1994)

  Ltr. Rul. 8937025

  Swaggart v. Commissioner, 48 T.C.M. 759 (1984)

  Ltr. Rul. 8350005

  Rev. Rul. 78-448

- **Double deduction of interest and taxes**

  Code Sec. 265(6)

  Rev. Rul. 87-32

- **Exclusion of the housing allowance**

  Code Sec. 107

- **Fair rental value test**

  Warren v Commissioner, 114 T.C. No. 23 (2000)

  Rucker v. David, 203 F. 3d 627,638 (9th Cir. 2000)

  Ltr. Rul. 8825025

  Reed v. Commissioner, 82 T.C. 208, 214 (1984)

  Rev. Rul. 71-280

- **Housing allowances for retired clergy**

  Rev. Proc. 92-3

  Rev. Rul. 75-22

- **Including interest on home equity loan**

  Ltr. Rul. 9115051

- **Minister who owns home outright cannot exclude parsonage allowance**

  Ltr. Rul. 9115051

- **Minister performing routine services**

  Rev. Rul. 57-129

Chapter 6, Business Expenses

- **Accountable expense reimbursement plans**

  Treas. Reg. 1.62-2

  Treas. Reg. 1.274-5T(f)

  Ltr. Rul. 9317003

  Ltr. Rul. 9325023

- **Accounting for business and professional expenses by independent contractors**

  Treas. Reg. 1.274-5(g)

- **Allocation of unreimbursed business expenses**

  McFarland v. Commissioner, T.C.M. 440 (1992)

  Dalan v. Commissioner, T.C.M. 106 (1988)

  Deason v. Commissioner, 41 T.C.M. 465 (1964)

- **Auto expense substantiation**

  Parker v. Commissioner, T.C.M. 15 (1993)

- **Club dues**

  T.D. 8601

- **Computer expenses**

  Bryant v. Commissioner, T.C.M. 597 (1993)

- **Contributions treated as business expenses**

  Forbes v. Commissioner, T.C. Sum. Op. 167 (1992)

- **Deductibility of spouse's travel**

  Code Sec. 1.162-2(c)

  Stockton v. Commissioner, 36 T.C.M. 114 (1977)

  U.S. v. Disney, 413 F.2d 783 (9th Cir. 1969)

- **Educational expenses**

  Ltr. Rul. 9431024

  Burt v. Commissioner, 40 T.C.M. 1164 (1980)

  Glasgow v. Commissioner, 31 T.C.M. 310 (1972)

- **Home-office expenses**

  Code Sec. 280A

  Rev. Rul. 94-24

  Rev. Rul. 94-47

- **Other business and professional expense deductions**

  Treas. Reg. 1.1402(a)-11(a)

  Bass v. Commissioner, T.C.M. 536 (1983)

  Rev. Rul. 80-110

  Rev. Rul. 79-78

- **Personal computer expenses**

  Code Sec. 280F

  Rev. Rul. 86-129

- **Substantiation of business expenses**

  Temp. Rev. 1.274-5T

  Code Sec. 274(d)

  Rev. Proc. 92-71

- **Temporary workplace**

  Rev. Rul. 99-7

- **Travel/Away from home**

  Rev. Rul. 83-82

  Rev. Rul. 75-432

- **Travel/Commuting**

  Treas. Reg. 1.262-1(b)(5)

  Rev. Rul. 94-47

  Rev. Rul. 90-23

  Walker v. Commissioner, 101 T.C.M. 537 (1993)

Soliman v. Commissioner,
94 T.C.M. 20 (1990),
Supreme Court (1993)

Hamblen v. Commissioner,
78 T.C.M. 53 (1981)

- **Travel/Mileage rates**

  Rev. Proc. 96-64

- **Unreimbursed business expenses**

  Gravett v. Commissioner,
  T.C.M. 156 (1994)

Chapter 7, Social Security Tax

- **General**

  IRS Publication 517

  IRS Publication 1828

- **Age not a limitation**

  Levine v. Commissioner,
  T.C.M. 469 (1992)

- **Exemption for certain religious faiths**

  U.S. v. Lee,
  455 U.S. 252 (1982)

  Varga v. U.S.,
  467 F. Supp. 1113 (D. Md. 1979)

- **Nullifying the exemption**

  Rev. Rul. 70-197

- **Opting out of social security**

  Code Sec. 1402(e)

  Treas. Reg. 1.1402(e)-3A

  Brannon v. Commissioner,
  T.C.M. 370 (1999)

  McGaffin v. Commissioner,
  T.C.M. 290 (1996)

  Hairston v. Commissioner,
  T.C.M. (1995)

Hall v. Commissioner,
(10th Cir. 1994)

Ltr. Rul. 9431024

Reeder v. Commissioner,
T.C.M. 287 (1993)

Keaton v. Commissioner,
T.C.M. 365 (1993)

Ltr. Rul. 9221025

Eade v. U.S., Dist. Court,
Western Dist. VA, Roanoke Div. (1991)

T.A.M. 8741002

Balinger v. Commissioner,
728 F.2d 1287 (10th Cir. 1984)

Treadway v. Commissioner,
47 T.C.M. 1375 (1984)

Olsen v. Commissioner,
709 F.2d 278 (4th Cir. 1983)

Holland v. Commissioner,
47 T.C.M. 494 (1983)

Paschall v. Commissioner,
46 T.C.M. 1197 (1983)

Hess v. Commissioner,
40 T.C.M. 415 (1980)

Rev. Rul. 80-59

Rev. Rul. 82-185

Rev. Rul. 75-189

- **Private insurance program participation**

  T.A.M. 8741002

  Rev. Rul. 77-78

- **Second ordination/social security exemption**

  Hall v. Commissioner,
  T.C.M. 360 (1993),
  10th Cir. (July 19, 1994)

- **Social security coverage for ministers**

  Code Sec. 1402(c)(2) and (4)

  Code Sec. 3121(b)(8)(A)

  Code Sec. 3401(a)(9)

  Rev. Rul. 80-110

  Rev. Rul. 79-78

  Silvey v. Commissioner,
  35 T.C.M. 1812 (1976)

- **Social security recipients must still pay social security taxes**

  Foster v. Commissioner,
  T.C.M. 552 (1996)

- **Taxability of fair rental value of church-owned parsonage for social security purposes**

  Treas. Reg. 1.1402(a)-11(a)

  Flowers v. Commissioner,
  T.C.M. 542 (1991)

  Bass v. Commissioner,
  T.C.M. 536 (1983)

Federal Tax Regulation (Reg.)

Treasury Decision (T.D.)

Private Letter Ruling (Ltr. Rul.)

Field Service Advice (F.S.A.)

Revenue Ruling (Rev. Rul.)

Revenue Procedure (Rev. Proc.)

Tax Court Memorandum (T.C.M.)

Technical Advice Memorandum (T.A.M.)

Index

A

Accountable plan, *43-44, 48-50, 53, 100-2, 149-58*
Administrative positions, *30-32*
Agency of a religious organization, *30-31*
Allocation of business expenses, *121-22, 169, 172*
Allowances, *53, 101-2*
Amended returns, *144-45, 148*
Annuities, tax-sheltered, *47, 66-67*
Assignment by a church, *31-32*
Automobiles,
    Actual expense method, *110-12*
    Allowances, *53, 101-2*
    Church-provided, *68-69, 112*
    Commuting, *113-14*
    Deductions, *108-114*
    Depreciation, *7, 110-12*
    Documenting expenses, *114*
    Interest expense, *119*
    Leasing, *112*
    Luxury, *110-12*
    Mileage rate method, *6, 109*
    Reporting business expenses, *114*
Awards, *53*

B

Birthday gifts, *59*
Bonuses, *53, 102*
Books, *53, 120*
Business and professional expenses,
    Accounting for, *100-2*
    Allocation of, *121-22, 169, 172*
    Allowances, *53, 102-3*
    Automobile, *108-14*
    Cellular phones, *67, 120-21*
    Clothing, *53-54, 118*
    Club dues, *56*
    Computers, *54, 119-20*
    Contributions, *117-18*
    Conventions, *54*
    Depreciation, *110-12*
    Dues and memberships, *56*
    Educational expenses, *6, 57, 118-19*
    Entertainment expenses, *58, 119*
    Gifts, *117*
    Interest, auto, *119*
    Moving expenses, *63, 119*
    Office-in-the-home, *60, 115-17*
    Personal computers, *54, 119-20*
    Record-keeping requirements, *102-3*
    Reimbursements, *53, 100-2*
    Section 179 deductions, *10, 120*
    Subscriptions and books, *66, 120*
    Telephone expenses, *67, 120-21*
    Travel expenses, *67, 104-8*

C

Cafeteria plans, *58*
Canada Pension Plan, *134*
Cellular telephones, *67, 120-21*
Charitable contributions, *117-18*
Child care, *55*
Christmas gifts, *59*
Citations, *175-79*
Clothing, *53-54, 118*
Club dues, *56*
Commissioned ministers, *27-28*
Common law rules, *34-36*
Commuting expenses, *113-14*
Compensation,
    Packages, *39-50*
    Reasonable, *39-40*
    Recharacterization, *49-50, 102*
    Reporting, *41-42*
    Worksheet, *42*
Computers, *54, 119-20*
Continuing education, *57, 118-19*
Contributions which reduce compensation, *117-18*
Conventions, *54*

D

Deferred compensation, *54-55*
Denominational pension plans, *63*
Denominational service, *30-31*
Dependent care, *5, 55*
Dependent educational benefits, *55*
Depreciation, *7, 110-12*
Disability,
    Insurance, *55-56*
    Pay, *65*
Discretionary fund, *56*
Discrimination of benefits, *52*
Documenting expenses, *102-3*
"Double deduction" of interest and taxes, *17-18, 26, 94*
Dues and memberships, *56*

E

Earned income tax credit, *4, 16-17, 139-40, 166-68*
Educational expenses, *6, 57, 118-19*
Educational assistance benefit plans, *57*
Educator expenses, *8-9*
Employee vs. self-employed, *36-38*
Entertainment expenses, *58, 119*
Equipment write-off, *10, 120*
Equity allowance, *58*
Estimated taxes, *136-39, 174*
Evangelists,
    Housing allowance, *28, 95*
    Qualifications, *28*
Exemption from social security tax, *130-33*
Expense allowances, *53, 101-2*
Expense reimbursement, *48-50, 53-54, 100-1*
Extension of time to file, *140-41, 146*
Extension of time to pay, *143-44, 147*

F

Fair rental value of parsonage, *2-3, 90, 91-92*
Federal Insurance Contributions Act (FICA), *123-25, 139*
First-year write-off of business expense, *10, 120*
Flexible spending arrangements, *58*
Foreign earned income exclusion, *9*
Forgiveness of debt, *62*
Form W-2, *137, 158, 174*
Form 656, *144*
Form 941, *137*
Form 1040, *20-21, 150-51, 160-61*
Form 1040-ES, *136-39, 174*
Form 1040X, *144-45, 148*
Form 1127, *143*
Form 2106, *103, 114*
Form 2106-EZ, *24, 103, 114, 169*

> INDEX

Form 2210, *142*
Form 2350, *141*
Form 2688, *141, 146*
Form 4361, *130-33*
Form 4868, *141, 143*
Form 8880, *170*
Form 9465, *143, 147*
179 expenses, *10, 120*
401(k) plans, *58*
403(b) plans, *47-48, 66-67*
Frequent flyer awards, *58*
Fringe benefits, *47-48, 53-69*
Furlough travel, *105*

G

Gifts
    Business and professional, *117*
    Personal, *59*
    Special occasion, *59*
Group-term life insurance, *38, 61-62*

H

Health club memberships, *56*
Health insurance, *36, 38, 59-60*
Health reimbursement arrangement, *10-12, 38, 59-60*
Highly compensated employees, *12, 52*
Holy Land trips, *105*
Home equity loans, *92-93*
Home office, *60, 115-17*
Housing allowance,
    Accounting for the allowance, *90-93*
    Advance designation, *86-89*
    Allowable expenses, *96-98*
    Amending the designation, *88-89*
    Clergy Housing Allowance Clarification Act, *2-3, 91-92*
    Cost to the church, *93-94*
    Denominational, *89*
    Designating the allowance, *86-89*
    Eligibility, *26-32*
    Evangelists, *28, 95*
    Excess, *15, 90*
    Fair rental value, *2-3, 90, 91-92*
    In general, *60-61*
    Limits on the designation, *87-88*
    Limits on the exclusion, *85-86, 91-92*
    Ordained, commissioned, or licensed ministers, *26-28*
    Parsonage owned or rented by church, *83-85, 96*
    Parsonage owned or rented by minister, *85-86, 97-98*
    Payment of, *93*
    Percentage of salary, *89*
    Reporting, *87, 89-90*
    Retired ministers, *94-95*
    Second mortgages, *92-93*
    Warren Tax Court Case, *1-2, 84*
    Worksheets, *96-98, 156, 172*

I

Income, reporting, *36-38*
Income tax rates, *4-5*
Income tax status of ministers, *34-36, 38*
Individual Retirement Accounts (IRA), *61*
Insurance,
    Disability, *55-56*
    Health, *36, 38, 59-60*
    Life, *38, 61-62*
    Long-term care, *62*
Integral agencies of a church, *30-31*
Interest,
    Auto, *119*
    Mortgage, *17-18, 26, 92-93*
Interim appointments, *106-8*
International travel, *104-5*
IRA, *61*
Itemized deductions,
    Contributions, *117-18*
    Mortgage interest, *17-18, 26, 92-93*
    Real estate taxes, *17, 26*

K

Keogh plans, *61*

L

Leased car, *112*
Licensed ministers, *27-28*
Life insurance, *38, 61-62*
Loan-grants, *62*
Loans to clergy, *62*
Long-term care insurance, *5, 62*
Love offerings, *59*
Luxury auto, *111-12*

M

Meals and entertainment, *119*
Meals, employer-provided, *62*
Medical
    Insurance, *59*
    Health reimbursement arrangement, *10-12, 38, 59-60*
Memberships, *56*
Mileage rates, *6*
Minimal fringe benefits, *62-63*
Minister,
    Administrative and teaching positions, *30-32*
    Assignment, *31-32*
    Denominational service, *30-31*
    Eligibility for treatment as, *26-32*
    Employee, *36, 38*
    Income tax status, *34-36, 38*
    Licensed or commissioned, *27-28*
    Nonqualifying, *33*
    Self-employed, *36, 38*
    Serving local churches, *26-28*
    Social security tax status, *33*
Missionary,
    Furlough travel, *105*
    Qualifications, *28*
    Social security tax, *65-66*
Moving expenses, *63, 119*

N

Nonaccountable plan, *53, 101-2, 159-74*
Nondiscrimination rules, *52*
Nonqualified deferred compensation plans, *54-55*
Nonqualifying clergy, *33*

O

Offers in compromise, *144*
Office-in-the-home, *60, 115-17*
Opting into social security, *133*
Opting out of social security, *129-33*

P

Parking, *63*
Parsonage allowance *(See housing allowance)*
Payroll deductions, *63-64, 69*
Penalties,
    Failure to pay, *142*

Pension plans,
    General, *10, 63-64*
    Denominational, *63-64*
Per diem, *106*
Percentage housing allowance, *89*
Personal computers, *54, 119-20*
Personal exemptions, *4*
Personal gifts, *59*
Pre-employment expense reimbursements, *64*
Property,
    Purchased from church, *64*
    Transferred to minister, *64*

R

Rabbi trust, *65*
Rates,
    Income tax, *4-5*
    Social security tax, *125*
Real estate taxes, *17, 26, 92-93*
Reasonable compensation, *39-40*
Recharacterization of income, *49-50, 102*
Record-keeping requirements, *102-3*
Recreational expenses, *65*
Reimbursements,
    General, *53*
    Social security, *65-66, 124*
Religious orders, *28-30*
Renting home, *85-86, 98*
Retired ministers
    Housing allowance, *94-95*
    Working after retirement, *78, 133-34*
Retirement gifts, *65*
Retirement planning, *73-80*
Retirement plans,
    Deferred compensation plans, *54-55*
    Denominational plans, *63*
    Housing allowances, *94-95*
    IRAs, *61*
    Keogh plans, *61*
    Limits, *10*
    Rabbi trust, *65*
    SEPs, *65*
    Tax-sheltered annuities,
        Section 403(b) plans, *47, 66-67*
Roth IRAs, *61*

S

Sabbatical pay, *65*
Salary, *65*
Salary reduction arrangements, *47*
Saver's tax credit, *7-8*
Schedule A, *22, 152, 162*
Schedule B, *153*
Schedule C, *163-64*
Schedule C-EZ, *23, 154*
Schedule EIC, *139-40, 166-68*
Schedule SE, *155, 165*
SECA, *123-34*
Second mortgages, *92-93*
Section 179 deductions, *10, 120*
Self-employed vs. employee, *33-36, 38*
Self-employment earnings, *125-27*
Self-employment tax deductions, *128*
Self-insured medical plans, *10-12, 38, 59-60*
SEPs, *65*
Severance pay, *65*
Sick pay, *65*
Simplified Employee Pension (SEP) plans, *65*
Social security,
    Both spouses are ministers, *127-28*
    Canada Pension Plan, *134*
    Computation of tax, *125-27*
    Deductions, *126*
    Exemption of ministers, *129-33*
    Form 4361, *130-33*
    Housing allowances for retired ministers, *94-95*
    Opting into, *133*
    Opting out of, *130-33*
    Reimbursement, *65-66, 124*
    Services in which exemption applies, *26-33*
    Tax rates, *125*
    Tax status of ministers, *33, 38*
    Voluntary withholding agreement, *128-29*
    Working after retirement, *78, 133-34*
Special occasion gifts, *59*
Spouse, minister, *127-28*
Spousal or children travel, *106*
Standard deduction, *4*
Standard mileage rate, *6*
Subscriptions, *66, 120*

T

Tax withholding, *26, 38, 69, 128-29, 135-36*
Taxes, real estate, *17, 26, 92-93*
Tax-sheltered annuities, *47, 66-67*
Teaching positions, *30-32*
Telephone, *67, 120-21*
Temporary workplace, *106-8*
TIAA-CREF, *94-95*
Tithes, *117-18*
Travel expenses,
    Furlough, *105*
    General, *67*
    Holy Land, *105*
    International, *104-5*
    Per diem allowance, *106*
    Spousal or children, *106*
Trust, rabbi, *65*
Tuition reductions, *68*

U

Underpayment penalty, *142*
Unreimbursed business and professional expenses, *102-3*

V

Vacation pay, *68*
Vehicle,
    Nonpersonal, *68-69*
    Personal use of church-owned, *68, 112*
Vestments, *118*
Voluntary withholding, *26, 38, 128-29, 135-36*

W

Wage continuation, *69*
Warren case, *1-2, 84*
Withholding,
    Exemption of ministers, *26, 135-36*
    In general, *69*
    Social security taxes, *128-29*
    Voluntary, *26, 38, 128-29, 135-36*
Workers' Compensation, *69*

10 Biggest Tax Mistakes Made By Ministers

1. Filing as self-employed for income tax purposes on your church salary, using tax benefits only available to employees, and leaving yourself vulnerable to reclassification by the IRS to employee status. Chapter 1.

2. Failing to have at least a modest housing allowance designated when living in a church-provided parsonage. Chapter 5.

3. Failure to understand the importance of the fair rental test for the housing allowance. Chapter 5.

4. Confusing the fair rental value of a church-provided parsonage (only includable for social security purposes) with the designation of a portion of your salary as housing allowance (providing an exclusion for income tax purposes). Chapter 5.

5. Failing to keep a log of miles driven for personal use vs. church purposes. Chapter 6.

6. Claiming office-in-the-home treatment — rarely justified under present law. Chapter 6.

7. Not documenting business expenses to reflect business purpose, business relationship, cost, time, and place. Chapter 6.

8. Failure of minister-employees to use an accountable reimbursement plan. Chapter 6.

9. Treating a minister's tithe as a reduction of salary except in relatively few instances where it is appropriate. Chapter 6.

10. Improperly opting out of social security because you don't believe it is a good investment. Chapter 7.

10 Tax and Finance Questions Most Frequently Asked by Ministers

1. **Income tax filing status.** Should I file as an employee (receiving a Form W-2 from my employer) or as an independent contractor (receiving a Form 1099-MISC) for income tax purposes? Chapter 1.

2. **Social security filing status.** Should I have FICA-type social security tax withheld from my pay or pay self-employment social security tax calculated on Schedule SE and pay it with my income tax return? Chapter 1.

3. **Qualifying for the housing allowance.** Do I qualify for the housing allowance? Chapter 1.

4. **Housing allowance exclusion.** How much can I exclude as a housing allowance for income tax purposes? Chapter 5.

5. **Structuring the pay package.** How should my pay package be structured to achieve the best tax benefit for me? Chapter 3.

6. **Proper use of accountable expense reimbursements.** Do the payments I am receiving from the church or parachurch ministry for expenses qualify as tax-free reimbursements? Chapter 6.

7. **Fringe benefit planning.** How do I determine which fringe benefits I receive are tax-free, tax-deferred or taxable? Chapter 3.

8. **Wise retirement planning.** What steps can I take now to insure I will have adequate funds to retire? Chapter 4.

9. **Paying income and social security taxes.** Should I have enough income tax withheld from my salary to cover my income and social security tax obligation, or should I pay quarterly estimated taxes? Chapter 8.

10. **Opting out of social security.** Under what conditions is it appropriate for me to opt out of social security? Chapter 7.

Zondervan Practical Ministry Guides
Paul E. Engle, Series Editor

SERVING AS A CHURCH GREETER
Greeters are the welcoming arms that people long to find in a church. This practical guidebook will help you reach out to people who need to experience the warmth of belonging to a church family. Includes discussion questions and tips for remembering names.

SERVING AS A CHURCH USHER
Your importance as an usher can't be overstated. Your impact is enormous both in meeting the needs of people and in keeping the church service running smoothly. Includes usher's checklist and resources for the offering.

SERVING IN YOUR CHURCH MUSIC MINISTRY
Worship is a slice of eternity that Christians can participate in on earth, and nothing can facilitate our experience of worship like music. This wise, concise guidebook will help you harness your God-given musical talent as a gift to the body of Christ, in a way that brings joy to both God's heart and yours. Includes instrumentalist survey and worship planning checklist.

SERVING BY SAFEGUARDING YOUR CHURCH
Church ought to be the safest place on earth. Here's how to fulfill that goal in practical ways, from developing a security structure and team to assessing interior and exterior building security, training ushers and greeters to be sensitive to security, forming an emergency reaction team, establishing financial accountability, and much more. Includes diagrams, checklists, and resources lists.

SERVING IN CHURCH VISITATION
Whether visiting people in their homes, in the hospital, or in a restaurant over a cup of coffee, the simple act of connecting with others is filled with powerful possibilities. The act of friendship is an inroad to hearts and lives that creates trust, value, and incredible potential for ministry. Includes self-assessment and do's and don'ts for various special-needs situations.

Pick up your copies today at your favorite bookstore!

Softcover

Serving as a Church Greeter	0-310-24764-0
Serving as a Church Usher	0-310-24763-2
Serving in Your Church Music Ministry	0-310-24101-4
Serving by Safeguarding Your Church	0-310-24105-7
Serving in Church Visitation	0-310-24103-0

GRAND RAPIDS, MICHIGAN 49530 USA
WWW.ZONDERVAN.COM

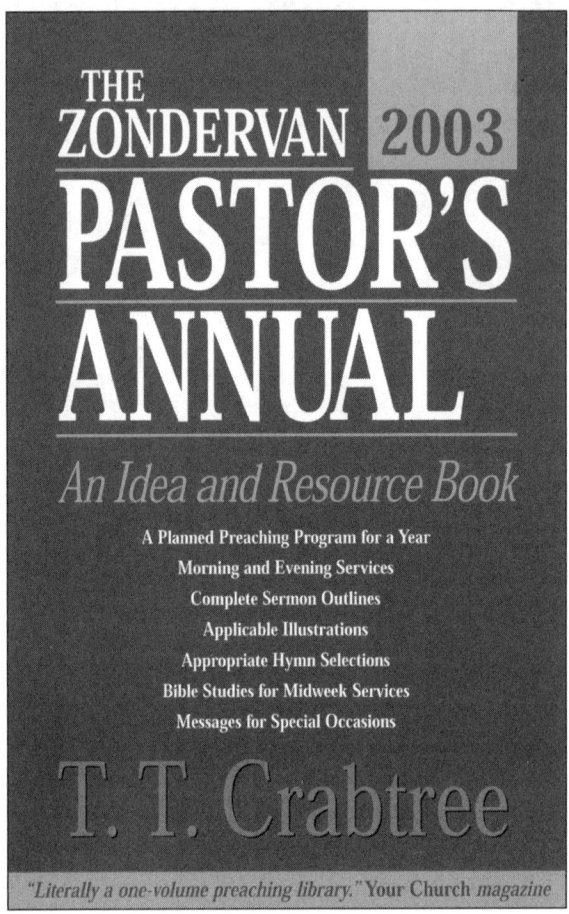

The Zondervan 2003 Pastor's Annual
T. T. Crabtree

This annual resource for preachers provides a planned preaching program for an entire year, including Sunday morning, Sunday evening, and midweek sermons. Besides the sermons, the Sunday morning services contain prayers and suggestions for music.

Also included in the book are helps for special occasions such as weddings, funerals, and youth meetings, and Scripture and topical indexes.

Softcover 0-310-24362-9

Pick up a copy today at your favorite bookstore!

GRAND RAPIDS, MICHIGAN 49530 USA
WWW.ZONDERVAN.COM